It's Not Always Depression

Hilary Jacobs Hendel is a certified psychoanalyst, and an AEDP psychotherapist and supervisor. She has published articles in *The New York Times*, including the piece 'It's Not Always Depression, Sometimes It's Shame', which was a #1 Most Emailed article for the paper, and professional journals. Her blog, *The Change Triangle*, is read worldwide. She runs a private practice in New York City and was the Mental Health Consultant for the Emmy- and Golden Globe-winning show *Mad Men*.

It's Not Always Depression

A New Theory of Listening to
Your Body, Discovering Core
Emotions and Reconnecting
with Your Authentic Self

Hilary Jacobs Hendel

Foreword by Diana Fosha

PENGUIN LIFE

AN IMPRINT OF

PENGUIN BOOKS

PENGUIN LIFE

UK | USA | Canada | Ireland | Australia
India | New Zealand | South Africa

Penguin Life is part of the Penguin Random House group of companies
whose addresses can be found at global.penguinrandomhouse.com.

Penguin
Random House
UK

First published in the United States of America by Spiegel & Grau 2018
First published in Great Britain by Penguin Life 2018
This edition published 2018
003

Printed and bound in Great Britain by Clays Ltd, Elcograf S.p.A.

A CIP catalogue record for this book is available from the British Library

ISBN: 978–0–241–97640–1

www.greenpenguin.co.uk

For Jon, whose love, wisdom, and
support made this book possible

For my mother, whose unconditional love
and kindness made me who I am

Foreword

by Diana Fosha

AS THE DEVELOPER of AEDP (accelerated experiential dynamic psychotherapy), a healing-oriented transformational model of therapy, I picked up the manuscript of *It's Not Always Depression* by Hilary Jacobs Hendel with a mixture of excitement and trepidation.

On one hand, *excitement:* Here was the potential for my work to take a quantum leap in its ability to help people change. Not only, as has happened to date, by affecting how therapists practice, and thus having an impact on the clients they see. But now, here, with this book, by going directly to the people, and sharing some "trade secrets." By making the ideas of AEDP more accessible, this book has the potential to benefit many more people—both those in therapy (with all different kinds of therapists) and those not in therapy at all. The prospect was exhilarating.

At the same time, I felt *trepidation*. Here was my life's work to date in a self-help book: Would it do AEDP justice? Or would the essence of AEDP somehow get watered down? Would the complex ideas of AEDP be turned into superficial fortune-cookie wisdom that would trivialize the years of work spent in developing a rigorous, healing-oriented transformational therapy? And if that weren't enough cause for *anxiety,* Hilary was a colleague I felt connected to. Would I find myself in the awkward position of not liking what she wrote? Or, with people's understanding of AEDP now out of my hands, would I have to live with an account of it that felt wrong or off?

I already felt some significant *safety.* Not only did I know Hilary Jacobs Hendel as a person of substance and a wonderful clinician to boot, I had also been truly wowed by two pieces she wrote for *The New York Times* about AEDP practice: those short, simple articles had showcased her enviable gift of capturing essence while writing simply and accessibly.

As I began reading the manuscript, *my breathing started to settle. My body relaxed* and *my mind became engaged.* What I was reading was apt and accurate. *I breathed a sigh of relief!* It was going to be okay.

As I kept reading, chapter after chapter, story after story, *I felt moved.* AEDP had a life of its own, separate from me. I had already experienced that with the contributions of my colleagues—faculty members of the AEDP Institute—who have extended the scope of AEDP through their work. However, here was a member of the next generation, someone trained by my colleagues, who had made the work her own and was now transmitting it not only to her clients, but through this book, to the public at large. *I felt a lump in my throat, and an uplifted feeling in my chest.* The intergenerational transmission was on.

You might have noticed the italicized words in the preceding paragraphs. They are all words describing either emotional feelings or bodily sensations associated with emotions. Emotion and bodily sensations often reveal us to ourselves. They contain biological wisdom and communicate what's important to us and to those around us. In the pages ahead, as you get familiar with Hilary Jacobs Hendel's book, you will learn to treasure the richness of emotions and what powerful guides they can be, pointing us toward doing what we need to do to heal old wounds and feel more effective and happy in our lives. Hilary does a wonderful job of teaching about emotions and the defenses behind which they hide. In her cases, she documents the toll that not being in touch with our adaptive emotions takes on us, and the benefits and advantages that well-processed emotions offer us. Those italicized words were crucial entry points into different aspects of my experience, all relevant to the task at hand.

We have a saying in AEDP: *Make the implicit explicit and make the explicit experiential.* In this foreword, I will make the implicit explicit and tell you about the basic AEDP principles that come to life in Hilary's clinical work. I hope to tell you enough about AEDP that you can understand the principles that underlie what you are about to experience. So here goes making the implicit explicit with respect to some fundamental AEDP principles.

Healing from the Get-Go:
Transformance as the Drive to Heal

The first core idea that animates AEDP is that healing is not just a desired outcome of treatment; it is a potential that is there from the start. We are wired to heal, to right ourselves, to grow and transform. This is not just a metaphor, a way of speaking. It is what neuroplasticity is about.

When we feel safe, or safe enough, the drive to heal comes to the fore. Unlike most therapies that focus on psychopathology, AEDP doesn't focus on what's wrong: it focuses on what's right. AEDP therapists are always on the lookout for this drive to heal, for which we have a special name: *transformance.* This is how I describe transformance, the motivating force of therapy:

> People have a fundamental need for transformation. We are wired for growth and healing. And we are wired for self-righting, and resuming impeded growth. We have a need for the expansion and liberation of the self, the letting down of defensive barriers, and the dismantling of the false self. We are shaped by a deep desire to be known, seen, and recognized, as we strive to come into contact with parts of ourselves that are frozen.[1]

What's beautiful, as well as convenient, is that the phenomena of healing are invariably accompanied by *vitality* and *energy*, which have clear somatic affective markers. These markers help us track and they help us see the manifestations of transformance and the strivings toward healing and well-being. And when we recognize those strivings in people, they feel seen.

Transformance and its positive somatic affective markers of energy and vitality are a direct translation of positive neuroplasticity in therapeutic action: it is what allows rewiring to take place.

Privileging the Positive, the Adaptive, and That Which Feels Right and True

While we are on the lookout for evidence of healing even amid despair and fear, we are also carefully attending to and working with what is positive, what is adaptive, and that which feels right and true. "Positive" in AEDP has a very special meaning. It certainly includes positive emotions, like *joy* and *gratitude* and *happiness*. However—and I cannot emphasize this enough—the way we define "positive" in AEDP encompasses those as well as anything that *feels right and true* to the individual. This is crucial to grasp, for we are often afraid of feeling our emotions because we don't want to feel pain. As you will read in the pages that follow, when we finally get past the protective barriers we built when we were children and we actually feel our genuine emotions, even when those emotions are grief or anger, we certainly feel *relief*. But we don't feel only relief; we feel something that we, and our bodies, have needed to feel for a long time. Similar to breathing a sigh of relief when a crooked picture is righted, when we finally feel the emotions that are true to our situation, it *feels right*. And we *feel good*.

Undoing Aloneness

Aloneness—unwilled and unwanted aloneness—in the face of overwhelming emotions is at the epicenter of AEDP's understanding of how emotional suffering and subsequent emotional difficulties develop. The implications of this understanding are clear: "being with"—i.e., being with a trusted other with whom we feel safe and known—is fundamental to healing and to being able to process our emotions in a healthy way. When we do not feel alone, when we feel accompanied, our nervous systems get upgraded. With help, we become better able to both *feel* and *deal*. Thus, a primary aim of the AEDP therapist is to undo the client's aloneness and be with the client on their healing journey.

As a result of what we know about attachment theory[2] and about how the autonomic nervous system works,[3] most experiential therapists seek to activate the social engagement system and establish safety and connection. Going further and taking a page from attachment research documenting how parents who raise resilient children behave, AEDP therapists lead with empathy, care, concern, validation, and authentic emotional presence. It is this that allows the work with emotions to be effective. As the saying goes, not only are two heads better than one; so are two psyches and so are two hearts. What's too overwhelming to deal with alone becomes much more manageable when we're in it together with a caring other. Undoing aloneness is the sine qua non of AEDP therapy: it underlies all the work with emotions that Hilary's work exemplifies so beautifully.

The Importance of Positive Interactions

Attachment theory teaches us that positive interactions between caregivers and those they nurture—interactions characterized by care, emotional engagement, contact, connection, help, and positive emotions—are the stuff of optimal brain development in childhood. They support the brain chemistry that in turn supports the positive neuroplasticity that operates in all of us throughout the life cycle.[4]

Long gone (mostly) are the days of the blank-slate shrink. The stance of AEDP therapists is characterized by connection, emotional engagement, and authenticity. AEDP therapists express genuine feelings of care and concern and a desire to help.

Working with Receptive Affective Experiences

Care, empathy, concern, validation, and authentic emotional presence are so important to the establishment of safety and connection. However, what good is giving if what is given cannot be received?

In AEDP, we not only focus on helping people express emotion, we also work to help people learn to receive emotions, and thus take in the good stuff. In other words, we work with *receptive affective experiences,* i.e., with what it feels like to *receive* love or care or understanding.

We all crave support, care, and understanding. We all yearn to be seen, to be felt, to be heard, and to be understood. And yet, when those experiences unexpectedly materialize before us, we often respond to them with reticence and distrust. AEDP works to help people overcome their blocks to taking in the good stuff that comes from good relationships, including the therapeutic relationship. We help people explore: What does *care* feel like when it's taken in? What does it feel like in the body to *feel understood*? In the process, we often understand why that which is so desired is often so blocked. In this manner, *care, love, empathy, admiration, understanding,* and *feeling seen* can be truly felt. And when they are felt, we can fully reap their benefits. With love securely in our hearts, and understanding securely in our bellies, we can more confidently meet the challenges of each day.

The Importance of Making the Most of Positive Emotions

"Undoing aloneness," "in it together," and "together with" apply not only to working with the negative painful emotions of suffering and their relief. AEDP therapists actively, explicitly, and experientially work with positive emotions between therapist and client; the therapist's own expressive range thus stretches beyond care, concern, empathy, and connection and expands into the explicit expression of *delight* and *joy,* as well as *pleasure* in the client. AEDP therapists thus go beyond empathy and validation to actual explicit affirmation. Furthermore, rejoicing in and the celebration of the client's positive qualities, strengths, talents, and achievements in therapy, and making sure the client is able to take that in, contribute to the effectiveness of AEDP therapy.

The Processing to Completion of Emotions Associated with Suffering: "Nothing That Feels Bad Is Ever the Last Step"

The above is a quote from one of the most brilliant experiential therapists, Eugene Gendlin, the creator of a method called Focusing.[5] It is also the title of a paper I wrote about how to help people process intense emotions.[6]

Emotions are wired into us by eons of evolution. Their purpose is not to scare us and overwhelm us and make us afraid to lose control. Emotions are wired into our brains and bodies and nervous systems to help us cope with our environments and thus enhance our adaptation. No matter how scary emotions may sometimes seem, if we allow ourselves to process and metabolize them, they will invariably take us to a good place: The core emotion of *grief* will lead us to eventual acceptance. The core emotion of *anger* will lead us to experiences of strength, clarity, and empowerment on behalf of the self and our need for what's just and right. *Fear* will lead us to seek safety. *Joy* will lead us to exuberance, energy, and an expansion of our willingness to connect and explore with zest. And this is a basic principle of experiential work with emotions: There is a pot of adaptive gold awaiting the complete processing of each core emotion. And that pot of gold is constituted of resilience, clarity, and improved capacity to know what we need in a way that can inform our actions.

As Hilary demonstrates, using the tools she describes in *It's Not Always Depression* helps you do precisely that. Even if you are not in therapy, the book might well undo your aloneness and teach you how to overcome blocks and inhibitions so that you can know what you are genuinely feeling. Once you know your deep feelings, they can guide you to that pot of gold of clarity.

This idea of processing an emotion to completion is shared by all the experiential therapies: EMDR (eye movement desensitization and reprocessing), Internal Family Systems, Gestalt, Focusing, Somatic Experiencing, Sensorimotor Psychotherapy, emotion-focused, etc.

And, indeed, when emotions are processed to completion, they release adaptive action tendencies, resilience, and clarity about what we need and thus what we need to do. Emotions processed to completion energize the system with intention, and the completion is accompanied by positive affect. We move from feeling bad to feeling good. And it is as important to process feeling good as it is to process feeling bad.

The Metaprocessing of Transformational Experience

If round one of therapy is how to get past defenses and anxiety, and round two is working to heal suffering and bring about increased effectiveness and resilience, in AEDP, there is a round three!

Round three of AEDP, *metatherapeutic processing* (*metaprocessing* for short), involves experientially working with positive emotional experiences as systematically and thoroughly as we work with negative emotional experiences.[7] Just as working with the negative emotions of emotional suffering allows them to transform into adaptive actions on behalf of the self, working with the positive emotions associated with change-for-the-better—e.g., healing or transformation—begins another whole round of transformation. Metaprocessing further broadens and builds[8] the change that results from processing the emotions of trauma through to completion. And it is this that rewires the brain and deepens and expands resilience and well-being.

AEDP's systematic focus on working with the *experience* of feeling good and the *experience* of change-for-the-better is a way of expanding, deepening, and solidifying well-being.

The Transformational Affects

Our experience with metaprocessing has revealed that when we explore the experience of the positive emotions associated with change-for-the-better, doing so gives rise to further rounds of transformational experience. And it turns out that each new transformational experience is accompanied by its very own wired-in emotion. We call these emotions the *transformational affects,* and they are invariably positive. AEDP describes the transformational affects in detail and works with them systematically. Much as our core emotions alert us to what we must deal with, and are specific to different kinds of challenges (for example, fear is an emotion specific to danger, and grief is an emotion that is specific to loss), the transformational affects alert us to important positive changes that are occurring within us. By attending to these positive changes, we are able to consolidate and make the most of the changes taking place, and thus further enrich our lives.[9]

The transformational affects include, but are not limited to: the *mastery affects* of joy, confidence, and pride; the *tremulous affects* associated with the positive vulnerability of having new and somewhat unprecedented experiences; the *healing affects* of feeling moved within ourselves, and gratitude to and love for those who help us; and the *realization affects* of wonder and awe at the changes taking place.

The Non-Finite Transformational Spiral

Exploring experientially the positive transformational affects leads to more positive transformational affects. And more begets more—jump-starting a transformational process that is not finite. This non-finite transformational process involves upward spirals of vitality and energy, and goes beyond healing emotional suffering to morph into *flourishing* and *well-being.*

Core State

The transformational process culminates in core state, a state of unifying integration and openness. In her book, Hilary calls it *the openhearted state.* The openhearted state partakes of both AEDP's *core state* and Internal Family System therapy's *core Self.* It is here that the process of change takes deep root, and it is here that the work of AEDP, IFS, and the work described in this book join contemplative traditions, East and West, to illuminate pathways to access the fundamental qualities of the mind that are there for the activating. The processes that characterize them lead to and often culminate in *generosity; wisdom; compassion for self and others; calm; acceptance; coherence; well-being; flow; ease;* and a deep *sense of knowing,* associated with the essence of *"This is me."*[10]

In closing, both AEDP and *It's Not Always Depression* start with our struggles and frustrations and end with us accessing our deepest gifts. This fundamental hopefulness grounded in scientific understanding and clinical experience is crucial, for one of the greatest challenges in mental health right now is combatting nihilism and educating the public about effective interventions. Education on emotions is a powerful force for eradicating the stigma put on those who suffer depression, anxiety, addictions, and other symptoms of psychological distress. Education on emotions has great power to change how we view ourselves and others. *It's Not Always Depression* will help people better understand why people suffer and will lead to a sigh of relief brought by understanding that "there is a reason for my suffering."

It's Not Always Depression also elucidates why and how emotion-focused therapies work. If you're a therapist learning and practicing AEDP, this book will help you grasp AEDP's essence by hearing it simply explained and watching it in action. If you are a client in therapy, especially in an AEDP, IFS, and other experiential therapy, *It's Not Always Depression* will help you better understand how your therapy works.

Read this book (and read it again). Also consider sharing it. While this is a self-help book that you can definitely work with on your own, you might consider having a book partner or forming peer groups to read it with: this way you can get support and witnessing for both your pain and your joy.

The bottom line is this: if you're a human, I recommend that you read this book.

Contents

1

Getting to Know the Change Triangle

What This Book Will Do for You

I FIRST ENCOUNTERED the Change Triangle[1] in 2004 at an academic conference on the science of emotions and attachment in New York City. There I was staring at a giant upside-down triangle projected on the auditorium screen. It was a representation of how emotions work and can lead, if mismanaged, to psychological symptoms like depression. Defenses, anxiety, and these very important things called *core emotions* were mapped out in such a way that something suddenly clicked. The elements of psychological experience, which had seemed random and chaotic, fell into place, like the final turn of a Rubik's Cube. I felt understood. I felt relief. I was excited. With all of my science and psychological education—Bronx High School of Science, a biochemistry degree from Wesleyan University, a doctor of dental surgery (DDS) from Columbia University, a master's degree in social work, and since then a certification in psychoanalysis—why had I not seen this simple map before? I had the thought then, *This should be basic education. Every one of us can benefit from understanding how our emotions work and how to work with them to feel better.*

When I saw videotapes of emotion-informed psychotherapy, I saw radical transformations that occurred in one session. For these patients, work that would have taken a traditional psychotherapist years to accomplish was achieved in an hour. I couldn't help wondering if it was too good to be true. Was this a method with scientific basis that could be taught and duplicated? My last decade of practice has proved that the answer is yes.

Having meticulously studied the last hundred years of psychological thought and the science and anatomy of the brain, and having practiced psychotherapy for more than a decade, I believe that the Change Triangle can help anyone, not just those in psychotherapy. My mission is to translate the theory behind the Change Triangle into a tool that everyone has access to, not just people training to practice psychotherapy. I've adapted the clinical literature and science to make the Change Triangle easy to understand and nimble enough to be used anytime, anywhere. I will explain how to use this important tool to help you feel better.

Life is tough. We all suffer. Modern humans experience more stress, burden, emptiness, anxiety, self-judgment, and depression than ever. Most of us don't know how to deal with emotions effectively. Instead we work hard to manage them through avoidance. That coping strategy is the very thing that leads to symptoms of mental distress such as depression and anxiety. Avoiding emotions just does not work in the long run. The Change Triangle is a map to moving past our distress so we can spend more of our time in calmer, more vital states of being. The Change Triangle is grounded in the latest scientific research on emotions and the brain. Despite its complicated scientific roots, it feels intuitively right and is a resource for managing emotions that none of us should be without.

Emotions are powerful forces that in an instant overtake us and make us feel things, do things, and react in ways that are often hurtful. In response, we use other parts of our mind to bury emotions, believing that won't affect us. But emotions are biological forces that move in accordance with physics. They cannot be ignored without consequences—hence the rising rates of anxiety and depression in the world. Our cultural and educational systems fail to equip us with the education, resources, and skills to understand and work with emotions, and our society lacks a basic understanding of how they function biologically. What our culture does teach us, quite well, is how to dismiss and avoid emotions. The Change Triangle is a challenge to this cultural norm.

Avoiding emotions has a multitude of costs. Emotions tell us what we want and need and what is bad for us. When we don't use our emotions it's like navigating a boat across tumultuous ocean waters without sonar or even a compass. Emotions also connect us to our authentic Self and allow us to feel intimately connected to other people. When we are out of touch with emotions, we suffer loneliness, because the connections to both ourselves and the people we care about are enriched through empathy, the emotional connector. A deeper connection to our most authentic Self comes through experiencing the seven universal, inborn, prewired core emotions: sadness, joy, anger, fear, disgust, excitement, and sexual excitement.[2] These core emotions help us to navigate life effectively, starting the day we are born and continuing until the day we die.

Emotions are survival programs deeply embedded in the brain and not subject to conscious control. In the face of a physical threat, fear is triggered. Let's say a wild dog was chasing you; fear makes you instantly move. Anger protects us by compelling us to fight in self-defense. Sadness is the core emotion we feel when we suffer losses, like losing one's hair, losing a cherished possession, and losing loved ones. When we succeed and connect with others in enriching ways, emotions such as joy and excitement propel us to engage further, so humans grow, expand, and evolve. *Emotions are immediate responses to the present environment.* Emotions stand in stark contrast to intellect. Our thinking brain allows us time to consider how we want to respond. Our emotional brain just responds.

Despite the fact that we truly need emotions to live effectively, they also cause us problems. What a fundamental conflict! From a biological perspective, we need emotions, but they also hurt us. The human mind has evolved in such a way that we have an incredible ability to ignore emotions to push through life. In fact, this ability helps us get things done. We need to work, feed our families, secure shelter, and take care of other basic needs. We use defenses so that we can carry on. But researchers now know that blocking emotions is detrimental to mental and physical health. Blocked emotions lead to depression, anxiety, and a wide variety of other psychological symptoms caused by chronic stress. Additionally, chronic emotional stress causes changes to our physical health by increasing the amount of stress hormones, called corticosteroids, coursing through our body. Emotional stress has been linked to heart disease, stomach pain, headaches, insomnia, autoimmune disorders,[3] and more.

Furthermore, the challenges of modern life—such as the pressure to succeed, the pressure to fit in, the desire to "keep up," the "fear of missing out" (FOMO), and the desire for good relationships and work satisfaction—evoke combinations of emotions that are often in conflict with one another. For example, Frank could not afford the kind of car he really wanted. Something as simple as Frank's thwarted car desire could cause a mixture of sadness, anger, humiliation, and anxiety. Needless to say, all those feelings together are hard to manage or bear without defenses. Life's challenges and conflicts create complex emotional cocktails.

Based on our genetics, natural disposition, and childhood experiences, we each navigate emotions differently. The type and amount of adversity we faced in youth directly affects how we feel today even if we cannot consciously perceive the connection. Furthermore, how our parents and caregivers responded to our individual emotions directly affects how we feel about and deal with our own emotions and the emotions of others in the present, now.

Some of us disconnect from our emotions to cope with the challenges we face. That has ramifications. We turn off. We shut down. We become numb. Eventually, we live in our heads with only our thoughts and intellect to guide us. We have lost our emotional compass. Alternatively, some of us cannot disconnect and instead become easily overwhelmed by emotions. That has ramifications as well. People who become easily overwhelmed expend a tremendous amount of energy managing their feelings, and that is exhausting. You might recognize yourself as someone who is quick to anger or who cries at the drop of a hat. Or maybe you recognize that you often feel scared even though intellectually you know there's actually nothing to fear. Some of us are easily hurt or insulted by others, taking even the smallest misunderstandings so personally that being around people becomes strenuous. When our emotions are so intense and easily set off, we sometimes react in ways we later regret, making our lives even harder.

Ideally, we create a balance between our emotions and thoughts. We need to feel our feelings, but not so much that they overtake us, impair our functioning and ability to be productive. We need to think, but not so much that we ignore our deep and rich emotional lives, sacrificing vitality.

The Change Triangle is a map to move us out of our defenses and put us back in touch with our core emotions. When we contact our core emotions, feel them, and come out the other side, we

THE CHANGE TRIANGLE

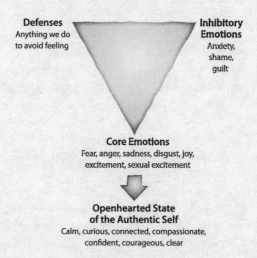

Defenses
Anything we do to avoid feeling

Inhibitory Emotions
Anxiety, shame, guilt

Core Emotions
Fear, anger, sadness, disgust, joy, excitement, sexual excitement

Openhearted State of the Authentic Self
Calm, curious, connected, compassionate, confident, courageous, clear

At any given moment, we will find our psychological state on one of the three corners of the Change Triangle or below it in the openhearted state.

experience relief. Our anxiety and depression diminish. When we are in touch with core emotions, our vitality, confidence, and peace of mind increase. Biologically, our nervous system resets for the better.

Working the Change Triangle makes the brain more flexible so we have much more control and power over how we feel, think, and behave. When people learn about the Change Triangle and understand how emotions work, they are transformed.

Although I first learned about the Change Triangle at a conference for professionals, it is a map that all of us can easily learn and begin to apply immediately. By the end of this book you will understand yourself, your loved ones, friends, and co-workers in a new way and be able to put that understanding to use. Because all of us are the same when it comes to how emotions work, the Change Triangle makes sense for everyone. You will be more informed about how to improve your relationships with both yourself and others. You will feel better and your life will be easier.

The Story of Me

I WAS BORN into a family of Freudians and a culture where mind over matter was the mantra. My mother had been a guidance counselor and my father was a psychiatrist. They believed that I could and should control my feelings with intellectual insight. Emotions were rarely discussed at home and, if they were, it was the goal to master them or "fix" them.

My clear memories begin around the fourth grade, when I started to feel self-conscious. My mother always told me I was beautiful and smart, but I didn't feel it. I felt stupid and ugly. When I looked in the mirror I felt that I came up short. I wasn't bullied and was friendly with the cool kids, but I always felt separate and insecure. As an adult, I realized that what I was feeling was anxiety and shame.

In middle school, I excelled academically. With each good grade and honor society mention my confidence grew. I developed the belief that if I worked hard, I would succeed and be recognized. With each success and recognition, I felt relief from insecurity.

Around that time, my seventh-grade English teacher had us read Freud and I became obsessed with psychoanalysis. In retrospect, it must have helped me understand myself in a way that made me feel in control. My passion for psychoanalysis continued to grow through high school to the point that my friends begged me to stop analyzing everyone. So I curbed my hobby of providing free—albeit unwanted—psychoanalysis and, instead, read voraciously on the topic.

By that time, I had decided I wanted to be a doctor like my father. I loved and was good at science, and I received a tremendous amount of positive attention for that decision. Up until my junior year in college, I never questioned my path, but I had never really considered what the day-to-day life of a doctor looked like.

In college I signed up for a course called Contemporary Psychoanalysis. Much to my chagrin, I realized that in fact it was an anti-Freudian course in feminism. For the first half of the semester, I sat righteously in the small seminar, me against ten radical feminists. Confident in my position, I argued fervently about why Freud was brilliant and his theories valid. After about five classes, I realized that my arguments were falling on deaf ears. In fact, my classmates had brought up some solid counterarguments and research that I found incredibly persuasive. The thought occurred to me that maybe I could learn something if I wasn't so busy arguing.

By the end of the course, I had started to question everything, including the values and beliefs of my parents, my society, and my culture. I started to consider why I had decided to be a doctor. As embarrassing as it was for me to admit at the time, I realized that my fantasy of being a doctor had everything to do with achieving a certain lifestyle and nothing to do with wanting to treat physical illness. When I imagined myself dealing with very sick people and having to deliver a dire diagnosis to their loved ones, I found the prospect too difficult—too anxiety provoking. I bristled at the responsibility. I didn't want to deal with such heavy issues of loss and death—topics we had always avoided in my family—on a daily basis.

I was too scared to abandon the medical track and I needed an immediate plan or I would be lost, out of control. Starting from

HILARY'S TRIANGLE

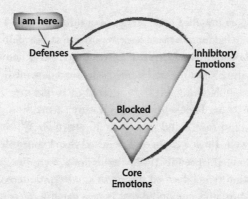

At this point my defenses were still working well, meaning I had no symptoms of anxiety or depression. But I was not aware of or in touch with my underlying emotions.

childhood and up until this point I had been driven by the desire to minimize my anxiety. I was making decisions, big and small, with the goal of having a long-term plan for my life to ensure I would be happy. I had many fears festering under the surface that I believed I could avoid if I just stayed on course to achieving a good career and finding a good husband. So . . . I decided to become a dentist.

In dental school, I met my first husband and I thought everything was working out perfectly. I had an amazing partner, I was ready to start a family, and my lucrative career was on track. Then step-by-step everything fell apart. I became a dentist but hated it and left the field a year after graduation. My decision to leave dentistry upset my husband, my in-laws, and my father terribly—I lost their approval and esteem. After six years of marriage, my husband and I were unable to manage the conflicts that had arisen between us. I was lost, alone, and afraid. Couples therapy didn't help. We had no way to solve our problems; our marriage ended.

I was single again, with two little children and no career. Everything I thought I knew and was confident about proved wrong for me. I loved my daughters, but I felt lost and without a compass. For the first time in my life I was off track and without a plan.

To support myself, I took a series of unfulfilling jobs. I rose up the corporate ladder to a management position at Maybelline Cosmetics, worked in the Garment District, started a home-based business selling vitamins, and headed sales for a new medical software company. Nothing felt right; nothing felt like me.

At that time, I took pride and pleasure in my stoicism, my toughness, and my "mind over matter" attitude. When things didn't go well, I made changes. I believed that I controlled what I wanted to feel. I proudly pushed aside fears, longings, and any other emotion that I deemed useless or counterproductive. Then my former husband announced that he was getting remarried. Although I was happy for him, I had an emotional reaction that blindsided me. I fell into a depression. I became overwhelmed by life. His marriage suddenly symbolized and sealed my utter aloneness in the world. I was afraid, and I was also ashamed that I was afraid. Fear begat shame, anxiety, and, in turn, depression.

It had never occurred to me that pushing myself, growing a career, raising children, and seeking a new partner would cause me to crash and burn. I thought I would be fine—after all, I always had been. But my emotional mind had another agenda. I was overwhelmed and I shut down. My lethargy grew until I couldn't leave my bed. I found refuge under my covers, lying in darkness, hiding from people and the daily demands of my life. It was the only place I felt safe.

My sister, Amanda, suggested that I see a psychiatrist to treat my depression. I was so checked out of myself that it never even occurred to me I had been suffering from depression, but once she suggested it, I knew she was right.

My psychiatrist suggested I take Prozac. She diagnosed me as having an agitated depression—a depression with lots of anxiety. She explained that stress made it harder for the body to manufacture a brain chemical called serotonin. When serotonin levels dip too low, depression results. When stress is relieved, serotonin production increases to its original levels and the depression goes away.

All I could say was, "Thank goodness for Prozac!" Four weeks later, I was up and around, functioning like I had been before, but I was forever changed by this experience. For the first time, I appreciated and respected my emotions for their power. I learned I had to pay attention to my feelings, to listen carefully to what they were telling me, and to take actions in accordance with what I was feeling. Still, I wasn't exactly sure how to tend to my feelings, how to act on them appropriately, or how to understand them. I started psychoanalytic psychotherapy and was able to discontinue taking Prozac after six months.[1] Having a place where I could talk about myself and my life was indeed helpful.

I decided to alter my priorities. Instead of choosing work based on what it paid, I would focus on a career based on my interests, and my interests had always drawn me toward psychology. I received a master's degree in social work and then enrolled in a four-year postgraduate program for psychoanalytic training.

As Luck Would Have It

Shortly before I began analytic training, a friend suggested that I attend a conference to hear an emotion-focused psychologist speak. Diana Fosha, PhD, had developed a new method called accelerated experiential dynamic psychotherapy.[2] AEDP has a healing-oriented approach instead of an insight-oriented approach. Insight-oriented therapy, like psychoanalysis or cognitive behavioral therapy (CBT), generally works with people's thoughts in the hope that through gaining insight, your symptoms will eventually improve. AEDP's healing approach means the therapy aims to change the brain and target symptoms at the level of emotions and the body, so instead of managing the symptoms, they disappear. AEDP, I learned, was much more directive than psychoanalysis; its methodology is specific and the results are predictably positive.

The word "healing" in relation to psychotherapy was jarring to me. It sounded like a new-age idea that my parents would have scoffed at. However, I got into psychotherapy because I wanted to make a difference in people's lives as quickly as possible. People were suffering and I didn't take that lightly. AEDP appealed to me because it is informed by the latest neuroscience and clinical theories of how people transform and heal from depression, anxiety, trauma, and more.

As I continued my psychoanalytic training, I delved deeper into the principles and theories of emotion, neuroplasticity, trauma, attachment, and transformation. Here was a path to change that did not require me to detach and stop feeling—tools I'd thought I needed to be a good analyst. With AEDP, I had a much broader range of ways to help relieve suffering.

AEDP gave me permission to be authentic and explicitly caring, and to not only focus on what patients were doing wrong (or what was wrong with them) but also on what they were doing right. This was a completely different world, one that included authentically connecting, healing, and transformation. This was a methodology in which emotions—be they emotions associated with difficulties or emotions associated with healing (AEDP's forte)—were central and important. The more I studied, the more I learned that emotion-oriented practice is not a weird fad of the moment. In fact, its cutting-edge scientific foundation made me think this was the wave of the future of psychotherapy practice.

When I left that conference, I understood myself in a new way. Emotion theory helped me understand why we become anxious and depressed, and the Change Triangle gave me concrete ways to move past those states of distress and misery. Not only was I wildly enthusiastic about what I'd learned, I knew I wanted to put it into practice immediately. I wanted my patients to have access to this simple, life-changing tool.

The Change Triangle Basics

THE CHANGE TRIANGLE is a map of the mind. The map takes you from a distressed state to calm and clarity.

No matter what is upsetting you, what symptoms of stress you are suffering from, what unwanted behaviors you have, or what aspects of your personality you want to change, the Change Triangle provides a logical, science-based path to follow for relief and recovery. Instead of resorting to mind-numbing coping tools like drugs, alcohol, or other defenses that rob us of our authenticity and aliveness, the Change Triangle offers us a positive path to dealing with challenges and also helps us understand what is causing us to suffer.

The three corners of the Change Triangle are core emotions, inhibitory emotions, and defenses. *Core emotions,* our inborn survival emotions, tell us what we want, what we need, what we like, and what we don't like. *Inhibitory emotions* such as anxiety, shame, and guilt block core emotions. They keep us civilized so we can fit in with the groups we love and need. And they serve another function: they are a stopgap or fail-safe mechanism to prevent core emotions from overwhelming us. *Defenses* are the mind's way of

THE CHANGE TRIANGLE

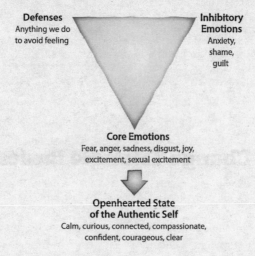

Defenses
Anything we do
to avoid feeling

**Inhibitory
Emotions**
Anxiety,
shame,
guilt

Core Emotions
Fear, anger, sadness, disgust, joy,
excitement, sexual excitement

**Openhearted State
of the Authentic Self**
Calm, curious, connected, compassionate,
confident, courageous, clear

protecting us from emotional pain and being overwhelmed by feelings.

What Are Core Emotions?

Core emotions are survival emotions. Each emotion has a specific wired-in program. The program causes physical changes to our body and evokes an impulse for action designed to help us survive or thrive in the immediate moment. Core emotions are meant to inform us about our environment so we live as adaptively as possible. *Am I safe or in danger? What do I need/want? What don't I want? Am I sad? Am I hurt? What brings me pleasure? What disgusts me? What excites me?* Because core emotions are hardwired in the middle part of our brains, they are not subject to conscious control. They can't be. Core emotions and their impulses work automatically, propelling us to act immediately. Nature intended for us to think only after we are "notified" by our core emotions. That's why core emotions originate from a part of the brain that

reacts faster than we can think and cannot be overridden consciously. And that is also why *we cannot think our way through a core
emotion; it must be experienced viscerally to be processed.* Core emotions
are brilliant: if we get out of their way, their innate programming
tells us what to do to live life adaptively.

The core emotions are

- fear
- anger
- sadness
- disgust
- joy
- excitement
- sexual excitement

Our core emotions are really a bunch of physical sensations. As we
grow up and with the help of our caregivers' empathy, we learn to
identify and name the emotions we feel: "I am sad, afraid, happy,
etc." But what we experience when we are sad is a heavy, sinking
sensation in the chest or a specific sensation in our eyes like pressure and tearing up.

Core emotions also contain physical impulses, which are designed by nature to be an immediate and adaptive call to action.
Did you ever reach into your refrigerator and pour yourself a glass
of milk without checking the date of expiration? One sip of sour
milk provokes an immediate reaction—you spit it out. Our taste
buds, threatened with poison, send a signal to our emotional
brain—the limbic system—to trigger disgust. Disgust, one of the
core emotions, causes nausea, a physical response in the body.

Disgust provokes an impulse for action that affects many muscles: the tongue retracts and the muscles around the mouth con-
tort. Disgust can affect the muscles in the GI tract, making us
throw up. Disgust evolved to mitigate the effects of poison as
humans foraged for food. Disgust is also provoked when human
interactions are toxic or poisonous. A consequence of being abused
is that the abuser evokes disgust. This is nature's intelligent way

of letting us know what is good for us and what is bad for us. Each core emotion has a specific action, and that action is meant to help us survive or thrive in that moment.

What Are Inhibitory Emotions?

Inhibitory emotions are a special set of emotions that block core emotions. Sometimes we block core emotions to get along with others and sometimes we block core emotions because they overwhelm us.

Your inhibitory emotions are

- anxiety
- guilt
- shame

Inhibitory emotions keep us connected, first to our parents and primary caregivers and later to our peer groups, schools, partners/ spouses, communities, religions, colleagues, friends, and the world at large. Humans are wired for connection—it is necessary for our survival that we care for one another. Therefore, preserving connections with parents or other caregivers is critical to a child's physical and mental development. If my mother leaves the room every time I am distressed, I will eventually learn not to show distress to prevent abandonment. If my anger causes my father to become angry and abusive, I will learn to hide my anger. Inhibitory emotions preserve connection by overriding core emotional expression.

After birth, we start learning which core emotions are acceptable to the people around us and which are not. "Unacceptable" emotions, by definition, provoke a negative response. For example, if a boy is told by his father to "man up" when he shows sadness, the boy's brain will consider that a negative response because his father has rejected this core emotion. If a little girl's excitement is met by her mother telling her to "take it down a notch," the girl's brain will learn to inhibit excitement. Future excitement will be tempered or at least conflicted. When a child tells her grandmother she is afraid of spiders and her grandmother replies, "Don't be silly," that child hears, "It is not okay to share my fear." In the future when she is scared, she might deal with her fear by herself instead of thinking she can go to someone for reassurance and comfort.

Any core emotion can evoke something negative, unwanted, and unbidden from our parents. Parents might respond to their child's core emotions with anger, sadness, or indifference. These negative responses are difficult for all of us to manage. People have a basic need for a positive response when we express our emotions. When our emotions are met with anything but interest and care, it signals to our brain that something unpleasant or dangerous is happening. Tone of voice, facial expressions, body posture, and language can all signal that our emotional expression is unwanted by our caregivers. When met with a negative response, we will attempt to curtail those emotions in the future. How do we do this? Our brains use inhibitory emotions, an emotional stop sign, to put the brakes on further emotional expression.

Anger NOT allowed!

When our brain senses core emotions that we previously learned were not welcome, inhibitory emotions will rise up to stop the flow of the core emotion energy, causing muscular tension and inhibiting breathing. The effect is like hitting the accelerator and the brakes on a car simultaneously. Core emotions push up for expression and inhibitory emotions push them down. The thwarting of emotional energy causes stress—sometimes traumatic stress—on our bodies.

Once we learn, even unconsciously, that a core feeling is unacceptable, the pattern of thwarting that emotion continues throughout our adult life, unless we actively work to change this dynamic.

In addition to helping us function in society, inhibitory emotions shut down core emotions when they become too intense. Emotions like rage, grief, and terror can be overwhelming. Sometimes we can't handle them. Our brain uses inhibitory emotions as a fail-safe way to shut down core emotions to protect us from being overwhelmed.

What Are Defenses?

Defenses are brilliant and creative maneuvers the mind makes to spare us the pain and overwhelming sensations that emotions can cause. They are anything we do to avoid feeling core or inhibitory emotions. In other words, defenses are emotional protection.

There are an infinite number of ways to guard against feeling. Defenses range from healthy to destructive. Some defenses are useful and adaptive, like choosing to watch a funny movie when we need a break from something stressful, or thinking of something positive to stop anger or sadness when we are trying to concentrate. Defenses, however, can become destructive when we are so out of touch with our feelings that our bodies and minds become adversely affected.

Are you aware of the ways you defend against emotions, confrontations, and conflicts? By definition, a defense is any thought, action, or maneuver we make that takes us away from being in touch with discomfort. Some common defenses are:

- joking
- sarcasm
- smiling
- laughing
- worrying
- ruminating
- vagueness
- changing the subject

- avoiding eye contact
- eye rolling
- mumbling
- not talking
- talking too much
- not listening
- spacing out
- tiredness
- criticizing
- perfectionism
- procrastination
- preoccupation
- irritability

- negative thinking
- judging others
- judging ourselves
- prejudice
- racism
- arrogance
- misogyny
- misguided aggression (i.e., getting angry at your partner when you're really angry at your boss)

- working too much
- numbness
- helplessness
- overexercising
- overeating
- undereating
- being secretive
- cutting
- obsessing
- addictions
- suicidal ideas

Can you add some of your own defenses to the list?

✓ _____
✓ _____
✓ _____

Can you add some defenses to the list that you've noticed in others?

✓ _____
✓ _____
✓ _____

When energy from emotions is diverted to defenses, there are many costs to our well-being. Defenses require energy; they deaden us by using up vital energy that could be used for relationships, work, and outside interests. Defenses keep our true, authentic Selves hidden and tempered. Most people don't feel good in the long run when they stay hidden. Defenses also make us more rigid, causing us to lose flexibility in thought and action.

For example, a married woman cannot tolerate when her stepson visits because it upsets her "routine." Her inflexibility hurts her because it strains her relationships and makes her feel tense. Her need to control the environment protects her from the underlying emotions evoked by her stepson's presence. If she could face the emotions her visiting stepson brings up, she would become more flexible and more generous. She might still choose to set the same limits and boundaries to protect her routine, but she will feel less tense and angry. Her relationships would benefit, as would she. Defenses cause us to feel trapped, inhibited, limited, and unable to reach our potential. Defenses force us to live in extremes of black and white, good or bad, where life lacks nuance. Too many defenses make it hard to wholeheartedly engage in life.

Additionally, defenses swing us into extremes of acting out in self-destructive ways. Since defenses block access to important emotions like fear that tell us to be cautious, overreliance on defenses causes us to engage in dangerous behaviors like thrill seeking, unprotected sex, and risky social behaviors. An "I don't care" defense prevents us from knowing who and what we value. When we are not aware of what we care about and why, we lose the ability to create the life we want and to feel our best no matter the circumstances life presents. For example, a young man believes he only cares about women for sex, yet when he is alone, he drinks excessively until he falls asleep. He isn't happy and he has convinced himself he doesn't care. Humans always do better when they are emotionally connected to others. The young man's "I don't care" defense protects him from his underlying emotions and needs for intimacy, but at great cost to his satisfaction and joy.

If someone hurts my feelings during a work meeting, it would probably be in my best interest to put off crying. A defense—like thinking of something funny—will keep the tears at bay. Defenses can be useful when we need a break from our emotions. Taking a break helps us calm down and rejuvenate and provides temporary relief from the pain or discomfort that some emotions bring. It is important, however, to return to our visceral experience and "check in" at some point to see if we are feeling any emotions that need validating and tending to. Ideally, we use our defenses only when we need them, not habitually, and certainly not all the time.

The Change Triangle in Action

When we know what we are feeling, we feel better. People who have full access to their core emotions have more vitality and energy for living because, by allowing emotions to occur, they are streamlining the neurobiological processes of energy efficiency and brain integration. The brain is integrated when the thinking brain, emotional brain, and body all work together the way nature intended. We do better in life and in relationships when we can think, feel, and deal with life as it happens. Working with our emotions allows us to return to a state where our biology is in balance, called *homeostasis,* which is one of the keys to a healthy mind and body.

The Change Triangle is a tool that helps us know our emotions and process them, but learning to use it perfectly takes time. Luckily, the Change Triangle also works even when we aren't yet able to process our emotions fully. As soon as we start using the Change Triangle it

- imparts immediate distance and perspective from our distress
- brings us an awareness of the way our mind is working
- helps us figure out if we are in a defense, experiencing inhibitory emotions, or experiencing core emotions
- helps us find and name our core emotions
- gives us direction, showing us what to do next to help us feel and function better

While I use stories from my practice to illustrate how I teach my patients to work the Change Triangle, you do not have to be in treatment to use this method. The Change Triangle can be used alone or with other therapeutic methods. It can be used sporadically to understand a big concern in your life or in daily practice to feel better and live the way you want. You can work the Change Triangle on your own, with a trusted friend, in peer support groups, with a professional counselor, or with your partner. You may find it very rewarding to learn about your emotions and your authentic Self with a partner who shares similar goals.

In time, when you ask yourself, *Where am I on the Change Triangle right now?* you will identify a location either on the top left corner in a defense, avoiding your emotions; on the top right corner, experiencing anxiety, shame, or guilt; or on the bottom, in touch with one of the seven core emotions.

Working the Change Triangle regularly means that you spend more and more time in an openhearted state—the state of your authentic Self. In an openhearted state we have a deep and grounded sense of peace and an ever-growing confidence that we can handle what life gives us. We feel in tune with our body, open to all emotions. We feel at home.

How do we recognize when we are in an openhearted state? With the 7 C's, as described by Richard Schwartz, developer of Internal Family Systems therapy (IFS):[1]

- calm
- curious
- connected
- compassionate
- confident
- courageous
- clear

At any given moment, we can access our openhearted state by being in touch with our core emotions, instead of allowing anxiety, shame, and guilt to block them. Working the Change Triangle repeatedly allows us to become progressively less anxious, less depressed, more vital, and more confident living our lives in the openhearted state.

Some lucky people spend a great deal of time in the openhearted state without much effort. Whether they had secure connections with their primary caregivers, less childhood adversity, or fewer traumas or they possess some innate, genetic calmness, they are the fortunate minority. The rest of us have to work a bit more (or a lot more) to reach those calm states. The Change Triangle can help us get there.

Putting It All Together: A Personal Example of Working the Change Triangle

When my former husband remarried I became depressed. Depression is not a core emotion. Depression is a defense because it blocks core emotional experience.[2] I felt down, I had no energy. I wanted to crawl into a hole. When I was depressed, I was also anxious. I sensed my anxiety in my core as a vibration, a persistent unsettled terrible feeling. So where was I on the Change Triangle? On both the defense and the anxiety corners.

If I had thought to ask myself what in my life was causing these feelings, I might have realized that my ex-husband getting remarried terrified me (core emotion: fear) because, until that time, I always felt he would be there for me. I knew intellectually

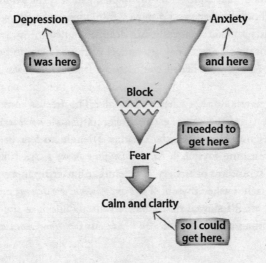

MY TRIANGLE
WHEN I WAS DEPRESSED
IN MY THIRTIES

Depression

I was here

Anxiety

and here

Block

I needed to get here

Fear

Calm and clarity

so I could get here.

that our relationship as husband and wife was over, but something about his remarriage made me feel absolutely alone. I had always had a partner—a boyfriend or husband—since I was fifteen. Being in a relationship, in retrospect, was also my defense against the terror of loneliness that was creeping into my consciousness. I was overwhelmed by fear, which caused too much stress for my mind and body to cope. That's why I started to exhibit symptoms of depression.

It may seem counterintuitive, but the antidote would have been to experience and engage with my fear, to bring it into full consciousness. To understand and explore it in a safe way, and, most important, to share it with someone who understood and could provide comfort and ideas for how to make things feel a little, if not a lot, more manageable.

While my depression was a low point for me—one that I needed a lot of support to overcome—the Change Triangle can also be used to move through less dramatic moments of distress.

Once I was anxious about a scholarly article I was supposed to write. I blocked the symptoms of this anxiety with two defenses. I had negative thoughts, a very common defense. I said things to myself like *Maybe I can't write this article after all*. I also felt compelled to play solitaire on my phone, which is the avoidance-with-technology defense. I'd moved from anxiety to defense unconsciously and automatically. My defenses pulled me away from the physical and emotional discomfort of my anxiety and delivered me to a place where I could escape from what I was really feeling.

Where was I on the Change Triangle? The defense corner.

Once I realized my negative thoughts (*I can't do this!*) were really defenses, I worked the Change Triangle to feel better. I began by asking myself, *What is happening in my body?* I noticed physical symptoms of anxiety, that familiar fluttering in my chest and stomach. I asked myself, *What core emotions are driving my anxiety right now?* I slowed down and ran through each of the seven core emotions asking myself, *Am I sad? Am I excited? Am I angry?*

Am I fearful? Yes! I realized I was afraid. Already, I felt some relief in naming my fear.

Fear feels similar to anxiety, but you can gain helpful information from fear. Anxiety is only inhibitory; its sole job is to block core emotions. Anxiety tends to paralyze instead of inform. But fear? We can actually deal with fear!

I imagined talking to the physical sensation of the fear: *What is it you are afraid of?* Then I listened to my body. I was patient with my fear, giving it ample time to answer—that's why slowing down is a big key to this process. My fear eventually answered, *I'm afraid of embarrassing myself, afraid of disappointing my readers.*

Ahhh . . . now I was getting somewhere. Fear, like all core emotions, includes hardwired adaptive impulses. Fear tells us to run away, as if we're in danger from a pouncing lion. Very adaptive, wouldn't you say?

To manage those impulses, I asked myself, *Do I want to act on my fear and run away? Or do I want to tolerate my fear, choose courage, and have a try at writing this article?* I reminded myself that even if my fears came true, I would most certainly survive. The important thing here is that once I noticed the emotion and its cause, I now had a choice about how to handle my dilemma.

So, how was I feeling after I worked the Change Triangle? Better. Naming my fear diminished my anxiety. Physiologically, giving language to experience calms the brain. It's neuroscience.[3] I felt calmer because I was clearer about what was upsetting me. I chose courage over fear and I wrote the article.

Our emotions are a compass for life. Anyone can live a life in touch with his or her core emotions and diminish anxiety, shame, guilt, depression, addictions, obsessions, and other symptoms. How? By getting to know the core emotions underneath and learning how to work with them. The Change Triangle is our guide.

FROM DEFENSE TO CORE EMOTION

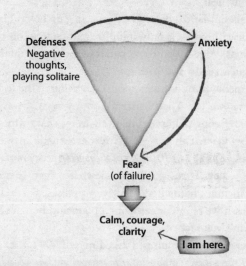

I noticed my defenses. I got out of my head and tuned in to my body and noticed
I was anxious. I searched for the core emotions triggering my anxiety and
realized I was afraid. I listened to the fear by focusing on how it felt in my body
(the physical sensations). Sensing the fear brought the impulse to consciousness:
I had an impulse to run away (avoid). My last step after working the Change
Triangle was to think through what solution would be the most beneficial
(adaptive for healthy living) to me and in line with my long-term wants,
needs, goals, and values.

How Comfortable Are
You with Emotions?

AS YOU LEARN and experiment with the Change Triangle, you will find that your emotional growth will increase, then plateau. At that point you'll have discovered another block to knowing yourself or others more deeply. You'll sense the block because anxiety and shame about yourself will arise. Or because you've gone into a defensive mode. You might notice avoidant thoughts like *This stuff is stupid* or *I'll do it later*. At that point, you have an opportunity to move past your defenses, anxiety, guilt, or shame to a new level of self-understanding. Emotional exploration unfolds like the layers of an onion. As you peel back one layer, a fresh layer emerges. Gaining understanding of emotions is a lifelong practice.

Quiz

This quiz will help you gauge your emotional tolerance. I'd like you to take it now, and then again later, after you've finished reading this book. When you retake the quiz, I hope that your score will have increased, indicating that you have grown more comfortable with these normal and natural experiences.

Directions: Rate your comfort level with each question.
Rate your comfort on a scale of 1 to 10, with 1 being "totally uncomfortable" and 10 being "totally comfortable." Go with your gut sense and don't overthink it. Circle the number that fits.

1 >   >   >   **5**   >   >   > **10**

(**1**=Totally Uncomfortable) (**5**=On the Fence) (**10**=Totally Comfortable)

How comfortable are you:

1. When people you care about direct strong feelings like anger and sadness at you?

1   2   3   4   5   6   7   8   9   10

2. When people you care about display strong feelings like anger and sadness in your presence but not directed at you?

1   2   3   4   5   6   7   8   9   10

3. When you are angry?

1   2   3   4   5   6   7   8   9   10

4. When you are sad?

1   2   3   4   5   6   7   8   9   10

5. When you are happy?

1   2   3   4   5   6   7   8   9   10

6. Staying in the present moment, just being with your thoughts and feelings as they arise?

1   2   3   4   5   6   7   8   9   10

7. Just being with and listening to someone who is expressing emotions without trying to help by "fixing" the situation?

1   2   3   4   5   6   7   8   9   10

Total Score: _____
Whatever your score, your emotional tolerance will build as you keep reading, experimenting, and tuning in to your emotions by working with the Change Triangle. Feel free to come back to this quiz to see how your answers change over time.

2

Releasing Core Emotions

Fran's Panic, Anxiety, and Grief

FRAN CAME TO therapy because she felt increasingly lonely. She was single. She had no desire to marry or have children. She worked in advertising and was very career focused. She described herself as "married to her job," but she had begun to feel a surprising sense of loneliness.

During her first session she told me that her parents had died in an accident when she was sixteen, and she had lived, from then on, with a loving aunt and uncle who had been good caregivers. She said she was not still grieving her parents, but she'd begun to feel their absence more and more. In that first session, she admitted that she had not been particularly close with her mother or father. She described them as "typical WASPs—stern and unfeeling." She had felt loved by them, but she had difficulty describing the ways they demonstrated their love to her.

Midway through our second session, Fran started to tear up as she talked about her inability to sustain romantic relationships. I asked her if she would mind taking a moment to acknowledge the emotion that was coming up. She looked at me blankly and then, without skipping a beat, she said, "I started knitting recently because I thought it would be nice to have a new hobby . . . something to fill my time when I'm not at work. I'm trying to cut down on the time I spend on Facebook." *Huh?* I thought. *Did I miss something?* Fran had thrown up a defense—changing the subject—when confronted with the core emotion of sadness.[1]

People's defenses against emotion are often unconscious; they become part of our social personalities. In that brief instant before Fran changed the subject, I saw her emotion. Tears had welled up in her eyes, and her mouth had turned down into a frown. Emotions are contagious—a by-product of special brain cells called *mirror neurons.*[2] Empathy caused my body to respond to her emotional state. I felt heavy in my chest. I recognized that Fran had tapped into her core emotional experience of sadness and almost

FRAN'S INITIAL TRIANGLE

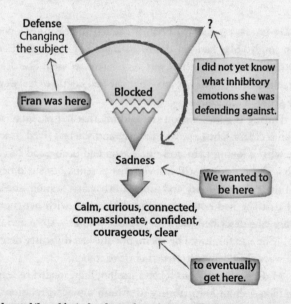

Fran changed the subject when her sadness (core emotion) started to emerge. This was how she protected herself from feeling it. At this point it was unclear why she needed this defense and I couldn't ask her, as she was not even aware that she was defending against her emotions. Fran needed to first become aware of her defense. Awareness would be the first step toward helping Fran reconnect with her core emotions, feel better, and tolerate more intimacy.

immediately shifted away from the emotion by changing the subject.

Defenses develop as protection. They are usually formed when we are young in an effort to save ourselves from overwhelming feelings. Fran's major trauma was the early loss of her parents. But because she had described her parents as cold, I suspected that her emotional repertoire might be limited. I asked her in our first session what emotions were "allowed" and what emotions were shut down in her childhood home, and how. Some parents inadvertently humiliate their children for showing certain emotions. They are dismissive, don't respond, or immediately go into "fix it" mode to stop emotion. It's worth mentioning that parents don't typically mean to cause harm to their children. It's just that emotions make parents anxious (our mind over matter culture enables that) and their defense is to help their children disconnect. Unfortunately, a child will erect a defense against an emotion if he or she learns that the emotion is unwanted. When a parent does not welcome a child's emotion, the child experiences that as a momentary break or rupture in the connection with the caregiver. These breaks are painful, and children erect defenses as protection from future emotional breaks.

Parents not only model ways to avoid and shut down feelings but they also model the "right" way to be. Fran told me that the discussions around her family dinner table were about facts, not feelings. Current events were fair game, but there was no discussion about how anyone felt in response. For example, she recalled a discussion about President Clinton's affair with Monica Lewinsky, but no one at the table expressed anger over the president's betrayal, nor did they express fondness for him despite his character flaws. The way her parents expressed emotion, what emotions were allowed or encouraged, and what emotions were shut down, shaped Fran's emotional repertoire, like it does for all children.

I thought that it might be difficult for Fran to feel sadness alone or in my presence. I also assumed, knowing how emotions from the present can trigger emotions from the past, that her sadness over romantic relationships might trigger a larger sadness from her past, such as the resulting grief from the loss of her parents. Current experiences that have similar emotional qualities to our past experiences are often linked in the mind. Loss connects to prior losses through brain cell networks holding past memories, emotions, physical sensations, and beliefs. In one second, we can go from feeling like the competent adults we are to feeling like a young child re-experiencing loss. Subjectively we feel like the trauma is happening again even though it's only a memory.

In that split second, when Fran experienced sadness and dropped down out of her head and into her body, where emotions live, she would have felt relief if she could deeply experience her sadness, even for a few seconds. Then BAM! Fran suddenly disconnected both from her emotion and from me—a person welcoming her sadness—by changing the subject. Fran defended against the sadness that was naturally emerging.

Since this was very early in our work together and we were still getting to know each other, I trod carefully. I wanted Fran to notice her movement away from emotion—that's all.

I listened as she talked about her knitting. "I joined a beginner knitting group. Once a week a group of us get together at a café near my apartment and we knit and give each other knitting tips."

"That sounds nice," I said, "and I want to hear more about it, but first, I wonder if you noticed that you were full of feeling a moment ago?"

"Really? I didn't notice."

"Well, I think I saw something, but I could be wrong," I said. "If we just rewind a bit, you were sharing how you were sure you would never find a partner, then your eyes welled up and you looked full of feeling. Did you notice that?"

She took a moment to check in with herself, a good sign that she was open to noticing her internal experience. I felt proud of her for her willingness to engage.

"Yes, I guess I did notice that," she reported, and the emotion came right back up. Her face showed sadness again, tears welled, and I felt the shift a second time.

"Do you know what emotion you are experiencing in this moment with me?" I asked.

Emotions benefit from being named and validated. Some people have an easier time identifying them than others, but it's a worthwhile pursuit and I wanted to help guide her. Also, I wanted her to know she was not alone—I was also feeling her sadness. I wanted us to stay connected. My intent was to give her a new and more intimate way to relate to others, starting with our relationship in therapy.

"No, not really, but the knitting really is great and I'd like to continue telling you about that, if that's okay."

"Of course it is." I was pleased that she noticed she was having a feeling. I would be able to use this moment as a reference point in future sessions. Over time, I would also teach her to recognize and name all of her core emotions. But first I said, "Before we return to knitting, I just want to let you know how great it is that you were willing to notice a feeling there. I know that takes courage. How was it for you that I noticed that?"

"It was okay."

"Maybe we can track that together from now on and just notice when an emotion comes up," I added. "Then we can decide whether we stay with it or move away from it, depending on what feels right to you." I wanted her unconscious mind to know we would handle emotions differently. Whether Fran was conscious of it or not, the mind responds well to feeling seen.

Over the course of Fran's treatment, our work moved along quite nicely. Six months in, she started noticing, even before I did, each time she defended against emotions. When she changed the subject she would announce first, "I know I am changing the subject, but I don't really want to go there. . . ." Her awareness, and her acknowledgment of it, was a huge milestone.

One beautiful summer day, Fran and I had our regularly scheduled session. At the start time for her appointment, I suspected that Fran would already be in the waiting room, as she was every Tuesday at noon. So I was surprised when I opened the waiting room door to find she was not there.

She finally arrived ten minutes late. Her face was puffy and flushed, as if she'd been crying. "I'm sorry I'm late," she apologized profusely, but I waved it away.

"Are you okay?" I asked. "You look like you've been crying." I had never seen her so emotional before.

"It's really dumb," she said. "I just saw a dog get hit by a bicycle. I was late because I tried to help. It was some teenager's dog. The bike came out of nowhere and ran over the dog. The dog was just lying there whimpering, its chest crushed and the owner was screaming. A policeman came to help. I think the dog was dead by the time I left."

"How awful!" I said.

"I felt so bad for the kid. She was screaming and crying. Then I started crying. It took me a while to pull myself together. I'm really shaken up."

"Of course you are. That sounds so upsetting."

Fran started to cry again.

"I just feel so bad for that kid to lose her dog so suddenly and right in front of her. I can still hear her screaming. It's so awful."

"So awful," I mirrored back.

"Enough of this," she said, wiping away her tears.

"Enough of what?"

"My self-indulgence. It wasn't my dog," she said solemnly.

She lifted her head and looked me in the eyes. She looked so sad. She seemed so young to me all of a sudden.

"I know," I said, "but your feelings don't care whose dog it was. You just feel sad . . . no need to justify it." I paused. "I see the feeling right there in your eyes. I can sense you trying to squelch this feeling. But these tears are important. There is more there."

And with that recognition she started to cry again, harder now, and she seemed scared. She started to rock back and forth, and her breathing became shallow. Her eyes widened. I started to think she was having a panic attack.

I switched gears to a more active and directive approach so I could help her get through her anxious panic. I stayed calm. Getting upset only worsens another person's anxiety.

"Do you feel me with you right now?" I asked. She nodded yes, and I moved my chair a little closer. "I'm going to help you feel better. Can you tell me what is happening inside you? Notice your heart rate."

"It's beating really fast," she said, gasping.

Calmly and gently I said, "This is a little panic attack." I used the word "little" to de-amplify her fear. The last thing I wanted to do was scare her more. My goal was to calm her mind and her nervous system as quickly as possible.

"You're going to be okay," I explained. "Something scared you and adrenaline just squirted into your system and once it's gone you'll feel better, but it will take a few minutes. Let's see if we can get you more comfortable. Look at me."

Our eyes locked. "Good! Now feel your feet firmly on the floor and let's take some deep belly breaths together. Breathe in for one, two, three, four, five, and six. Good! Breathe deeper and deeper into your belly. Let's hold for a beat and now exhale slowly, like you're blowing on hot soup to make it cooler. You're okay. I'm right here with you. This will stop soon."

Things to Know About Panic Attacks

- Adrenaline is released into the bloodstream.
- Because of adrenaline, the heart beats faster and breathing becomes shallow and harder.
- It's a scary experience, so if a person doesn't understand what is happening, they may fear they are having a heart attack and will die.
- It is not a heart attack.
- We don't die from panic attacks.
- The body will return to a normal state after the adrenaline is metabolized, which takes several minutes.
- The worst that happens is you faint and then start breathing normally again.

In time her breathing became more regular and she was able to take deeper breaths. "How is your heart rate now?"

"It's slowing down," she said.

"Good. Just stay with me and let's keep breathing."

Fran panicked because the grief over seeing a dog killed connected to her past grief over her parents' death. The flood of emotion was too much for her. It scared her and triggered the release of adrenaline, leading to panic.

Once she recovered, I asked, "Has this ever happened to you before?"

"I used to get panic attacks when I was a teenager."

"Do you remember how old you were when you got your first one?"

"Not really. I just remember I was at school and I was crying in class for some reason. The next thing I remember, I ended up in the nurse's office. She was really nice." She paused. "I must have been about sixteen because I was in a new school in Florida. It was after my parents had died."

"That must have been such a hard time."

"Lots of people lose parents," she said.

"Yes, and I imagine it was rough on you." I sensed she was struggling with something. "I could be wrong, but I sense a conflict here, about acknowledging that it was hard."

She nodded.

"Can we name all parts of the struggle?"

Fran thought for a minute, then said, "I think a part of me likes your sympathy and encouragement to indulge myself in the pain of what I went through, but I feel some embarrassment admitting that. Another part of me says not to wallow and that it's no big deal and that I should just move on."

"That makes perfect sense. I hear at least three different parts. One part of you wants my sympathy, another part feels some embarrassment, and another part wants to move on and ignore any sadness you feel toward yourself for what you went through. That part doesn't like my empathy and it says, 'It wasn't that tough, it was no big deal.'"

Parts

I use the word "part" to refer to a discrete aspect of a person's experience.

- A part can refer to each side of a conflict: "A *part* of me felt this and a *part* of me thought that."
- A part can refer to a childhood experience that lives on in the brain as a memory or as trauma: "This *part* of me feels ten years old."
- A part can be an emotion, belief, image, or thought: "A *part* of me felt sad."

Fran nodded and lit up. "Exactly," she said.

"What's it like for you to name all the sides of your conflict?" I asked.

"It feels right. It's true," she said.

"What does 'true' feel like, physically?"

"It feels calm."

There is never only one right way to intervene as a therapist or as a person exploring the root of defenses and emotions. At this juncture, I was aware that I had several choices. All of them involved helping Fran move down the Change Triangle by calming her inhibitory emotions, in this case anxiety, and moving toward experiencing grief, the core emotion. I could have brought her back to the moment before she had the panic attack, or I could have brought her back to being sixteen years old at a new school, or I could have just stayed in the present moment. Each of these moments was emotionally loaded and each of them would have given us an opportunity to do important work. Whether we are in the distant past or the recent past or the present, the goal is always the same: to know where we are on the Change Triangle and work our way down to knowing what core emotions we are having. In this case with Fran, I chose to focus on the present moment.

"What do you experience inside that lets you know something is true for you?" I asked her.

"I'm not sure what you mean. I don't think I notice anything."

"The sensation may be very small and subtle, hardly noticeable at all. Just turn your attention inside to your heart, belly, limbs, back, and head. Scan your whole body slowly, very, very slowly and see if you can notice and name some sensations that you're experiencing."[3]

"Well, I don't feel anxious."

"Can you put positive language on it? You don't feel anxious. What does that feel like inside?"

"I guess I feel still."

"Great! What else?"

"A little lighter."

"Where do you notice this lightness?"

"It kind of starts here"—she pointed to her stomach—"and radiates up and out."

If you observe yourself for fifteen seconds or so, many sensations start to emerge. The more you notice, the more you will continue to notice. Emotional observation has similar goals to a meditative practice. The observer aims to notice things in himself without judgment. The only goal is to be open and aware of physical experience. This skill, which all of us can learn with practice, is critical for psychological wellness.

I knew that Fran and I were laying the groundwork that would allow her to process whatever trauma was unresolved from when her parents died—even if I didn't know exactly how we would get there. By witnessing Fran's panic attack and helping her through—without judgment—she learned that I could handle her intense feelings and be there for her.

The following week, Fran informed me that she was thinking a lot about our last session and how she had suffered not only from the loss of her parents but also from having to move, switch schools, and make new friends. She acknowledged that those extreme changes didn't leave her much time or energy to grieve.

"What do you feel as you share that with me now, Fran?" I invited her to name her emotional experience and, for the first time, she took me up on my invitation.

FRAN'S MID-TREATMENT TRIANGLE

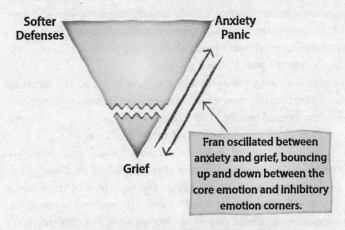

Softer
Defenses

Anxiety
Panic

Grief

Fran oscillated between
anxiety and grief, bouncing
up and down between the
core emotion and inhibitory
emotion corners.

**Fran had an unconscious conflict about experiencing her grief.
The fear of her grief raised her anxiety. She felt she had to avoid
anything that might connect her with her sadness.**

"I feel sad, but just saying that makes my heart start to beat really fast in my chest."

"So let's slow way, way down and stop right here. Can you turn all your attention to your heart?" Sadness had again raised her anxiety and caused her heart to race and her breathing to become shallow.

When an inhibitory emotion like anxiety comes up, the goal is to lower it immediately. Eventually, Fran's brain would permanently reset and stop triggering anxiety and panic in response to sadness. Fran needed to feel safe to experience her grief. I told her, "Just turn all your attention to the physical feeling of anxiety in your body. Keep me with you. Keep breathing deeply. . . . What do you notice now?"

"It's calming down," she reported. Just noticing the physical sensations of anxiety calms them.

"Great job. On a scale of one to ten, with ten being the worst anxiety you have ever had and one being a state of peace, where is your anxiety right now?"

"I'd say a three."

"Pretty low, but let's see if we can get it even lower. Just stay with the anxious feeling a little longer, breathing nice and easy. At the same time, can you remember a place you have been where you feel most calm and peaceful?"

"I love my bed. It is my safe place."

"Great. So just imagine being in your bed. Feel the sheets on your skin. See the room all around you. Now what do you notice?"

She exhaled deeply. "I've calmed down."

Now Fran was ready to tap into her deep grief.

Fran had moved from her defense in our first session—changing the subject—which is at the top left of the Change Triangle to working with anxiety at the top right of the Change Triangle. For months Fran and I worked on teaching her body not to panic so she could stay with the core emotions that spontaneously emerged within the course of our sessions. The goal was for her to feel her sadness on a physical and emotional level rather than a purely intellectual one. Some of my patients tell me they "know" they are sad, but when I ask them, "How do you *know* you're sad?" or "What happens physically that lets you know you are sad?" they don't have an answer. *Experiential work helps a person have an emotional experience in the here and now.* This is more powerful than merely talking and reflecting about a prior emotional experience, which is a more emotionally distant, intellectual exercise. Only through having an experience of sadness can we move past grief. Experiencing emotions fully in this way leads to ever-growing confidence that we can tolerate our core emotions.

When core feelings (sadness, anger, joy, etc.) get pushed down by inhibitory emotions (anxiety, shame, guilt) we develop defensive behaviors, from changing the subject to avoiding intimacy, as a way to avert emotional discomfort and emotional conflicts. But there is a cost to avoiding emotions. Maintaining defensive behavior requires energy that could otherwise be available for other vital behavior. In Fran's case, maintaining her defenses took her energy away from creating intimacy in her life.

When our defensive behavior becomes more damaging than

helpful, we can choose to feel our emotions. Why do we need to experience our core emotions physically? Focusing awareness on a sensation stimulates nerve cells to fire, facilitating the flow of emotions. When we learn to let our core emotions flow, our everyday distress that is caused by blocked emotions is ameliorated, we feel calmer and more balanced, and our courage and self-confidence grow.

About a year into our work, Fran began the session with a big statement: "Sunday was the anniversary of my parents' death."

"That's very important," I said.

Anniversaries bring up memories, some of which may be completely unconscious. Memories are recollections of physical sensations, sounds, smells, thoughts, images, or even impulses that our mind has stored.

"I've never talked about it to anyone before, although I think on some level I'm always aware of when it's coming."

"What do you feel when you hear yourself say that it's the anniversary of their death out loud?"

"It's actually a relief—and it's sad. I feel sad about it." Her words hung in the air. Her eyes and mouth turned down.

"Fran, I hear you feel both relief and sadness. Both are so important. Which experience should we be with first?" When two or more emotions are present, it's best to notice what emotion is front and center in the moment, and that is the one we should start with.

"I feel the sadness. It's like a weight in my chest but it also feels like a hole." As she focused on the physical sensation, I watched as her eyes filled with tears.

"Can you stay with this sadness and let whatever happens happen? I'll be here with you." She nodded. I had a spontaneous image of our hearts connected by a long cord. I remained quiet. The arc of her frown deepened and her lip quivered. Her eyes filled again with tears.

Fran covered her face with her hands and bent forward over

her lap as sobs convulsed her body. Her wave of grief finally broke free.

"Hmm. So good to let this sadness go," I said, wanting her to know she was not alone.

She poured out her grief, her body wracked with sorrow. I explained, as she cried, that this grief was a form of her love and connection to her parents.

"That's it. . . . Don't hold it back. Let it come," I whispered.

As her crying subsided, Fran straightened up. She looked at me. I looked right back at her, showing as best as I could the love and caring I felt for her in that moment. She took a couple of deep breaths. A twinge of pain crossed her face, which I sensed ushered in a new wave of grief.

"There is more," I said. "It's okay. Let it come."

And with that she began to cry again, covering her face but this time staying upright. In about two minutes, the wave was over. Fran once again looked into my eyes, making sure I was still there, still nonjudgmental. I was. The feeling in the room lightened.

Fran took a deep breath, gazed upward, and exhaled slowly. She refocused her eyes on me, and we sat in silence for another moment. She let go of another, bigger exhale. Finally, she said, "I feel better." I smiled. "I feel like a huge weight has lifted," she said.

"Tell me," I said. "What's it like?"

In the moments that followed, Fran tapped into the innate biological healing process that occurs after we experience a full wave of core emotion. Fran accessed this healing process by staying attuned to her physical sensations and allowing them to flow till they naturally stopped. What follows universally after a deep release of core emotion is gold. Fran and I were going mining.

"Wow! That was intense but I feel okay now, lighter."

"Can you stay with this 'lighter' experience and get to know it?" I sat back relaxed in my chair to let her know she shouldn't rush. I wanted her to give herself lots of time to notice all the subtleties of her experience.

She reported, "I realize I have needed to do this for so long. I always knew it but I also didn't know it."

"And what does that realization feel like inside?" I asked.

"It's like a surprise. Like I can't believe I finally let it out and I feel good. I feel lighter and like I can breathe."

I was proud of what this woman had courageously done and asked her again to peel back another layer of self-knowing. "What does it feel like in your body? This is so important."

Slowly and calmly she replied, "I feel light. I feel calm. I feel tired. But there is something else. I feel a little shakiness and, like, tingly in the back of my neck going up to my head."

When two people slow down and exist together, there is so much physical and mental activity we can observe. People have all sorts of meaningful physical sensations that we never pay attention to because we are too busy moving and thinking to notice. These sensations, however, mark change.[4] Slowing down sets the stage for change and transformation because these sensations can be allowed to flow. Whirrs, whirls, vibrations, tingles, and streaming sensations are common physical manifestations of core emotional processing and healing. Fran was experiencing healing emotions![5] They usher us into the openhearted state where we have access to our C's: calm, curious, connected, compassionate, confident, courageous, and clear.

"Can we stay with these tingles together?" I said, hoping she would feel safe to explore these new and strange sensations. I wanted her to lean in to them and follow them.

Fran focused inward. After about thirty seconds she said that they were subsiding. I asked her to notice what was left in their wake. "I feel calm," she said.

"Let's stay with calm. What is it like? I'm not looking for anything in particular, but let's notice all we can. . . ."

Ninety percent of the time, when I ask, "What's it like?" or "What else do you notice?" my patients will notice more emotions, more sensations, leading to more insight. The more we notice, the more we get to know the nuances of our emotional experiences and the more confidence we gain to repeat the process on our own. Wellness is a by-product of our ability to tolerate our internal experiences.

Fran was quiet. She was paying deliberate attention to her internal experience. She looked up at me, again tearful, but these were very different tears. Her face was peaceful and soft. "Thank you," she murmured with tenderness.

"Tell me about the 'thank you,' Fran."

Gratitude is a healing emotion. Like all emotions, it is very helpful to know what it feels like and to feel it deeply. It connects people in a very positive way. It may seem strange that I would encourage her to express gratitude toward me, but each emotion was an opportunity for Fran to experience and get to know it. Then, when she felt that emotion in the future, she would recognize it more easily.

"No one has ever been with me the way you have. I feel safe and I feel cared for. Thank you so much."

"I'm very touched by you, Fran," I shared. Then I asked her, "Can we put a word to the emotion you feel?"

She thought for a moment. "I feel grateful."

"Can we stay with gratitude a little longer? You have worked so hard today, and I am sure you are tired, and this, too, is so important. I am really asking if you have had enough for today, so feel free to tell me."

"We can stay here. I'm okay."

"Great. So, what does gratitude feel like physically? Scan your body from head to toe and let's just notice everything you can."

She checked in again. "I feel calm. (Pause) I feel warm here (she pointed to her heart). I feel grounded like I am taller and sitting up straighter."

"Great noticing," I affirmed. "Just stay with all this sensation for a moment . . . really get to know it. . . . This is the gold you've worked so hard for."

After a little while, she looked up at me and shared more of her emerging insights. "After my parents died I went underground. I acted like I was the same, but I wasn't. I realize I have been protecting myself from being hurt again for all these years. I

FRAN'S TRIANGLE AT THE END OF THE SESSION AND SHOWING HER MOVEMENT FROM DEFENSES TO OPENHEARTED STATE

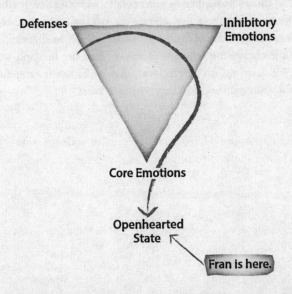

Defenses ——— Inhibitory Emotions

Core Emotions

Openhearted State

Fran is here.

Fran's defenses were lowered and her anxiety was calmed, so she was able to fully experience the grief that had been stuck in her nervous system. Fully experiencing her grief allowed her to enter the openhearted state. In the openhearted state, Fran felt calm and spontaneously gained insight into how her trauma had affected her.

have been terrified that anyone I love will die. Life has risks, but you have to take risks to live." She took a deep long sigh.

"Wow! I'm in awe of you! And that sigh you just made, if you tune in to that big sigh, what is it telling us?"

"I can breathe. And I'm okay," Fran assured us both.

Fran was in the openhearted state of her authentic Self.

In the months following this breakthrough session, Fran began dating. For the first time in her life, she wanted to fall in love and have an intimate relationship. She used our sessions to talk about the multitude of feelings that were triggered by dating, including her biggest fear: falling in love with someone only to have him die.

Bad things do happen to good people, as Fran knew firsthand, but we worked to help her tolerate the risks of loving and living openheartedly. I helped her get to know her fear intimately. Over time she obtained a reflective distance from her fear and worry. Fran was learning, on a deep level, that while loss is exceedingly painful, she could and had survived such pain.

You Can Change at Any Age: Neuroscience and Neuroplasticity

Psychotherapy works by going deep into the brain and its neurons and changing their structure by turning on the right genes. Psychiatrist Dr. Susan Vaughan has argued that the talking cure works by "talking to neurons," and that an effective psychotherapist or psychoanalyst is a "microsurgeon of the mind" who helps patients make needed alterations in neuronal networks.

—Norman Doidge

WHEN FRAN BEGAN treatment she was totally blocked off from her emotions. Her ability to connect intimately with others was hampered. At the end of treatment, she was transformed. None of this would have been possible if brain cells did not move and grow. In fact, all of psychotherapy is predicated on the fact that cells in the brain, called *neurons,* have the capacity to move and form new connections with one another in predictable ways under controlled conditions. Without brain cell reorganization, learning and brain change would be impossible.

When the brain is exposed to new information through experiences, brain cells fire and make new connections. For example, in grade school I learned that 2 + 2 = 4. The brain cells involved in that learning arrange in such a way that when I see 2 + 2 again, I can easily compute that it equals 4. If learning like this did not happen, each time I was asked to compute 2 + 2, it would feel like I was learning it for the first time.

Our bodies can learn as well as our minds. When we play sports or learn a musical instrument, our brain tells our muscles to move our bodies in specific ways. The movements of the muscles in our bodies become honed to perform better. It's a feedback loop from the brain to the muscles in our body and back to the brain again.

The more we practice, the more efficient our brain cell associations become, which allows our muscles to perform more quickly and with greater precision. Conversely, if we stop practicing for many days, we can lose the gains we made the week before.

Emotional learning happens similarly. When it comes to learning, the general rule is that brain cells that fire together, wire together.[1] When we have an experience, information comes to our brain through one or more of the five senses—seeing, hearing, smelling, tasting, and touching—stimulating brain cells. Those stimulated brain cells start firing and join up. Different elements of that experience will wire together to form a memory. Ever hear a song that takes you right back to a specific place and time? The song we heard is linked to whatever image we saw.

All of us can be transported by our memories. A visit to our old neighborhood, a disagreement with someone in our family, hearing an old song, being kept waiting, somebody leaving on a trip, getting the flu—anything can bring us back to a childhood state. In those moments, we are living some blend of the past with the present from a neuroscience perspective, because old and new brain cell networks are simultaneously activated.

We all have many experiences every day, but the lasting memories that shape us tend to have a large emotional component. Emotions signal to the brain that something integral to survival is happening, and so the brain files it away for later reference. The stronger the emotion evoked by each experience, the stronger the connection between those associated brain cells. The more frequent the experience, the stronger the associations. The less time between similar experiences, the stronger the associations. Patterns established in childhood repeat and become reinforced. That is the reason why the past affects us so much and why it takes longer to change the feelings and beliefs we acquired in childhood: childhood experiences—reinforced over years of life—form very strong brain cell networks.

When a patient of mine has an intense reaction to something, I suspect it might be linked to an earlier experience. When I ask my patients to think back to the first time they had a similar feeling, they often land in childhood. Childhood experiences tend to stick. Brains are programmed to remember painful or dangerous events so we avoid them in the future. From an evolutionary perspective, that aids in survival, and it also explains why we learn and remember deeply as children.

We Cannot Change the Past, but We Can Change How We Feel About the Past

Every important memory has four components.[2] They are

1. the **emotion** we feel
2. the physical **sensations** evoked in our bodies
3. the **images** or pictures we see in our mind's eye that capture the memory
4. the **belief** about ourselves that the experience left: a conviction created about our core sense of ourselves

When Fran found out her parents were dead, her mind made a snapshot. The emotions she felt were grief (an extreme form of the core emotion sadness) and fear. The image she saw was herself alone and sad. The physical sensations were the sense of the floor dropping out from underneath her. The beliefs instilled at that time (what she consciously or unconsciously learned) were *I am alone in the world* and *People I need will leave me.* These kinds of learned beliefs shape our future interactions.

When neural networks that were formed in childhood are associated with current experiences, we are vulnerable to experiencing those past memories again with the same intense feelings. When Fran witnessed a dog that was hit by a bicycle, it triggered neural networks associated with the past trauma of when her parents were hit by another vehicle. A bike doesn't equal a car. But to Fran's brain, it was similar enough that the two experiences paired.

What Is the Difference Between a Memory and a Traumatic Memory?

When we think of a memory, it is clear that the event is in the past. When we recall a traumatic memory, the past and the present become harder to tell apart. A traumatic memory can make us feel like that event is happening all over again, causing us to feel the same emotions and bodily sensations, see the same images, and hold the same beliefs about our Self. Our goal is to turn traumatic memories into ordinary memories. We don't want to be triggered to feel emotions or physical sensations, see images (flashbacks), or hold upsetting beliefs about our Self that stem from trauma.

My patient Mary was traumatized by her father's enraged reactions whenever she broke something like a dish. Mary, now thirty-six years old and in a relationship with a kind man who would never yell at her, still reacted to accidents like she did with her father. Mary knew her fearful reaction was "crazy," but she could not stop it. A dish breaking transported her back in time, through the associated brain cells to the traumatic memory from age seven. The twenty-nine-year-old neural network still lit up and led to her unconscious expectation that she was about to ignite her father's (or her partner's) anger.

The four components of Mary's experience were

1. **emotion:** fear
2. **sensation:** trembling throughout her upper body and arms
3. **image:** her father's wide eyes and bulging facial veins
4. **belief:** "I am not safe."

Most of us experience strong reactions in response to the following emotionally fraught events: when loved ones leave, when we make a mistake, when we lose something, when we receive criticism, or when we need to ask for help. These experiences shape us, especially in childhood, when we lack rational coping skills to understand context or the emotional state of our caregivers and are unable to soothe ourselves. Each of these experiences typically evokes strong reactions and emotions. In the present, these old networks can often be triggered. This can cause an outsized reaction to the current situation as we forget the skills we have as adults to cope, solve problems, and talk with the people in our life about our feelings.

Some people suffered regularly in their childhood because of parents' personality traits or family circumstances. Common traumatic lessons or debilitating beliefs typically learned in childhood include: *I can't count on someone to comfort me; I will be hurt; No one cares about me; My feelings don't matter; I am not safe; I am bad; I am ugly; I am disgusting; I am stupid;* and *I am alone.*

When my sister got married, she agreed to spend every Thanksgiving with her in-laws. Up until then, I had spent every Thanksgiving since birth with her. Thanksgiving meant a great deal to me. After her marriage, each year when Thanksgiving came around and she talked about heading down to Memphis, I had the same "poor me" feeling tinged with anger, jealousy, and sadness. I believed in that moment that my feelings didn't matter. I would overreact. The hurt part of me wanted her to feel guilty for leaving me on Thanksgiving. I could hear how the tone in my voice changed so she would know I was upset. Inside I was having a mini-tantrum. I did not want to behave that way. I love my sister and I wanted her to be happy. I just couldn't get over my own hurt.

It became clear to me that in those moments I felt like I was six years old again. I could visualize the young me alone in my pretty nightgown. It's not like I could even correlate the experience of my sister "abandoning" me with any other specific memory of abandonment at age six. It was just a feeling I had. Once I figured this all out, I could give the part of me that was six years old compassion and understanding by imagining I was hugging and giving her comfort. When I did comfort my younger Self, I felt relief. I no longer had the same mood shift despite the fact that my sister continued to spend Thanksgivings with her husband and away from me. That's an example of networks communicating (the six-year-old me and the adult me), the brain reorganizing/integrating, and brain change resulting.

That's why psychotherapists are always harping on the past. It's because our childhood experiences are so powerful, especially those loaded with negative emotions. Childhood neural networks are strong and tight. But we can change the way we react by liberating the stuck emotions—like Fran's grief or Mary's fear about breaking things—and reorganizing our neural networks. Conversely, if we never address our blocked emotions, our traumatized neural networks stay entrenched.

How are the four components—emotion, physical sensation, image, and belief—important to brain change? Ideally, we want to minimize old unhelpful emotional responses that we had as children to minimize suffering in the present. We can use the Change Triangle to liberate buried emotions from past memories and transform the components of that traumatic memory network.

To change the brain, we have to create a new path, or new neural network, within it. Imagine you are hacking your way through thick brush, exploring the jungle for water when you come across a creek about fifty feet from the cabin where you live. Since the creek is the closest place you have found for drinking water, you begin to visit it every day, several times a day in fact. In time, a smooth brush-free path is carved out, which makes it easy to access. You take this same path every day for a year and pretty soon it is a clear road requiring no work at all to traverse.

Each time we want to change a previously habitual reaction in the brain, we once again have to grab our machete and hack our way through the brush. Then we take this same path repeatedly until a new clear road is carved, which again takes weeks, months, or years depending on how diligently we stay on the new path.

Fran and I created a new unencumbered road to experiencing her sadness without the anxiety that used to take her away from her grief. The process that we repeated again and again looked like this: When grief came up, she stayed with it. She turned her undivided attention to the physical and emotional experience of sadness. As soon as she noticed anxiety, such as muscular tension or an increase in heart rate, we stopped what we were doing and used techniques that calmed her anxiety. Grief *dysregulated* Fran's nervous system because grief and anxiety were intertwined. Imagine two pipe cleaners wrapping around each other. One is anxiety and one is grief. We needed to help Fran untwist those pipe cleaners in her brain so her sadness was free to be expressed unencumbered by anxiety. Once we lowered the anxiety that arose, we switched back to sadness to make room for it to come up. Each time we did this, we were teaching her nervous system to further tolerate the experience of sadness and separate it from anxiety.

Fran did this again and again: staying with her sadness, calming any anxiety, staying with sadness, calming anxiety. Over time her body relearned that sadness was not equivalent to danger. In the session where she had the breakthrough, all the prior work we had done paid off and Fran stayed regulated as her grief came up and out. Her brain changed. Fran's body went from being dysregulated by sadness to being *regulated.* She could experience sadness and stay calm. The Change Triangle was the guide for that work.

My patient Harry experienced a great deal of rejection from his parents, who were preoccupied with their own lives. Harry formed a neural network in childhood around rejection. When he started dating as a teenager, rejection from a girl would send him reeling into a dark mood where he was consumed by negative thoughts of *I'm not good enough,* and *I'm a loser,* and *I'll never find a girlfriend.* His teenage dating experiences were connected with his childhood experiences with his parents. As Harry grew up, these same feelings were triggered anytime he asked a woman on a date.

Now thirty years old, Harry met a woman at a party and he asked for her number. She explained she had just ended a serious

How to Tell If You Are Dysregulated

"Dysregulation" is a great word to describe being upset because it reminds us that "upset" is a biological state. We know we are out of whack because we feel it. When we are upset/dysregulated, our nervous system is not running smoothly. We are not calm. We are not in the openhearted state. Our body's physics, chemistry, and biology have been compromised. Some people who suffered a great deal of trauma never know what it is like to be regulated. They are never calm. Instead their bodies and minds are on constant alert for danger.

relationship and was not ready to date yet but would like, in a few months, to get together for coffee. Harry experienced this moment as another rejection even though her response had nothing to do with him. The decision to decline his immediate request was based on her life. To help Harry, we needed to rewire his rejection brain cell network. Then he could feel and act appropriately to the current context.

The Change Triangle is an effective way to alter brain cell networks by working with the emotional components of a traumatic experience. Releasing stuck emotional energy causes neural networks to rewire and allows our past wounds to heal. The resulting new neural networks are updated to suit our current life so we can stop responding to things as we did in the past.

Experiment: Slowing Down

WE CANNOT BEGIN to notice our emotions and body state, let alone work with them through the Change Triangle, without first slowing down. Slowing down leads to relaxation—if not at first, then with some practice.

Belly Breathing

Deep belly breathing[1] is a skill I teach everyone I work with. It is one of the greatest calming tools we have. When you first start experimenting with slowing down, you will become aware of things happening inside you. It is important to keep breathing when experiencing something new or uncomfortable.

Belly breathing actually stimulates a major nerve in the body called the *vagus nerve*. When stimulated, it sends a message to the heart and lungs to slow down, and this is a powerful and reliable way to calm and soothe anxiety. Here is how to do it:

Inhale slowly and deeply through your nostrils, breathing into what feels like the bottom of your belly. Feel your belly come out. You should strive to look like a Buddha—belly out as far as possible. It helps to place your hand on your belly to make sure it is

THE VAGUS NERVE

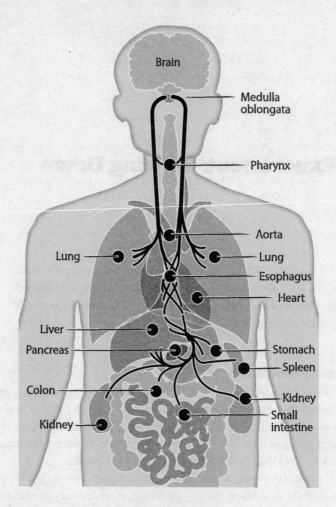

expanding as you inhale. This actually takes practice over weeks. Most of us breathe into our chest, technically the top of our lungs. We are trying to retrain how we breathe from chest breathing to belly breathing.

When you've inhaled fully, hold your breath for a beat.[2] Now exhale fully through pursed lips, as if you are blowing on a hot spoonful of soup. Pursed lips help you control the airflow out so you can create maximum relaxation. Tune in to your body as you exhale so you tailor the speed to what feels most relaxing inside. Your exhale should take approximately twice as long as your inhale. As you exhale, imagine your entire body going loose and limp. Repeat this five times.

Can you name two things you notice after practicing belly breathing? Just check in to your internal world and notice any shifts, however tiny or nuanced, in your emotional state or in how your body feels. Try to put words on any change you notice. (Use the emotion and sensation word lists at the end of this book to help you put language on your experience.) Most of all, remember that there are no wrong answers. These experiments are about noticing and naming your unique emotional and physical responses, in this case to breathing.

1. _____

2. _____

Learning and using proper breathing techniques is one of the most beneficial things that can be done for both short- and long-term physical and emotional health. Belly breathing helps to relax the nervous system, reduces stress and tension, lowers blood pressure, and calms the mind. Practicing belly breathing also massages and tones the internal organs, particularly the digestive system.

Getting back to proper breathing isn't hard but it does take practice. I recommend setting a reminder to practice deep belly breathing at least twice a day. You can do it as you are waking and going to sleep. You might find it helps you fall asleep at night.

Use this breathing anytime you notice anxiety and when experiencing core emotions. Breathe nice, long, deep belly breaths as the wave of emotion peaks and then ultimately calms and releases.

Consciously Looking Out

You need just two minutes to practice consciously looking out. Set aside quiet time at home for practice. Or you can do it when you're stuck in traffic, waiting on line at the grocery store, or walking to your car. Noticing what you see, hear, and smell helps bring you into the present moment. Slowing down and being in the present moment will also help you tremendously when you are trying to name feelings, emotions, and sensations that you encounter when working the Change Triangle.

Look out into the world. Notice colors and name three you see right now:

1. _____
2. _____
3. _____

Notice textures in your environment. Name three textures you see right now:

1. _____
2. _____
3. _____

Notice sounds around you. Name three sounds you hear right now:

1. _____
2. _____
3. _____

What was this like for you? Check in with your internal world and notice any shifts, however tiny or nuanced, in your emotional state or in how your body feels. Can you name two things that you notice now about how your state has shifted from doing this experiment? Try to find words for any change that you notice and write them down below:

_____

_____

These experiments are designed to bring you more into the present moment. You might feel more awake. You might feel more unsettled. You might feel more connected to the present. You might notice that nothing has shifted at all. Whatever you notice is fine. This is a practice in observation that has no right answers. The only goal is simply to notice the nuances of our internal reactions and try to find words that best fit our experience. You can use the emotion and sensation word lists at the back of this book to help you find language to describe what you notice.

If any of these experiments cause you to feel too unsettled or uncomfortable, take a break. Breathe in a way that is calming for you. Or try the following experiment in grounding, which is often calming.

Grounding

Standing or sitting, plant your feet on the floor. Sense the floor against the bottom of your feet. Keep feeling the floor underneath you for about thirty seconds. It's that simple.

Can you name two things you notice internally when you stand or sit quietly, turning all your attention to the soles of your feet? Just check in with your internal world and notice any shifts, however tiny or nuanced, in your emotional state or in how your body feels. Try to put words on any change you notice.

1. _____

2. _____

Now, combine grounding with breathing. Notice your feet on the floor as you take four or five deep belly breaths. Notice as you breathe in as much air as possible for one, two, three, four, or more seconds. Hold for a beat. Now exhale slowly through pursed lips (like you're blowing on hot soup) all the way to the end of the breath, maybe for eight to twelve seconds. Take your time.

Again turn your attention to the soles of your feet. Feel the ground underneath you. What do you notice now?

Can you notice two additional changes in your internal state? Just scan your entire body from head to toe and notice any shifts, however tiny or nuanced, in your emotional state or in how your body feels. Try to put words on any changes you notice.

1. _____

2. _____

Each time you slow down and notice your external or internal world, you are creating and promoting positive brain change. You're taking care of yourself. Whatever you experience during any of these exercises, you'll soon be able to map them on the Change Triangle, which will tell you what you need in order to feel better.

Imagining a Peaceful Place

Once you've created it, a peaceful place is yours to use whenever you want. You can go to your peaceful place when you need a break from stressful experiences. If you are working with the Change Triangle and your anxiety rises, take a break and imagine your peaceful place. If you are working with a part of you that holds guilt or shame and you start to feel too uncomfortable, go to your peaceful place. You can do this at work or in your relationships when you get upset about something and want to calm down. Add your peaceful place to your toolbox of existing calming strategies.

Slow down again by being still, feeling your feet on the floor, and taking four or five deep belly breaths.

Now, think of any place, real or imagined, where you feel peaceful and calm. It could be the beach, the mountains, your bed, or a place from a movie or book. Try imagining a few different settings that bring up peace and calm for you. Really take your time. Find the image that relaxes you the most and imagine you are there. You can add people, pets, and things you love, doors and locks to keep out others who upset you, or anything you want to enhance the peacefulness of this fantasy.

If you have trouble with visual fantasy, imagine a song that relaxes you or brings you back to a happy time. You can even imagine a comforting smell like your grandmother's cooking or a loved one's perfume.

Notice how you feel inside when you imagine experiencing your peaceful place, sound, or smell.

Can you put a few words on this experience?

1. _____
2. _____
3. _____

Mental Blocks When Imagining a Peaceful Place

If you sense you are blocked from imagining a peaceful place, it's okay. It happens. We all get blocked at times. Don't judge.

If you are willing to stick with this and experiment a little bit more, see if you can imagine what you would need to overcome the block to finding a peaceful place. The beauty of fantasy is that we are not limited by the confines of reality. You can imagine anything you want; the sky is the limit. For example, let's say you feel guilty imagining yourself in a peaceful place because someone you love is suffering illness or struggling and you feel you can't be peaceful if others are not. You can imagine a judge or God who grants you temporary permission. Or perhaps you cannot stop your mind from ruminating on your problems. Maybe you can imagine putting all those problems in a box for a minute or two. Then see if that helps you imagine a peaceful place. If you find it impossible, just notice that without judgment. You can still remain curious and open to how your experience shifts with practice.

3
Identifying Trauma

Sara's Depression and Navigating Conflict

> People disconnect from their emotional experience, afraid of
> being overwhelmed, humiliated, or revealed as inadequate by the
> force of feelings, only to pay the price later in depression,
> isolation, and anxiety.
>
> —Diana Fosha

MY RELATIONSHIPS WITH patients run parallel to their relationships in the outside world. In fact, I encourage my patients to use
our relationship as a template to help them understand how they
feel about and connect with others. In a session, we can safely experiment with new and more satisfying ways of relating. Most of
us have difficulty dealing with conflict, but there are many skills
we can learn that make interpersonal conflict immeasurably easier
to navigate.

We handle conflict with others in many ways. We tell adver-
saries that we are pissed off, avoid the issue, stew and plot revenge,
shove our angry feelings down and get depressed, or worry our
needs are more than our partners can handle, or vice versa. Many
of us have trouble asking for what we want or need when those

things are in opposition to what our friends, family, or partners desire. These are difficult dilemmas for all of us. The good news is that once we take care of the underlying feelings that hinder us from accepting our truth, sharing it, and advocating for our well-being, everything gets easier.

Sara and I had been working together for five years and we'd come to know each other very well. The scars and wounds from years of emotional abuse left her suffering from depression and anxiety. Getting through the day took most of the energy she had, leaving little energy to avail herself of the simple pleasures in life like engaging with friends.

From the time she was a toddler and could say, "No!" Sara was yelled at nonstop. If Sara didn't like a particular meal her mom made, her mother yelled. If Sara was sick, her mom would yell. If she looked at her mother with the "wrong" expression, her mom would yell at her. In fact, Sara was often interrogated for hours over a particular expression. "What were you thinking?" Sara's mother would ask. "Why would you do that? Do you hate me?" Sara would cower in the corner, praying that her mother would run out of steam and the tirade would end. As Sara grew older, her mind became vigilantly obsessive about what she could do to prevent her mother's rages and how she could stop them once they started. Her brain's ultimate solution was to shut down all of her own thoughts and feelings and mirror her mother's in an effort to please her and maintain maternal connection.

This continued throughout her childhood. Sara's father was loving but largely absent. When he witnessed the tirades, he was powerless to help. Because to survive she had to block her core emotions, Sara developed symptoms, including anxiety, obsessiveness, perfectionism, cutting, head banging, low self-esteem, and depression.

Sara was thirty years old when I first met her. My heart broke for what she had endured. Helping her feel safe and secure with me would create the foundation from which all emotion and trauma work would stem. During the first year we worked together, her nervous system was on such high alert that she walked on eggshells with me. She was terrified that she would displease me in the same way she had been terrified of displeasing her mother. If I had an expression she couldn't read, she assumed displeasure and felt rejection. She would withdraw into wordless panic. She would fold—collapsing her head over her knees and closing her eyes—and shut down right in front of me. Biologically she was exhibiting part of the fight, flight, or freeze system that we all have.

As she thawed from her freezes and could once again communicate, Sara told me she felt both a desperate need for me to comfort her and a mortal fear of my anger right before she shut down. Needless to say, therapy wasn't easy for Sara, but she was deeply committed to getting well. Over time, we built up a trust. I was predictable and calm, which was helping her brain entertain the possibility that she was safe with me. Our work deepened.

SARA'S TRIANGLE AT THE BEGINNING OF TREATMENT

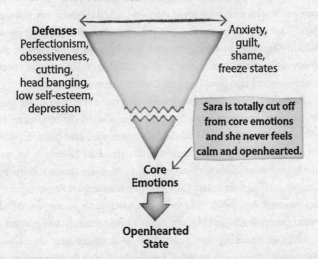

Defenses
Perfectionism,
obsessiveness,
cutting,
head banging,
low self-esteem,
depression

Anxiety,
guilt,
shame,
freeze states

Sara is totally cut off
from core emotions
and she never feels
calm and openhearted.

Core
Emotions

Openhearted
State

When I first met Sara, she fluctuated between defenses and high states of anxiety. She had no access to her core emotional experience and was always dysregulated; she was never calm, confident, or any of the other C's.

Our second year of work was spent getting to know and working on the many traumatized parts in Sara's mind. All of us have many parts. It is helpful to get to know those parts as though they were separate people with their own beliefs and feelings. Understanding that we are made up of many parts helps us understand our conflicts and why our feelings can be complicated and inconsistent. Once we see our minds as a blend of past and present, child and adult parts, our mind's mysterious ways become easier to understand.

When Sara was upset, I encouraged her to speak from her upset part. Sara would often say, "I feel two years old," "I feel five years old," or "I feel like a teenager." Each of these was a different part. We got to know and care for the many young parts that inhabited Sara's mind.

During the third and fourth years of treatment, we worked on self-care and self-compassion—concepts she struggled with from the beginning. For Sara, to offer herself compassion and care—or, as I like to say, to become her own good mother—meant she had to relinquish the fantasy of someone else rescuing her. Sara did not want to be the one who gave care or compassion to her younger parts. Her young parts wanted me, not her, she repeatedly explained. But only by being her own good parent would she be able to develop self-reliance. She would be able to calm and soothe herself around the clock, not just when she was with me.

Because Sara had difficulty with care and compassion, we cared for her younger parts together until she was ready to assume the role herself. It seems natural that a person who had been deprived would easily accept compassion and care. But people who were mistreated have difficulty accepting care, even though they also long for it. They feel that they can't risk being let down again. If Sara opened her heart and let down her guard, she feared she would be crushed, and the anticipated devastation was too great. In addition, getting the protection and safety one has always longed for evokes a deep grief for the Self who endured so much neglect. Accepting compassion is often a painful and fraught process.

By our fifth year of treatment, my attachment with Sara was quite secure. She had identified her younger, traumatized parts and was comfortable communicating with them. Also, Sara developed a capacity to assert her position. She could be direct with me about what she did and didn't want to talk about. She didn't fear my anger as much. She even provoked some conflicts by standing her ground. She consented to try medicine for her obsessive and intrusive thoughts, something she had been reluctant to do before. This was an improvement because it showed her growing desire to feel better and that she was developing a belief that she *deserved* to feel better.

We had traveled around Sara's Triangles hundreds of times with the goal of increasing her capacity to stay present, diminishing toxic feelings of shame and anxiety, and making room for her core anger, sadness, and fear. We met one day on the eve of my vacation, after she had missed a session the day before. Sara missing sessions had been a common occurrence for her in the previous months.

I welcomed her in, and she greeted me with a big smile.

"I'm sorry about yesterday. Are you getting annoyed with me for missing sessions?" she asked nervously, her hand rising up to stroke her hair in an act of unconscious self-soothing.

We were seeing each other twice a week. Sara often missed the early morning appointment because she couldn't, or did not want to, get out of bed. Yet she liked having the option of coming in if she wanted or needed to.

"Well, I'm not annoyed," I reassured her, "but I have been thinking about it and I do want to talk about the sessions." My discomfort about her paying for two sessions and only coming for one was mounting.

I noticed Sara biting her lower lip; her breathing became shallow and noticeably labored. She began shifting her body around on the sofa. I didn't want Sara to leave upset. If she did, I worried I would feel guilty during my vacation and be concerned about her. I didn't want her to have to wait two weeks till I returned to get some peace of mind. However, since Sara had brought it up, I went with it, trusting that we had built up enough of a secure relationship to get through the talk.

"I know you like having two sessions, but on the other hand, you only come once a week these days." I stammered as I spoke, careful to say the right thing in the right way to avoid evoking more anxiety.

She laughed a nervous laugh and smiled. With a high-pitched voice, she said, "I know." The grimace on her face showed me her pain.

"You might not want to pay for twice a week," I said. "So maybe when I get back we can talk about the whole thing and figure out what's best."

"But if I decide I still want to keep the two sessions per week, is that okay?" I knew this was hard for her because she still held a deep fear, albeit a diminished one, that I would one day reject her, like her mother had repeatedly.

"Yes, you can keep two sessions a week. I just want to get curious with you to understand why you don't come if you want the second session. And just to be absolutely clear, I am not annoyed. I just want to do what's right for you and explore what it means to pay for something you don't use. It's an opportunity to learn more about you."

"Okay, that sounds good," Sara said.

"Also, I'm going to raise your fee in September since it has been a couple of years and that might affect whether you want two sessions a week or not," I added, thinking I might as well give her all the news now so we didn't have to have two hard discussions.

She asked me about the new fee and I explained it was a function of a few things: how many times per week we met and how long the sessions lasted. We currently had a fifty-five-minute session, but since I started working with Sara, I had phased out fifty-five-minute sessions. Sessions were either forty-five minutes or sixty minutes, depending on what each patient needed.

"I definitely like fifty-five minutes," she told me. I was proud she asserted herself.

SARA'S TRIANGLE WHEN SHE ASSERTED HER NEEDS AND WANTS

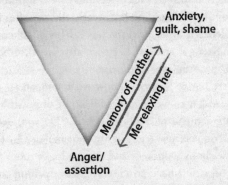

Anxiety,
guilt, shame

Memory of mother

Me relaxing her

Anger/
assertion

Sara now had access to anger and could assert her wishes, but doing so often triggered anxiety, thrusting her back up the Change Triangle to the inhibitory corner.

Asserting one's needs is adaptive to living. For Sara, assertion triggered a slew of old memories of her mother getting angry when she had any needs at all. Old memory networks fired up and brought on those same feelings she had when she was little. The guilt, anxiety, and shame backlash from asserting her desire to keep the fifty-five-minute session thrust her back to the inhibitory corner of the Change Triangle.

Helping Sara meant moving her back down the Triangle from states of shame, guilt, and anxiety to the core emotions that lay below. Knowing and validating her core emotions would tell her what she needed and wanted.

"Good to know," I said. "The point of collaborating is because it feels better: more connected and less alone. Two heads are better than one. I think it is worth it to tolerate the feelings that talking about this brings up. Out in the world with other people, you'll want to be able to talk through problems. This is good practice. I'm confident we can do this!" Assurance and affirmation are two great interpersonal ways to increase comfort and safety and to lower anxiety. "Can you share what talking about this brings up inside you right now—just to validate the emotions that are coming up?"

I sensed she had a lot of feelings by the scared look on her face, the way she was holding her breath, the way she closed her eyes to avoid looking at me, and the way her body looked stiff and frozen. When Sara got anxious, her normally pale skin became gray.

"Ummmm," she said nervously.

I try not to assume I know what someone is feeling, so I encouraged her to welcome a wide range of possible experiences by offering a menu of likely reactions. "Do you feel small, are you scared, do you notice anger, are you anxious? Just tune in to your body without judgment and make a lot of room for all your feelings, because I have no idea what's happening to you. I want to know so I can help."

She paused for maybe fifteen seconds. "I don't know. It's a lot. A lot of jumbled stuff."

"It is a lot," I affirmed. "And it may help if we just take a deep breath and slow . . . way . . . down together and feel the connection between us. Can you let yourself stay close and connected to me while we do this together?"

"Okay," she said tentatively.

"It might feel better if we just validate each emotion you notice; we don't have to go into it. Just validate what you're experiencing."

"I guess I am a little upset and maybe a bit angry."

"Great! I'm so glad that you let me know. I hear you're upset and maybe a bit angry. Anything else you want to share?"

Typically, she would withdraw into miserable states of anxiety and shame, then need to recover for several minutes before naming her emotions. She was handling this stress in a new way, bouncing back to connect with me and herself much more quickly, and I was thrilled for her.

"Maybe confused," she said.

"Can you put aside the confusion for a moment and really validate and honor what you are actually feeling?[1] Try to speak from that place of anger or upset, and remember that I am not your mother, I am Hilary, and we have a whole history together of working things out in a way that you always say feels good afterward. Remember? Your anger doesn't scare me or threaten me. I like it when you tell me what you're feeling so I don't have to guess, and then we can talk about it to make things better. Sara, can you let your anger speak? Tell me, 'I am angry because . . .'"

She looked up with a little smile on her face. "Oh, I don't know," said Sara.

"You have every right to your feelings."

"But I really don't know why I'm angry," she said. Sara typically wanted to understand why she was feeling something. Asking why we feel something is not so useful. Instead, I teach people that *feelings just are.* The better approach is to radically accept the emotion we notice and to learn through experiencing it what the emotion is telling us: What evoked it, what does it feel like in the body, and what is the impulse?

To help her in that moment, I suggested that we focus on her body's sensations. The body is always the place to turn to for deep emotional knowing. I wanted to see what we could learn.

"What tells you inside that you have anger?" I asked.[2]

"I don't really feel very connected to you. Like I want to . . ." Her eyes closed and she flopped back against the cushions of my sofa, pinching her mouth closed, which altered her breathing and stopped the flow of her emotions. Sara was fighting to stay present and not get swallowed up in bad feelings. Her confession of anger triggered her anxiety again.

"Sara, what do you want to do? What is the fantasy if you don't shove it down?" The more aware of and comfortable with our impulses we are, the less we will fear them and need to block them.

She winced. I said firmly but with kindness, "Stay with me, Sara! It's going to be okay."

She needed to experience over and over how expressing her anger made her feel better, not worse, so her brain could form new

SARA'S UNCONSCIOUS
CONFLICTS ABOUT ANGER

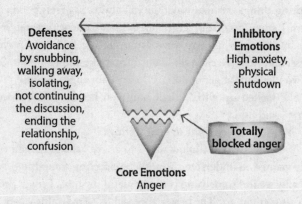

Defenses
Avoidance
by snubbing,
walking away,
isolating,
not continuing
the discussion,
ending the
relationship,
confusion

**Inhibitory
Emotions**
High anxiety,
physical
shutdown

**Totally
blocked anger**

Core Emotions
Anger

Sara inhibits her anger with fear/panic/anxiety/shame. She runs away
to stop these painful feelings. But it costs her the relationship as she
needs to avoid the other so those bad feelings don't resurface.

and healthier connections. She needed to get to the bottom of the
Change Triangle, but she was instead bouncing back and forth
between her defenses and anxiety.

I continued, "What does the anger want to do?" She was still
silent. "It's all okay. What does the anger want to do to me? Let's
do this for you!"

"It wants to snub you or something, like not talk to you."

"Great!" I said. She nodded with her eyes still closed, afraid to
see my reaction. Her unconscious brain was still confused as to
whether I would react to her with anger like her mother or with
kindness and compassion as I always did.

"If you didn't snub me, which is a way you avoid your anger,
what would the anger want to do or say to me right now? Let the
angry impulse come out at me in fantasy."

Knowing what our angry impulses want to do or say to the
people who hurt and angered us, and then using our imagination
to express our anger in a fantasy, is a prime way to release blocked
emotions and practice healthy ways to process anger.

She was struggling with what to share, so I said, "I know, even if you show me your anger, that you deeply care about me and need me not to abandon you. Even if you feel and show me your anger, I still want to stay connected to you. So let's honor this important anger together."

This helped bolster her confidence to share. "Okay. I guess maybe it wants to get up to leave."

She was trying, and I was proud of her. This, however, was another way her clever unconscious mind avoided dealing directly with her anger. Leaving was a defense against experiencing her anger.

"Yes! But leaving is a way to avoid the anger," I explained. "Leaving is a way *not* to deal with the anger."

Sara's anger felt so big inside. She was very young when her traumas began, so I imagined Sara's anger originating from a baby or very young child part of her. If you've ever seen an angry baby or child, you might recall the look of abject fury on their face and the full body contorting. To a baby or young child, anger feels huge and overwhelming, especially when they are left alone to cope.[3]

That's what Sara's anger felt like to her, which scared her. Sara felt her baby part's anger plus the anger that she'd been blocking from then on—the sensations and the energy felt overwhelming. So, as Sara wrestled with whether to trust that her anger wouldn't destroy either of us, her anxiety went up. The Change Triangle predicts this: *if you stop using protective mechanisms, you will feel more vulnerable and your anxiety will predictably rise.* Then, when nothing bad happens but instead you have a new and positive experience, the brain rewires with a new, more realistic program, especially if this happens over and over again.

When Sara's anxiety rose, I helped her calm it down with a variety of techniques from breathing to talking about TV. In general, anxiety calms by staying connected to someone safe and with whom we can be honest about our feelings.

"Don't forget to breathe," I said. "Can you let yourself feel your anger and see what it wants to do?"

"I guess maybe it would yell at you," she finally said.

How to Lower Anxiety During Conflict with Another Person

1. Take a break and promise to come back to finish the conversation after one or both people feel calmer and more connected again.

2. Practice deep belly breathing together.

3. Talk about something different and lighthearted.

4. Hug each other and remind yourself about the good times and that you'll get through this.

Ways to Work with Anxiety on Your Own

1. Get out of your head by turning all your attention to the soles of your feet. Feel the ground underneath them.

2. Practice your deep belly breathing.

3. Take a walk outside and observe the scenery. Name three colors, name three sounds, name three textures.

4. Remind yourself that you are anxious and therefore it is not a good time to draw conclusions about the future until you are calm.

5. Remind yourself that you are anxious and the feeling is temporary.

6. Focus on the anxious body sensations with compassion and curiosity—and without judgment—until they subside. Remember to breathe deeply as you focus.

7. Imagine a peaceful place or a time when you felt confident.

8. Imagine something soothing like beautiful music, or hot sun on your skin, or being hugged.

9. Do some exercise like jogging or yoga, or go to the gym.

Hallelujah, I shouted to myself, she got it! She stayed with me and expressed the impulse of her anger. This was such a major milestone for Sara's mental well-being.

"What would it want to yell? Imagine it with the full force that you feel. You can imagine it inside, or share it out loud with me, whatever feels better." I wanted Sara to become aware of what her anger (the raw emotion, not her rational self) wanted to do to me. It would help her get comfortable with her natural impulses. Talking about our impulses doesn't hurt people. Sharing what her anger wanted to do to me would not hurt me. Only acting thoughtlessly on impulses can cause harm.

"I guess it would say, 'I'm angry that you brought this up today because you're going away and . . .'" She stopped.

If you remember, Sara actually raised the topic by starting the session with, "I'm sorry about yesterday. Are you getting annoyed with me for missing sessions?" This is a great example of how internal parts of us don't necessarily communicate. We want to foster awareness and communication between our disparate parts so our brain can function optimally. I chose not to bring this to Sara's attention in that moment.

"Stay with me, Sara. You're doing great! What else? What else? This is good!" I said with a lot of energy and enthusiasm to support her anger. "You're pissed that I brought this up today because I'm going away," I repeated.

She was laughing now and had a big smile. This was transformation in process. Something that was toxic was now digestible and even fun.

"What else?" I asked.

"Ahhh, nothing," she said, looking down and to her right, a gesture I empathically felt as her embarrassment.

I waited for her to share more.

"I guess . . . I don't know. I mean the thing about raising the fee. . . . You know I usually get over it, but it is kind of a reminder that I pay you for this. And I am a little angry because the reminder is unpleasant."

"Yes. What else? You're doing great and I know this is hard.

And I'm so glad that you are telling me that it pisses you off." She nodded yes. "Is there more? I really want to give you the opportunity to honor all of your anger."

"That's probably it for anger. But I am also worried that you're telling me I should not come here anymore. You know, like, are you trying to get rid of me?" She struggled to get this out. I noticed her eyes were closed again and her breathing was labored and shallow. Each time she moved to talk about her concerns, I saw her fear.

"It sounds like you have a question for me. Can you be direct?" I wanted her to practice being direct, being assertive.

"Are you trying to wean me off coming at all?" she asked directly and boldly.

"Would you like me to answer it directly?" I asked permission so she could own her courage and desire to know my truth.

"Yes," Sara answered.

"I am definitely not weaning you off therapy," I reassured. "I love seeing you, Sara, and I have no desire to push you out whatsoever."

"Do you have desire to push me to one session?" It was great that she fired off another concern by asking a direct question without any prompting.

"No," I said. "However, I do have the desire to discuss your coming for one session and paying for two." She laughed and relaxed a bit.

"Okay, I think I can handle that." She smiled.

Often when "negative" feelings are processed, "good" feelings more easily shine through. She now saw me for who I was and she could infer my true intent. I was no longer her mother in that moment. The old lens was gone.

"Now I'm worried again," she said. Her hands covered her face as she leaned way back on the sofa.

Having touched the bottom of the triangle with core emotion, she jumped back to the anxiety corner of the Change Triangle. Sharing honestly triggered her old neural networks, so her anxiety rose again in response to the anticipated imagined backlash from her mother, the one living in her head.

I said, "Wait! Wait! What's happening? Don't go away. Everything is okay. What happened? Can we just rewind to right before you felt overwhelmed again and notice what happened?" I wanted her aware of all her heretofore-unconscious triggers. Once she was aware, her nervous system could relax by teaching her brain that the past was over and now she was safe.

I asked, "Do you notice how frightened you get by the thoughts and feelings that you want to share with me? Your thoughts and feelings don't threaten me as long as we can talk about them so I can clarify and share my thoughts and feelings. That's what healthy relationships look like."

Looking at me directly, our eyes locked. "You're so good," she told me.

"I'm just maybe not that bad," I said. My funny, self-deprecating tone elicited a laugh from her. She leaned over sideways and lay down on the sofa, her feet still touching the floor. She snuggled the pillow on my couch like she often did.

She alternated frequently between sitting up and looking alive, to slumping down almost in a fetal position, to snuggling a sofa pillow for security. Each time she recovered from the slump and sat up, she smiled and she looked brighter and calmer. For brief moments following the expression of core emotions, she was in that calm and peaceful openhearted state. Then something else would trigger her and she'd move back to anxiety or defense on the Change Triangle. But each time we circled up and down, her brain was firing and wiring, making new updated connections.

Sara often thought I was the only person in the world who had the capacity to understand her or treat her kindly. I would remind her there were millions of kind and understanding people in the world to befriend. But she had to take the time and expend the energy to get to know potential friends to find out if they were kind and understanding. If she met someone who was mean to her, she never had to see him or her again. Many people, especially those who don't feel entitled to set boundaries, forget they have the power to say no to things that are bad for them.

Now that she was feeling much more present and relaxed, I wanted us to reflect on what had happened internally during moments in the session when she struggled to stay present.

"What happens when you get so afraid?"

"Everything gets all jumbled up and confusing. I think it's a feeling of rejection—not that you're actually rejecting me—but it feels that way," she said.

"What does that part of you that feels rejected hear from me so we can validate it?"

Sara explained, "I don't hear anything. It's just total panic and I just shut down."

It is not uncommon for people to shut down defensively when they feel angry. The shutdown response protects them either from being internally overwhelmed by emotions or from upsetting a caregiver who can't deal with their anger. With Sara, I understood the shutdown as an emotional expression of overwhelming shame, guilt, and anxiety that was evoked by being treated so badly by her mother. Her core emotions of anger, fear, and sadness were buried by these inhibitory emotions to both protect Sara from her mother's wrath and maximize their connection by being pleasing.

"Do you think a young part of you is pissed off at me and that terrifies other parts of you? Is that possible?"

"Yeah, that is definitely possible." She was smiling and nodding yes, a signal that I was on the right track.

For Sara and all people who suffer childhood trauma, we want the brain to stop signaling danger when there is none. This will allow the body to stay calm and openhearted with all the adaptive benefits that state brings, like clear thinking.

"Is there some way you can check in to your young parts so you can sense what age they are and what they are experiencing now?"

She focused inward for several seconds. "She is three years old and angry and wanting to push you away but also desperately needing you."

Relating to her anger as if it were a real three-year-old child visiting from the past allowed the present-day adult Sara to hear her three-year-old, comfort her, talk to her, and, perhaps most important, give her compassion. In contrast, when young parts overtake us, they can frighten us and make us feel out of control.

Using mental energy, a person can work to gain separation from child parts and actually visualize them, identifying their age, what the part is wearing, where the part is, and more. Imagining parts allows communication between the part and the person's present-day openhearted Self. When our young parts merge with our present-day Self, they obscure access to the openhearted state.[4]

Without separation between the Self and a young, traumatized part, the Self loses its ability to talk to and help parts calm down. During a session, I can usually tell when a child part has emerged because my patient will look, behave, or sound younger. She might change positions or play with her hair or speak in a young voice. Some people prefer being in their child parts, and separating from them never feels right. But it is best to do the work to separate your younger parts from your present-day Self to help you become more self-confident, become more resilient, and have healthier relationships.

In our session, I validated Sara's three-year-old part and insisted that she could push me away as much as she wanted and I wouldn't go anywhere.

"Okay!" Sara smiled, nodding. Then she closed her eyes to communicate with her three-year-old part, something she had practiced numerous times in our sessions.

"The three-year-old Sara has every right to be annoyed," I said.

For many years now that young child part had been controlling her life by avoiding conflicts. The capacity to separate from the three-year-old shifted the power to her adult self. She was learning that she could deal with conflict. Most of us are blind to the fact that we are being unconsciously hijacked by childhood states of fear, anger, sadness, anxiety, and shame and that these states are currently controlling our feelings and behaviors negatively.

TRIANGLE OF SARA'S
THREE-YEAR-OLD CHILD PART

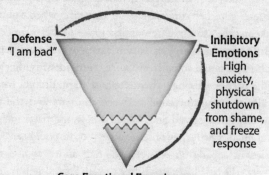

Defense
"I am bad"

Inhibitory Emotions
High anxiety, physical shutdown from shame, and freeze response

Core Emotional Experiences
Rage from being abused and abandoned emotionally
with impulse to physically attack back at mother

We can diagram this on another Triangle that shows the child in relation to her core emotions, inhibitory emotions, and defenses.

As Sara gained some distance and perspective from her child part, she relaxed and had more access to her present-day open-hearted Self with its characteristic qualities: calm, curious, connected, compassionate, confident, courageous, and clear.

She continued, "But the child also wants to be picked up and held."

"So can you find a way to imagine that?" I wanted Sara to use fantasy to heal her past trauma. "Could you imagine being a loving mother to the three-year-old part of you as you visualize her now? See if you can sense what might feel right for that young part and also feel right for you, the present-day Sara."

She closed her eyes and focused inward for a while and said, "I told her it is fine to be angry with Hilary and that you love her and won't abandon her."

I asked, "Can she receive that or are the words still too adult for her?"

Sara nods yes. "She understands a little bit. It's just hard. She doesn't want to be held." Sara flopped facedown on my sofa again and snuggled the pillow. "I'm glad you understand," she said.

"I really do," I replied.

As our work carried on, Sara's young parts grew calmer and calmer. Their fear and desperate longings waned. Consequently, Sara asserted much more freely with me in session. She stopped freezing up. She let me know what she did and did not like. In her daily life, Sara began asserting herself more with friends and co-workers and took more control over her life.

We Are All a Little Traumatized: Small t and Big T Trauma[1]

> Tell me what you fear and I will tell you what has happened to you.
>
> —D. W. Winnicott

FRAN'S STORY ILLUSTRATED how trauma can result from overwhelming emotions and from feeling alone. For many reasons, Fran did not have enough internal or external resources to move through her grief. Instead, Fran's brain blocked it—her grief was too much for her at that time. The sudden death of her parents was a big T trauma, meaning that she experienced a major catastrophic event that affected her for decades.

Other big T traumas include rape, war, accidents, natural disasters, physical and sexual abuse, and witnessing or being the victim of a crime. But there is another type of trauma that helping professionals call small t trauma, which is caused by repeated, sometimes seemingly inconsequential events that build up over time and eventually lead the sufferer to develop symptoms of traumatic stress. We all have some degree of small t trauma, and we all have the capacity to heal from it.

Sara's story is centered around small t trauma. Until I met her,

Sara believed she had a normal upbringing. She also believed her mother yelling at her was actually good for her. Sara believed that if she had not been yelled at, she would not be a good person. This is a great example of how trauma leads to false beliefs about ourselves and how abuse and emotional neglect—however small—lead to shame. When I suggested that Sara should stop emotionally beating up on herself, basically perpetuating her mother's treatment of her, she dismissed the idea, fearing that she'd become someone terrible without upholding those harsh standards.

Small t Trauma

Many events can lead to small t trauma, including

- a shortage of affection
- a shortage of eye contact
- lack of emotional understanding
- emotional abuse: being yelled at, called names, manipulated, taken advantage of, threatened with abandonment, etc.
- being bullied by parents, siblings, peers, or others
- being ignored
- having overbearing parents
- getting too much attention (intrusion), overstimulation
- not succeeding in school
- losing a job
- feeling we could not measure up to our parents' standards or our siblings' accomplishments, i.e., not book smart, athletic, extroverted, or socially adept
- feeling "different" or alone for any reason, including but not limited to feelings about gender, mental or physical disability, mental or physical illness, sexual orientation, learning disability, body type, weight, socioeconomic status, cultural issues, etc.
- moving
- divorce
- a parent remarrying
- blending families
- infidelity

- adopting or having a child
- being adopted
- conflict or estrangement with family members
- legal troubles
- physical or mental illness
- physical injury
- having a sick parent or sibling or a family member die
- having a parent who is incarcerated for a crime
- being incarcerated
- having a family member who suffers from addiction
- having a depressed parent
- having a parent who was traumatized or who has a mental illness or personality disorder like narcissism or borderline personality disorder[2]
- poverty
- oppression
- racism
- misogyny
- being the target of prejudice or judgment
- emigrating
- inability to meet social expectations (religion, community)

Add your own small t trauma not mentioned above:

- _____
- _____

Small t trauma is something most of us develop on a sliding scale depending on life experiences. Small t trauma happens from events often hidden or unacknowledged within an apparently normal life. Small t trauma occurs from emotional abuse. Small t trauma also results from neglect—both subtle and overt. A first-born child can suffer neglect when a new sibling comes along. An "easy" child who lives in a household with a child who has a disability or illness can feel neglected. Small t trauma results from subtler forms of harm that occur when we are not adequately tended to, responded to, seen, cared for, protected, or rescued. In other words, small t trauma stems from a subjective sense of pain and hurt. It doesn't matter that your parents, siblings, relatives, teachers, and clergy were well-intentioned or that you appeared to be cared for and loved.

Infants and children are particularly susceptible to having small t trauma. Their brains are immature and are not yet rational. With limited capacity to soothe and calm down, babies easily get overwhelmed. Young brains react intensely to hurt and discomfort. For example, a baby whose caregivers leave him sitting in a dirty diaper for too long becomes uncomfortable, then upset. The baby cries to get attention. If no one comes, emotional intensity builds and the baby needs defenses to cope. A baby moves up instead of down the Change Triangle, from core emotions through the anxiety corner and then to developing defenses. If no one comes to soothe the baby, defenses like dissociation are formed to cope with overwhelming emotions.[3] However, if the caregiver soothes the baby's cries, the baby will return to a calm state and will not develop defenses.

It is also true that some babies and children cannot be soothed. A child, due to temperament and genetics, may be inconsolable or constantly having tantrums despite an emotionally available parent. These are painful and challenging circumstances for all with no right answers.

If you are a parent reading this and recognize yourself in these vignettes, I want to encourage you not to lean in to self-blame or blaming others. Nor do I want you to feel guilty. Mostly I want you to identify with your own childhood and the small t traumas you might have experienced. As parents, we all do the best we can under our circumstances. I hope you use this information for hope, healing old wounds, and preventing new ones in yourself and the children in your life.

Small t trauma experiences, like big T traumas, leave a mark because they evoke powerful emotions that are hard to manage, especially when we are young and vulnerable. Sara plummeted into frozen states of panic at the thought that she would displease me. When I ask my patients to try to put in language the emotional and physical experiences that come up during sessions, they describe a phenomenon like a black hole, going blank, going into altered states, getting dizzy, feeling numb, coming out of their bodies, and other unsettling perceptions. These strange feelings are scars from early small t or big T trauma. They can be healed by working the Change Triangle: moving over defenses; calming anxiety, shame, and guilt; and processing the core emotions so the body returns to a natural homeostatic (balanced) state of relaxation.

My patient Martin was raised in a wealthy family by two high-powered lawyers who loved him but had little interest in children. Martin needed more attention than they gave him. The emotional neglect led Martin to develop shame and a belief that there was something wrong with him. Core emotions of rage and sadness underlay his shame.

Stephanie had a brother who bullied her and her sisters. As a child, she was often overwhelmed by fear and anger. That fear and anger were eventually hidden under anxiety and a belief that home could not possibly be a safe place.

Bruce's mother was a contemptuous woman who made Bruce think he had ruined her life. Bruce felt like his mother hated him. He needed to experience his disgust, rage, and sadness, which were defended by shame and anxiety, in order to feel better.

Maria's second-grade teacher was incredibly mean. She pointed out her pupils' failures publicly and doled out harsh punishments with abandon. Maria was terrified to attend school. When no one took her fears seriously, she covered up her terror by dissociating.

Connie is gay and transgender and uses the gender-neutral pronouns they/them/theirs.[4] Connie had been secretly cutting themself for years. Cutting was both the symptom and the defense. They cut to avoid the overwhelming blend of shame, anxiety, rage, and fear about their confusing sexuality and identity and feeling different from those around them.

Michael was the youngest of three kids and he had mild Tourette's syndrome. He remembers being scared and lonely for most of his childhood; he felt separate from his siblings and the other kids in his class. As an adolescent he started using drugs to "treat" or numb his fear.

Mary, whose father humiliated her and her sisters for small transgressions like breaking a dish, has symptoms of small t trauma. Now living with her boyfriend, she fears severe humiliation and panics at even the thought of making minor mistakes like forgetting to do an errand—or worse, breaking something like a glass. Mary's boyfriend can't understand why Mary gets so uptight that she won't even talk to him. He doesn't care if she breaks a dish. Mary can't speak up in these moments because she is frozen in fear.

People who suffer because of past trauma and childhood adversity are not at fault and not to blame. Suffering symptoms of trauma is not a sign of weakness. If anything, it is a reminder of our humanity and our biology.

Awareness Is a Prerequisite to Healing All Trauma

When we compartmentalize and dissociate aspects of our experiences, like the way Fran dissociated her grief over her parents' death and Sara buried her anger, our original emotions are often forgotten, yet that neural network still functions as a live wire. The emotional energy from that time is still stuck in the brain. When the dissociated network in the brain sees something familiar in the environment, the neural network that represents that traumatized part is ignited. What happened in the past feels like it happens again in the present. These forgotten moments can continue to impact your life, but it is not necessary to dredge up long-lost memories in order to heal. What *is* necessary is to gain an understanding of the emotional impression that is left and to process those emotions with the Change Triangle.

We often hear of combat veterans suffering from PTSD flashbacks. A car backfiring triggers a terrified part, and the veteran hallucinates gunfire. The veteran feels like he is in peril, even though he is actually safe. One of the goals of trauma treatment is to help a person feel safe when he is safe.

If we are going to heal from trauma, depression, anxiety, and other psychological symptoms, we must learn to be aware of our emotions and of our body's responses.

Setting aside time to be present with yourself by meditating or simply grounding your feet on the floor and breathing deeply helps foster calm and awareness. By taking that time you will

- transition from noticing thoughts to noticing feelings and sensations
- transition from thinking about the past and worrying about/ predicting the future to being in the present moment
- transition to being fully present and connected to your body
- transition to a slowed-down, aware state

All of these transitions help make it easier to monitor your internal world and for you to work the Change Triangle. Over time and with practice, you will get better at noticing your internal world and you will need less preparation.

There are two ways of being aware. One is a general awareness about your state. If you ask yourself, *How am I?* you will tend to notice your general wellness: *I am good!* or *I am exhausted!* The other kind is a more focused awareness. Focused awareness occurs when you bring all your attention to a particular sensation and just observe that sensation. It requires you to adopt a stance of radical compassion and curiosity toward yourself and all that you notice—no judging. Focused awareness requires quiet, calm, patience, and a willingness to not predict what will happen next. As a result, you need courage and confidence to observe a feeling and let it play out naturally, remembering that it is just a feeling—it can't kill us, even though it might be incredibly uncomfortable. If you have trouble with that confidence, have a trusted partner sit with you while you let these feelings play out. You can talk and share what you observe as it is happening. Getting familiar with the way emotions behave demystifies them and helps us feel less afraid, therefore opening us to new emotional experiences.

What Is the Relationship Between Trauma and the Change Triangle?

Traumas evoke big emotions. Painful experiences are a fact of life, and many of us move through these times without scars. However, when we lack necessary resources, like a calm and secure other person to comfort and bolster us, our brain uses defenses to cope. We may suffer symptoms of trauma: depression, generalized anxiety, low self-esteem, etc.

When we repeat mistakes, make consistent bad choices, act in self-destructive ways, cannot get along with others, or fail to reach our potential, small t trauma offers a possible explanation for our being stuck or our compulsion to repeat: old neural networks might be unconsciously and adversely influencing our choices and actions.

When you discover you are using a defense or you have the sense that something in you is holding you back or preventing you from thriving, you have a great opportunity to uncover and heal the original trauma behind it by working the Change Triangle.

We Are Wired for Connection: The Science of Attachment

> Young children, who for whatever reason are deprived of the continuous care and attention of a mother or a substitute-mother, are not only temporarily disturbed by such deprivation, but may in some cases suffer long-term effects which persist.
>
> —John Bowlby

WHY DID SARA have trouble believing she was safe with me despite my constant reassurance? How we were treated in childhood is a main influence on our ability to safely connect to people. Patterns of connection are established early in infancy and throughout childhood. Remember that neurons that fire together, wire together. Our prior experience with others informs what we come to expect from others in the future. What we anticipate from others and what we believe they can and cannot provide have a huge influence on how we think about and behave in our current adult relationships. All the wiring in our brains is unconscious; we don't even realize that our past is influencing us. We see our assumptions as reality. But they are not reality. We are only seeing life through our particular lens.

Because Sara's mother often yelled at her, Sara's brain now expects all people to yell at her. Her mother expected Sara to meet her emotional needs, so now Sara thinks that anticipating and meeting emotional needs is her job in all relationships. Even though, intellectually, Sara might understand that is a totally unreasonable expectation, her brain tells her that she must put others first or else something bad will happen—because, with her mother, it did! Even though her conscious mind may think otherwise, her brain is wired to her past.

Humans are naturally social; we need other people to survive. We are driven to seek and stay near those who care for us.[1] Under ideal circumstances, our caregivers are accessible and able to comfort us when we become distressed. Babies and children do well when caregivers can share their joy and excitement. In general, every time a baby expresses a core emotion and a caregiver responds in a way that validates it, emotions are allowed to flow and mental health is bolstered. In contrast, every time a baby/child expresses a core emotion that a caregiver rebuffs, inhibitory emotions and defenses are activated as the child blocks his emotional expression to please his caretaker.

Attachment theory, developed by John Bowlby in the 1950s, explains how our immediate environment and early relationships either foster or disrupt our ongoing ability to connect, attach, and feel secure with others. When caregivers are reasonably available to meet our needs for food, physical comfort, and emotional bonding, we feel secure.[2] Babies and children feel safe and secure when the people around them are kind, responsive, encouraging, empathic, and trustworthy. When babies and children feel safe and secure, they strive, take risks, and explore the world around them confidently. With a secure base to which to return, children feel free to engage in life, propelled by their unencumbered energy and excitement.[3]

Secure children become secure adults who form satisfying attachments to others. Conversely, when caregivers are not available to meet our needs, we learn we cannot depend on others for comfort and help, and core emotions like fear, anger, sadness, and disgust naturally arise. To make matters worse, when the baby/child experiences those emotions, they need their caregiver for comfort and soothing. When the caregiver fails to provide soothing, the child is left to cope alone. Anxiety and shame then arise signaling danger, aloneness, and unworthiness. The combination of core emotions plus inhibitory emotions is too much for the baby/child. The brain must manage this feeling of being overwhelmed, so it compartmentalizes it out of consciousness as a way to protect the mind and the connection with the caregiver. This sets the stage for the creation of small t trauma and the birth of traumatized parts. When I met Sara, she could not feel her anger. It had been totally dissociated from her Self. All she was aware of was anxiety and feeling bad about herself.

Babies and children without soothing from a caregiver can accommodate alone using defenses to help them cope, but they cannot thrive. The way a child brain deals with aloneness and overwhelming emotions generates defenses and small t trauma.

BABY/CHILD'S EMOTIONS NEED TO BE ACCEPTED

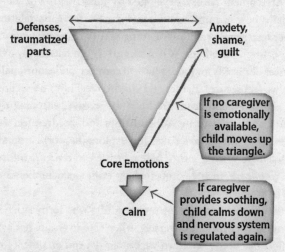

From the perspective of the Change Triangle, the baby/child gets anxious and develops shame from the lack of caring, which makes it impossible for the baby/child to process core emotions.

Energy that would otherwise be devoted to exploring the world has to now be diverted inward. The child survives, but there are costs. Children, like Sara, whose caregivers were not available for soothing, grow up to be adults whose brains tell them not to rely on and trust others. Like Sara, these adults are prone to distress and problems in relationships, not to mention higher levels of anxiety and depression.

Researcher Mary Main conducted experiments watching how toddlers responded when their parent left them in a simulated playroom and then returned after some time had passed.[4] This experiment, called the Strange Situation Protocol, showed that children and adults have two main attachment styles: *secure* and *insecure*. Main subdivided the insecure type into three subcategories: clinging, avoidant, and disorganized (a combination of both clinging and avoidant). These learned coping patterns linger and influence how children connect to others when they grow up.

People in these categories describe their relationship experience in specific ways.

> **Secure:** I'm self-sufficient AND I am also comfortable with intimacy. I want interdependent relationships. I generally feel loved and accepted. I am comfortable expressing my emotions and providing comfort for someone in need.

Since security fosters exploration and expansiveness, securely attached people tend to fare well in both work and love, and are resilient in the face of inevitable adversity.

> **Clinging:** I'm overly dependent. I want excessive intimacy. I cling to relationships. I often find myself doing anything not to be abandoned even if it goes against what I want and need. I am preoccupied by my relationships.

People who cling are so desperate not to be left that they often choose partners indiscriminately. It is as if they cannot calm themselves down enough to objectively evaluate if their partner's behaviors are kind and healthy for them. People who are in this clinging category often lose their sense of self in the process. They have relationships but are not fulfilled by them. Both their work and love lives suffer since their main goal is to please others. They often have trouble identifying their own needs.

> **Avoidant:** I'm uncomfortable with intimacy. I prefer to withdraw into my own interests and myself. I am good at putting up walls and protecting myself from others. I'm excessively independent of everyone else; I do not need other people. I often appear distant. I do not feel comfortable sharing my feelings.

This style is the opposite of clinging. People who fall into the avoidant category are physiologically agitated even though they might appear calmly aloof. When I first met Fran, her attachment style was avoidant. These people do not rely on others in relationships. They do not look to other people to provide comfort and care. Their love life lacks depth but they often excel at work—feeling it is a safe place to pour their energy.

> **Fearful-Avoidant:** I fall into terrible states of aloneness and despair. I lose myself. I don't know who I am sometimes and feel like I am disappearing. I want to avoid people and they scare me when I am near them. I am not worthy of a loving and caring relationship. I want to hurt others or myself sometimes. I feel damaged and broken. Although I crave closeness, I am afraid of being hurt by others.

This last class is the style most associated with people who suffer from extreme symptoms of trauma. It is the attachment style that develops when a child mortally fears their parent, creating the worst dilemma imaginable.

You may be wondering how a child can both cling and avoid at the same time. Main described strange behaviors like a child walking backward toward her parent. Picture a child approaching her parent back first; it poignantly and vividly demonstrates the child's dilemma of both wanting and fearing that parent. These people struggle in work and in love because they experience major anxiety in social situations. This style most closely described Sara when I first met her.

Babies and children need to feel emotionally safe to grow and thrive . . . and so do adults! When I feel safe with a partner, it is because I believe he will treat me kindly. I believe he will give me the benefit of the doubt when I ask him to. I believe my partner will be there for me when I need him. To feel safe, I need consistent love (within reason) and I need to believe that my partner thinks highly of me and will be my advocate when I ask. I must believe my partner would not abandon me or hurt me on purpose.

Sadly, many of us don't have this kind of connection. A lack of safety and security has many ramifications. How loved and accepted we were by others directly correlates with how much we love and accept ourselves. If we received little or no compassion when we felt bad, we will give ourselves little or no compassion for our internal suffering. If we had to block our caregivers out of our minds because they did not respect our physical or emotional boundaries or they demanded too much closeness or were too distant, we in turn have trouble letting people into our hearts and minds for fear of that happening again.

Our childhood degree of safety and security affects how our nervous system develops. The brain becomes more susceptible to trauma in insecure environments in part because of the aloneness the baby/child experiences.

It can be helpful to identify which category, secure or insecure, you fit into.

1. Do you take full advantage of what human relationships have to offer? If not, what gets in the way? You? Them?

2. How closed or open do you feel in the presence of others? What influences how much you let someone in or how much you let

someone else affect you? What behaviors help you open up and
what behaviors shut you down?

How you answer those questions can help you identify what you
need to create more security both internally and in your relationships. I have worked with many people who were insecurely attached when they began therapy but, by the end of our work, they
had become *earned secure*. Earned secure describes people who used
to have an insecure attachment style but were able to change and
become securely attached in adulthood.

For example, in the first year Martha and I worked together
she made it a point to remind me she wanted the shortest therapy
possible. She had no interest in "spending the rest of my life in
therapy like Woody Allen." She needed my reassurance that she
could stop therapy whenever she wanted. Her former therapist
made her feel guilty for wanting to stop coming. Martha felt
trapped by her guilt and did not want to feel trapped again by me.
Also, preemptively, she told me not to share anything about my
life with her. And, when I showed her empathy or any positive
emotion, she seemed to cringe.

In the beginning of our work together, I treaded very lightly.
My approach was to identify and ask about some of the avoidant
maneuvers she made, but I never pushed her too much because it
only activated her defenses. She needed distance from me to feel
safe. When we had more connected moments, I asked her what
they felt like. Her answers were always conflicted. She liked it but
also worried she would feel obligated to take care of me if we got
too close. I asked her what "getting close" meant for her. Martha
said it was dangerous for her to take me in. She needed to maintain some sort of wall between us. When I asked her how she did
that, she replied, "It's literally like I feel a wall between us and I
feel comfortable with it there." The more we talked in depth
about her experience with me, the more it became evident how
much work she did protecting herself from some presumed intrusion. When I asked her who first intruded on her, she unhesitat-
ingly replied, "My mom!" Being psychologically intruded upon

happens when someone doesn't respect our personal boundaries, like not taking no for an answer, or when someone doesn't understand what a healthy boundary is because they never experienced one.

In time, Martha felt safer to both open up and let down her wall so she could see me more clearly. What did she need to see? That I explicitly did not want to intrude on her. That I would listen and obey if she said, "No!" If I unwittingly came too close, she let me know. She began to trust that I could respect her boundaries. She noticed that I demanded my own boundaries be respected in return. We talked about what it felt like to be respected, putting language on how the experience of respect felt physically—relaxing in her core. We processed the anger at her mom that her young parts had for not being respected. And then, she began to trust that other people could also respect her boundaries. She got more comfortable demanding her boundaries be honored. Martha moved from being avoidantly attached to having a secure attachment. Martha now falls into the earned secure category.

To become secure, we must build confidence that we can

1. set and enforce boundaries
2. ask for what we want/need
3. handle the expected ups and downs that all relationships bring

Every one of us can learn new skills and grow our capacity to manage relationships effectively. Skills that can help are: pausing before we react, getting curious about the origins of our triggered emotions, breathing and grounding to calm our emotions and reactivity, working the Change Triangle, and learning other ways to calm ourselves so we can thoughtfully reflect on the ways our relationships are helping or hurting us. Ultimately the goal is to communicate our wants, needs, fears, and boundaries confidently and effectively.

By slowing Sara down in painful moments, I taught her to notice when she was triggered by conflicts between us. Once she knew she'd been hijacked by feelings from childhood, she had tools that could help her. She could breathe to calm herself. She could slow down and identify her parts that were triggered. She could remind herself about the real nature of our relationship, based on actual experiences she had had with me. She could intellectually assess that she was safe in present-day reality and not in danger, like she had been in the past. She could talk to her younger parts, let them know they were safe, and calm them. More and more she was able to stay in her adult openhearted state, where she could see me and her young parts simultaneously and calm herself down. *This is true for all of us: when we get triggered, we can use emotional skills to calm down.* The calmer we can become, the more our thinking will be rational and grounded in present reality. Then we can distinguish past from present and solve problems appropriate to the current context.

Interdependence—when two people are both independent and reliant on each other—is a hallmark of a secure relationship. People who have interdependence in their relationships are equals. They depend on each other and also function separately and independently of each other. People who have interdependent relationships recognize both their own needs and the needs of their partner and strive to bring both into balance.

If you find someone you believe is trustworthy and emotionally available, you have an opportunity to heal insecurities and move toward building a secure relationship. You have to *want* to change and grow, however. It takes courage to trust when every bone in your body, primed from past bad experiences, warns you not to trust. But you have to take chances in order to grow. A secure partner, friend, or therapist is there, wanting to talk about problems and conflicts and build bridges. Secure others are willing to repair whatever hurt they cause. By repeatedly repairing small breaks and ruptures in a relationship, we learn to trust more and more. It is difficult to weather the mini-ruptures that are a normal part of working things out. Sara and I, over the course of our sessions, had many ruptures in our connection. Every time there was a break in our connection, I made sure we repaired it. I did this by explicitly letting her know my intent was to understand her and stay connected, no matter what. I was implementing skills that anyone can use during difficult conversations. Even though it may not feel natural, developing the habit of consistently repairing small ruptures that happen from miscommunications and lapses in trust eventually leads to greater trust and intimacy.

Experiment:
Giving Yourself Compassion

AS ATTACHMENT RESEARCH and theory tell us and as we intuitively know, we all need to be accepted and loved unconditionally to function best. We must learn to relate to our pain in the same way: to accept, soothe, and treat ourselves with kindness, especially when we hurt. And to be clear, we not only hurt when we are sad or fearful, but also when we are angry, disgusted, or upset in any way. Some of us even hurt when we feel joy, excitement, and pride in ourselves, if it brings anxiety or shame with it.

Self-compassion does not come easy for most of us. However, people who relate to themselves with compassion and acceptance feel better. Just think: When you are upset, do you generally feel better when you are treated with understanding, acceptance, and compassion or harshness and judgment? Our brains calm down when we feel safe, seen, and accepted.

Think of a recent event or memory that brought up hard feelings.

Write it down: _____

_____

Ask yourself what you would say or do to comfort a beloved friend who experienced the same thing and felt the same way as you. Write down what you would do or say here:

_____

_____

Once you access the compassion that you imagined giving to someone else, experiment with turning that compassion inward toward that part of you that was suffering recently. Actually try directing the comforting words or imagining the comforting actions you wrote above to that part of you that was hurting. Give yourself unconditional permission to take in that compassion.

Breathe deeply. Use your imagination to breathe in the compassion and breathe out any distress. Notice your body and mind's response to this. If you find the exercise challenging, that is fine. It just means you are really doing it. Self-compassion can be very difficult!

Write down two words that describe your response to this experiment (your thoughts, feelings, or any bodily sensations you notice). Many people feel warm or more relaxed when they let in self-compassion.

1. _____
2. _____

Experiment: Self-Parenting

AS WE WORK with our emotions, we must practice more and more adopting an accepting and loving stance toward what we find inside.

Picture a secure and calm parent comforting an upset child. The way a parent holds her child allows the child to feel his emotions safely and, ultimately, feel better. These caregivers have essential knowledge that their children lack:

1. Emotions are temporary.
2. Emotions don't kill us.
3. Having a calm and available caregiver helps us move through our emotions.

Do you remember a time when you were young and someone hurt your feelings or shut you down, causing you to feel bad? Use your imagination to see your present-day adult Self approaching your young hurt Self. Imagine parenting that hurt part of you in whatever way feels right. Maybe that younger part of you needs a hug or just some encouraging words. Really see and listen to that young part of you.

You are not trying to change the past. What's done is done.

You are trying to change how you'll feel in the future. You are working to heal small t trauma. As an adult, having survived your past, you can provide comfort and compassion to the hurt parts of you. You now have that essential knowledge about emotions. The goal is to use your imagination to bring compassion and safety to a painful emotional moment no matter how long ago it occurred. You are trying to securely connect to a hurt part of you and parent that hurt part of you the way you needed.

There are several ways to give and experience comfort to parts of yourself using your imagination:

- talking
- verbal reassurance
- hugging
- swaddling/wrapping yourself in a blanket
- making eye contact
- giving a pat on the back or shoulder
- offering a glass of water or something to eat like cookies and milk

Can you think of two more possible ways to offer comfort?

1. _____

2. _____

What was this exercise like for you? Can you write down two things you notice inside yourself right now? They can be thoughts, emotions, or physical sensations.

1. _____

2. _____

Core
Emotions

Bonnie's Rage

I RECEIVED A voicemail from Bonnie, a new patient, explaining that she wanted to come in to talk about some things related to her parents' divorce. When we spoke on the phone, she told me that she was a twenty-five-year-old graduate student who'd gone to "regular" therapy for about two years when she was an undergraduate. The news that her parents were divorcing came as a surprise. She felt depressed. She had no idea that they were unhappy. She had had a traditional upbringing in an upper-middle-class family. She grew up in a suburb of New York, and described herself as a shy kid who didn't like conflict. Bonnie also told me during our initial phone conversation that she had been depressed on and off throughout her childhood, but it never impaired her ability to function at school. She was, however, sometimes socially withdrawn.

The week following her initial call, we met. Bonnie had a gentle demeanor. She smiled when I greeted her and followed me into my office. She looked around the room eyeing the sofa, then the club chair, and chose the chair—the farthest away that a person can sit from me in my office. I noticed this and wondered what meaning the distance held for her. I noticed her posture—prim and proper. She was working her back and leg muscles to sit up straight. I knew from years of sitting in that chair myself that Bonnie was not letting herself relax.

It's normal for a first-time client to be nervous. Without judgment, I look for signs of anxiety and address them to help my patients feel more comfortable from the start.

Gaining awareness about one's body in space helps illuminate a story of our wants, needs, traumas, and relationships. For example, think of the classic posture of people who feel good about themselves in contrast to that of people with low self-esteem. People who feel good about themselves generally stand up straight and tall; people who don't generally slump, as if they are trying to hide or make themselves smaller.

"So, welcome," I announced with a big smile. "I'd like to share a few thoughts before we begin. Much of this you may know or expect but I want to make these few points explicit because they are so important for our work together."

She met my eyes and I continued. "First, I want you to know this is a judgment-free zone. I approach all you share from a stance of curiosity and compassion. I will encourage you to approach yourself in the same way. Judgments close us down and make us feel bad. Judgments are not helpful here. Second, your safety and comfort come before anything. If at any time you don't feel right, or you feel upset or distressed, or I say something that you don't like, I want you to let me know. Is that something you think you can do?"

"Yes," she said, nodding her head.

Since I didn't know how much she tended to accommodate other people, I wanted to press this a little more. The importance of setting a boundary is key in therapy and life. Many people find it hard to say no if they don't like something. It feels too confrontational.

"How would you feel comfortable letting me know if you were distressed or displeased? Can you come up with something you could say or a hand gesture?"

"I guess I could say, 'I'm not feeling well.' "

"Would you be willing to practice that once or twice now? I don't mean to put you on the spot, but it is important to me that we communicate honestly. Are you willing?"

I saw her hesitate, then she declared, "I'm not feeling well."

"Well done! Once more just for the practice."

"I'm not feeling well," she said with even more oomph.

"Awesome!" I said. "The last thing I want you to know is that you do not have to take care of me or my feelings at all. I take care of my feelings and me. I am here to help you with yours when you need it. Okay?"

"Actually that is nice to hear because I do tend to take care of other people. I'll try not to do that with you."

"That is something you know about yourself?" I asked.

She nodded.

"That's terrific! So, if you find yourself concerned about me for any reason or thinking I am judging what you are telling me, maybe you could let me know and we could get curious about it together in the moment it is happening."

"Okay." She gave me a big smile, yet she still felt far away.

"What do you notice is happening now for you as we begin?"

"Not much. It's been really hard since my parents told me they were splitting up."

"Please feel free."

Bonnie's face flushed. Her eyes filled with tears. The corners of her mouth tightened. "It was about three months ago. They asked me to have dinner with them and they told me they were getting divorced. They said they hadn't been happy for some time, and now that I was grown they'd decided to split up. It was mutual. They were going to sell the house and each would buy a new one in the same area. They said it would be okay." She raised her voice. "But it's *not* okay for me. I've lived in that house my whole life!"

So much was happening in that moment, both in and out of her awareness. I could see that Bonnie was experiencing multiple emotions. I did not assume sadness just because she was crying. People cry for many reasons. The expression of sadness, anger, fear, disgust, anxiety, shame, guilt, or any combination of these could lead a person to cry. I wanted to help her know what she was *specifically* feeling as she was feeling it. Why? Because knowing what we are feeling helps calm the emotion(s) in the moment and mitigates any anxiety around that emotion. Knowing the specific emotion helps us know what to do next that is adaptive, helpful, alleviating, productive, and good for us.

Bonnie said it was "not okay" that her parents were getting divorced. But that was a thought, not an emotion, and it was vague. My aim was to help her know her experience with much more specificity.

"I know what 'not okay' means to me, but what is it like for you?" I asked.

"It's really hard," she replied.

"Can you tell me more? Like what is the hardest part?"

She was quiet for a while. I wasn't sure if she was thinking, if she was editing her thoughts before she said them, if she was not thinking at all but had gone blank instead. She seemed somewhat blank. Finally she said with a smile, "I don't really know."

"What was happening just now when you were so quiet?"

"I was just thinking."

"Does it feel okay to share with me what you were thinking?" I was very gentle now because she seemed reluctant or unable to say.

"I was just thinking how it all sucks and I wish this wasn't happening." More vagueness! Was she angry? Sad? Scared? Disgusted? Anxious? Ashamed? Guilty?

"Yes. It sucks," I mirrored back. This was a perfectly valid sentiment, and yet it did not really tell me anything about her personal experience. I can imagine many reasons why it might suck when your parents get divorced. My parents divorced when I was nineteen and I know the ways it sucked for me. However, I didn't know what it meant to her. Assumptions frequently undermine effective communication.

Specificity is a key ingredient in working with emotions and the mind. If you can elicit a specific feeling, image, memory, body sensation, or belief to work with, healing can occur. I began to think she might be using vagueness as a defense that both blocked her from dealing with her true emotions and protected her from any unconscious anticipated negative consequences that might come with knowing exactly what she was feeling.

"Bonnie," I said softly, "I get the sense that you are struggling with whether to share more with me."

"Yes!" she said emphatically.

"Maybe you could articulate both sides of your struggle: the side that wants to share and the side that doesn't."

She started to cry again. "If I say something I feel trapped by it. Like that is all I'll be."

Even though I did not understand very well what she meant, I could see it was important to her.

"And if that is all you'll be? Then what?" I asked.

"You'll judge me for it," she said.

"I see," I said, nodding. "So of course you are finding it hard to share with me if you think I will judge you for what you say. Thank you for letting me know. It's really so important."

I understood that her vagueness was a defense against being trapped and judged.

BONNIE'S TRIANGLE AT THE START OF TREATMENT

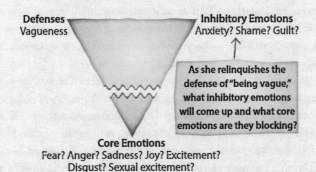

Defenses
Vagueness

Inhibitory Emotions
Anxiety? Shame? Guilt?

As she relinquishes the defense of "being vague," what inhibitory emotions will come up and what core emotions are they blocking?

Core Emotions
Fear? Anger? Sadness? Joy? Excitement?
Disgust? Sexual excitement?

Bonnie was afraid to speak or she'd feel trapped. I was afraid to speak because each time I asked her something I'd be trapping her further. How could we untangle ourselves from this interaction that might have deep meaning from her past? After thinking and feeling in silence for a few moments, I began again. "Something about answering a question with specificity makes you feel trapped?"

She nodded yes as she grabbed some tissues out of the tissue box. She looked so young now. There was something jerky and awkward about the way her body moved for the tissues.

"Let's slow way, way down now. Something very important is happening." I paused until she visibly relaxed. "I wonder if you can imagine the part of you that feels trapped coming out and sitting on the sofa so you can get an image of that part of you through your calmest and most confident Self. What do you see?" Then I waited for a long while, maybe a minute.

After a while she said, "I see myself as a little girl." She sighed a big sigh and her shoulders shifted downward, signifying relief.

Our brains have the ability to visualize traumatized parts of us by imagining them outside of ourselves in order to see them through our present-day adult eyes. Doing this does many things: the distance she just created between her present-day Self and her young trapped part immediately calmed her. Externalizing parts of us that hold uncomfortable feelings so we can talk to them is a reliable way to immediately relieve shame, guilt, and anxiety. Imagining isolating a part of us is the most efficient way to learn more about and heal traumatized aspects of ourselves. Many people can do this from the very first session, but some cannot. It takes focus, patience, and a willingness to try.

"Great!" I said. "So just notice what it feels like now to have that part of you sitting with us over there." I gestured, pointing to the sofa where the imaginary little Bonnie was sitting. "Keep looking at the little girl until she comes into greater focus. How old is she; what is she wearing; where is she?" I wanted her to bring up a memory as vividly as possible so we could work with it. The longer she stayed with this part of herself, trying to see it

Therapeutic Benefits of Visualizing Young Parts of Us as Separate Beings

- creates distance from emotions held by those young parts, which produces immediate relief
- helps us relate to, learn about, and communicate with young parts so we can soothe and help them
- makes it possible to heal young parts by witnessing their emotions and allowing their stuck emotional energy to flow again
- helps build bridges of communication, integrating the young parts back into our consciousness, which leads to calming of our nervous system

through her present-day eyes, the more it would come into focus. We were lighting up a part of her brain—a neural network—that held a traumatic experience in childhood.

"This is weird. I see myself at eight years old. I am wearing a leotard. I am in my kitchen. I remember that my father had just whacked me on the head for saying I wanted to stop ballet lessons. He called me ungrateful. I hated ballet. I hated the other kids and the teacher and I didn't want to go anymore."

I was moved by her plight. In the memory she recalled, Bonnie was expressing a true want directly to her parents. She was not only hit for doing so but her character was attacked when she was called ungrateful. I thought to myself that her dad had unknowingly slapped the directness right out of her in that moment. This is small t trauma.

The lessons her father taught her in that moment were:

1. It is not okay to tell someone how I feel or what is important to me.
2. People (because the mind of a child equates their parents with all people) don't care how I feel.
3. If I tell you what I want or what is important to me, I will be hurt and humiliated.

This memory helped me gain more understanding of why she felt trapped by me when I asked her how she felt about her parents' divorce. In her mind, telling me how she felt about the divorce equaled telling her father how she felt about ballet.

A part of her got triggered, transporting her into a past reality. I ceased to exist in that moment. Instead, she saw me, through the eyes of her eight-year-old part, as her father. There was another part of her here in the room with us too: a part that protected the eight-year-old. The protector part chimed in and said, "No way! We won't dare tell Hilary or else we will be hurt the way Dad hurt us." I was her dad in that moment and she was eight years old.

For Bonnie to feel free to be direct and have her needs met, that protector part of her had to learn she was safe now with me and that I was not her dad. But that eight-year-old was stuck in the past. We had to help her see that I was not her father and that she was no longer eight years old with no resources to protect herself. She needed to relearn that she was safe now because as an adult she could defend, protect, or stand up for herself. As a child she *was* trapped. As an adult, she was not. As an adult, she could defend herself by saying, "I don't like that!" or "You can't talk to me that way!" or "I am out of here."

I prepared her to work with this memory, to heal the eight-year-old part and move Bonnie from being stuck in the past to the present, where she was indeed safe.

I said to Bonnie, "As you sit here now with me visiting this scene, what feelings come up toward little Bonnie or your father?"

I was trying to access the core emotions that went with this memory. The eight-year-old Bonnie had to thwart her anger and sadness—both natural, core feelings evoked when people are physically attacked. But now I was asking her present-day adult Self to see what feelings she had toward her father or her eight-year-old part. I wanted Bonnie, as an adult, to safely feel the feelings that she wasn't allowed to have as a young child. Experiencing those feelings would help set her free—the memory would no longer have such an emotional charge. Liberating the stuck anger would help lift her depression. Then she wouldn't need the "vagueness defense" that she currently used for self-protection, which affected her ability to communicate her needs and wants effectively.

Why Is the Defense of Vagueness a Problem in Life?

Vagueness . . .

• keeps our truth hidden

• keeps us confused about what we mean and what we need/want

• makes it difficult to work out relationship conflicts since we are not saying what we want/need or object to

• makes it hard to tell what we really feel about something

• makes it hard to find our core emotions that are linked to specific circumstances

Bonnie answered my question about what feelings came up toward her father from that memory. She was able to answer now because we moved aside the young part that was trapped in the past. The eight-year-old had been in the forefront of her mind and she had been acting from that part of her since the beginning of our session. Once we moved that part to the sofa, adult Bonnie was able to feel safer in the present, able to see me as me and not her father, and therefore was able to share her emotions with me.

"I am angry at my father."

"Great noticing. Your anger is important!" I said.

The recognition of core anger was a milestone for Bonnie. When I am in a session and my patient accesses old anger, I think, *Jackpot!* My goal, then, is to help someone experience it fully.[1]

"Bonnie, what is happening in your body that lets you know you are angry right now? Be on the lookout for anything you notice and let's try to put words on it that describe these physical sensations." When people are just learning to tune in to their bodily experiences or are uncomfortable sensing their bodies, it's helpful to have a menu of words to choose from. "As you scan your body from head to toe, notice what sensations are there. Notice energy you feel, temperature changes, tensions, pressure, vibration, and anything you sense that lets you know you are experiencing anger." This invitation kept her in the present moment, in her body, and asked her to focus inward.

After about twenty seconds she said, "I notice, like, a fiery pit in my stomach."

"Great! What else do you notice? Let's really slow down so you can sense even the smallest nuance."

"There's, like, some energy moving upward." Bonnie's hands were clenched into fists. I wanted her to become aware of this as well. It was meaningful—the anger with its impulse was expressing itself through her fists.

"Great job. . . . I hear you notice a fiery pit in your stomach and it has energy moving upward. Is that right?"

"Yes," Bonnie said.

"Just stay with that sensation with a sense of curiosity—we want to welcome the anger and see what it wants to do. This anger is so important. Notice your hands. Feel into them. What are those fists telling us?"

Her concentration broke and she looked up at me. "This doesn't feel right," she said, grimacing.

Bonnie was feeling the core anger in her body. But then something shifted. An inhibitory emotion had arisen. How did I know? Because she stopped staying with the anger to tell me that it didn't feel right.

Bonnie had bounced from the bottom of the Change Triangle, the core emotion corner, to the upper right corner, where we find inhibitory emotions. This was a sign that we should stop what we were doing and tend to the emotion coming up.

The underlying core anger pushing up for expression was in conflict with the inhibitory emotion pushing down to stop it. Gaining awareness of this conflict in experiencing anger toward her father was a key therapeutic moment. This conflict had been happening in Bonnie's unconscious for years, yet it had exerted a hidden influence—the vagueness defense.

BONNIE'S TRIANGLE DURING ANGER PROCESSING

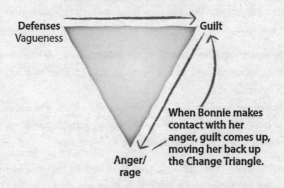

Defenses
Vagueness

Guilt

When Bonnie makes contact with her anger, guilt comes up, moving her back up the Change Triangle.

Anger/
rage

With the defense of vagueness put aside, Bonnie moved from the top left (defense) corner of the Change Triangle to the top right (inhibitory) corner. She was able to then move her guilt aside so she could access her core anger toward her father. Then guilt arose again, inhibiting the experience of core anger, and moved her back up the Change Triangle to a guilty (inhibitory) state. The anger did not yet feel safe to experience.

"Okay, let's stop what we are doing. You did great. You noticed so much about your anger and how you are experiencing it now. Even more important, you let me know something we were doing didn't feel right for you. I really appreciate your honesty. Thank you," I said. "Let's get to know the part of you that doesn't feel right being angry. What does that part of you say?"

"I feel bad, I don't want to hurt my father," she explained.

"When you feel bad, what feeling is that? Can we put an emotion word on it?"

"I think it is guilt. It's bad to hit people!"

Who said anything about hitting? I wondered. Now we knew the impulse emanating from the anger. The anger wanted to hit her father. But before we went there, I had to help her with her inhibitory feeling of guilt.

Let's look at the Change Triangle again: We addressed the vague defense, and she was willing to give it up—momentarily. She then was able to access her core anger. When the anger became too close or intense, and the impulse to hit her father started to break through into her consciousness, Bonnie became blocked by guilt. Our goal was to help her put aside the guilt so she could freely experience her anger all the way to its natural end point. This would

1. release the blocked energy of her anger to help her brain integrate that neural network so she no longer was affected by that memory as much or at all.
2. rewire her brain so that, in the future, she would have access to her anger—she could use it freely for healthy assertion and limit setting without excessive guilt prohibiting its expression.

I continued, "You are so right! It *is* bad to hit people in reality. But we are pretending now. What we are doing is NOT a dress rehearsal for something you would do in the outside world. This is just for us to do in here only. We are just playing with fantasy. Where is your dad right now?"

"I think he is at work." She smiled.

"Do you believe that if you *imagine* hitting him he will actually get hurt?" I asked to test her sense of reality.

"No," she emphatically declared.

"Good! So if guilt is for a crime, what is the crime in fantasizing about hitting your dad?"

She thought for more than a few seconds. "I guess there is no crime, but it seems like it is not okay to do that."

"Can you say more? What is not okay about having a fantasy about hitting?"

"Isn't it bad to think bad thoughts?"

"Where did you learn that?"

"I'm not sure. My mother used to scold me for saying I hated my brother sometimes. She said, 'You don't hate your brother, you love your brother.'"

"Exactly! Just like you weren't allowed to express thoughts about hating ballet without consequences. It makes so much sense that you learned 'bad' thoughts were dangerous. So conjuring vivid fantasies about hitting your father like I am inviting your anger to do seems 'bad.'"

"I guess that makes sense."

"I think in terms of whether something is ultimately constructive or destructive; will it help solve the issue at hand or make things worse? Processing anger the way we are doing is constructive on many levels. It helps you feel better, because you are not holding the anger inside. Plus, it might very well help your relationship with your parents by alleviating some of the anger you have toward your mother and father. Using a fantasy, you express anger safely in here, where no one actually gets hurt with harsh words or violence. You get it out of your system, so to speak. Once the anger is out, your body calms down. When our body is calm, it's easier to be more rational, thoughtful, and kind when you finally do talk with your parents about how you feel. Our brains can problem-solve better and find constructive ways of addressing our feelings when we are not suppressing emotions or in the midst of them.

"Fantasy is a very safe way to discharge the energy associated with anger. When it comes to processing emotions, the brain doesn't really know the difference between fantasy and reality,[2] which is really very useful in this work we are doing. Does this make sense?"

"Actually it does. But I still feel like I'm a bad person if I hit my father."

"Yes. So don't hit him in reality. Are you willing to try to ask the guilty part of you to move aside so we can get to know the part of you that is so legitimately angry at being hit when you were little? Is the guilty part willing to trust us for a little while? If the guilty part of you starts to feel upset with what we are doing, it can come right back and let us know how it is struggling. Are you willing to try?"

"I'll try," she said. I took her willingness and ran with it. I had the confidence to push her because, having done this many times before, I knew that if she could allow the anger to express itself fully, she would experience an immediate transformation and sense of relief.

"I know this sounds hokey, but can you ask the guilty part of you if it is willing to wait in the waiting room? Listen to it for an answer." It's important to communicate with parts respectfully to create internal safety. Internal safety is equivalent to a safe and secure relationship with a friend or parent. Internal parts feel better and are more willing to be known and communicate if they aren't judged, criticized, or abandoned.

After waiting a few seconds, I asked, "What does the guilty part say?"

"It says it will wait in the waiting room but will come in if it doesn't like what is happening."

"Fair enough," I said. "Can you thank that part of you for trusting us?"

She did, and we moved back to her anger.

When I first begin working with someone, they rarely feel free to experience their anger—to feel its physical sensations and impulses. We have all been socialized to think anger is bad and destructive, but some of us find anger and other emotions more threatening and scary than others. Bonnie, however, was ready.

Once Bonnie had moved aside her guilty part, I asked if she could still detect the anger physically. It was crucial that she still had access to the sensations of anger in her body instead of just remembering the anger. Feeling it physically was the way to begin experiencing it. And experiencing it was the first step to releasing it.

"Can we return to the scene in the kitchen just after your dad has hit you? Do you still sense your outrage on behalf of your younger self?"

"Yes. I feel a tension in my stomach and that same energy rises up."

"Great. So just stay with the sensation. As you stay with it, notice if the sensation has an impulse toward your father." Her hands were forming into fists again.

After several seconds passed I inquired what was happening inside her.

"What do you notice the anger wants to do?"

"It wants to hit him!"

"Can you let yourself imagine that? We are just honoring what the anger wants to do. I know you would never actually hit your father and that you love your father, but the impulse of the anger is to act. That's what anger does. It wants to attack back. It is fiercely protective of you. What do you imagine?"

"I want to slug my father."

"Great job! Let yourself see that. Where does the anger want to hit him exactly?" I was excited for her. I sat on the edge of my seat. My voice was stronger now, more energetic. I matched her angry energy.

"Right between the eyes, just like a quick punch to knock some sense into him."

"Good, let yourself feel the contact between your fist and his face. Make it vivid, like a movie." I paused to let her do this. "Where is he now? Did you hit him?"

"Yes, he's on the floor."

"Look at him, what do you see? What is he doing now?" I wanted her to walk through this fantasy step-by-step until the end. At this point, we both had no idea where this would lead. This was a new experience emerging on the spot yet dictated by the biological properties of emotion.

Bonnie reported, "He is stunned. He is looking up at me."

"Now check back into the anger in your body. What do you notice now?"

"Something in my upper chest," Bonnie reported.

"Just stay with it and see if there is an impulse."

"Yeah! It wants to yell."

"Great!" I encouraged and affirmed her.

Learning to stay with emotional experience helps release what is stuck, and it develops future capacity to stay with anger and other core emotions and process them fully. This would serve Bonnie immeasurably, as she would be able to use her anger to assert wisely, to set firm limits and boundaries in the service of creating healthy relationships.

"If we could hold a microphone up to the sensation in your chest and it could speak, what would it want to say to your dad?"[3]

"What the fuck is wrong with you?"

"Great. What if the anger didn't ask a question but instead made a statement and expressed it with the force that matches the sensation in your chest?" A question is a minor avoidance of anger. I wanted Bonnie to be direct.[4]

She shouted, "YOU FUCKING ASSHOLE! All I wanted was to quit ballet class when I was eight years old. That is not a crime. That is a normal request. How would you like it if I told you what you had to do and with whom?" Bonnie looked up at me. I sensed she was just checking to make sure I was okay in the face of her shouting.

"Great job! Now, check back in to the physical feeling of the anger again to see if there is more."

"You shouldn't have done that!" she screamed at her father. "That was wrong!"

"What is he doing now?" I asked.

"His head is down. He looks ashamed." There was sadness in her voice. The anger had shifted.

"How is it for you to see that?"

"I feel sad for him. It's kind of pathetic and he knows that now. That actually feels good for me even though I now feel bad for him."

"Let's just check one more time if you notice any more anger inside. What do you notice?"

"It's gone," she answered.

"What is in its wake? If you just scan your whole body from head to toe. What do you notice now?"

"I feel calmer."

Processing the anger in this way, she moved through the core emotion into the openhearted state characterized by those C words: calm, curious, connected, compassionate, confident, courageous, and clear. Core emotions are so important because they are the doorway to the openhearted state of the authentic Self.

"What does calm feel like in your body? Can we put some language on even the subtlest of sensations?" I asked.

"I feel lighter." And with that recognition she took a deep breath and sighed.

I directed her back to her body again. "What is that big sigh telling us if you tune in to it?"

"That I feel relieved. Like I just let go of something big. That must be why I feel lighter inside."

"So just stay with the feeling of lightness inside . . . just get to know it and notice what happens as you stay with it."

"It feels calm. I realize I am really angry with my parents for getting a divorce. It really screws things up for me. I like seeing them together as I always have. But I also understand that they want some more adventures before they die."

"It's both feelings: anger for how it screws things up for you and understanding for their needs."

"Yes!" she said with a big nod that told me she had recognized something deeply true for her.

"And what is that like to acknowledge?"

"Better. I am still unhappy that they're divorcing but I don't feel as tight or shut down now."

"Wow! That's amazing. You came in today finding it very hard to share with me. Then we were able to move aside the part of you that protected yourself by being vague so no one could pin you down. Then we were able to access an old memory where you learned it was not safe to speak your mind. Then you accessed the emotions you couldn't have in the past but were able to feel today with me. Then you allowed yourself to process your anger at your dad in a safe way in which no one was hurt. Then you felt some sadness and compassion for your dad. Then you felt calm and light and you just had this amazing insight that you are angry about the divorce but also understanding. We did so much! You are a star. What is it like for you that we could do this today?"

"That *is* a lot. Amazing! I feel happy."

"What does happy feel like for you?"

She laughed. "I'm also tired."

"Of course you are—you worked hard. We could stop now or

just spend one more minute on what happy feels like inside because that's what you just worked so hard to get to, and those happy emotions are like vitamins for the brain."

She described the feeling to me. "Happy feels like I am calm, at peace. I feel open in my chest and stomach."

Bonnie and I saw each other for a year to work on various other places she was stuck. She used her newfound ability to welcome her emotions. For example, she was able to talk to her parents about the divorce. She also shared that she felt more engaged in the world. Her relationships were more gratifying both personally and professionally. Her fears around conflicts diminished greatly as she felt more confident to tolerate both her emotions and the emotions of others. "They are just feelings," she replied during the last weeks of her therapy. Her depression also lifted.

Processing core emotions is a repetitive process of checking in to your whole body, noticing sensations, listening to the sensations for the impulse, seeing what the impulse wants to do, imagining that impulse carried out in a fantasy, and checking in again . . . repeating these steps again and again as needed until the energy from the emotion is released and one feels subjectively calm. It is simple in concept, but allowing one's Self to go through the experience feels anything but simple at first. The process requires the patient's trust, both in herself and me; courage; and willingness to let emotions flow without judgment.

Why We Need Anger and How to Use It Adaptively

Bonnie had trouble asserting herself because she had to disavow her anger to survive her childhood. Her connection to her father was more important when she was little. But as an adult, without the use of her (core) anger, she was vulnerable. If we cannot feel our anger, we cannot protect ourselves with appropriate and adaptive actions, such as saying no and setting limits and boundaries for how people can treat us.

What works best for us is having access to anger and learning how to channel it constructively. We do this by forming a healthy relationship with it. We must confront any fears we have of our anger and learn their origin. We need to work through any conflicts we have with the concept of anger. Lastly, we need to learn how to assert ourselves effectively. This leads to confidence and comfort in taking risks with other people.

Some of my patients worry that if they let themselves get angry, they will rage out of control. That concern is important. To address it, we explore where and when that belief originated. A question I sometimes ask is, "Have you ever lost control and become violent to yourself or others?" If the answer is yes, which is rare, it is important to move more slowly, working on impulse control first, until the patient feels safer experiencing his anger *without* taking action. On the other hand, if a patient has never lost control of his anger, it is unlikely he will lose control in the future. The fear is real, however, and in most cases it comes from a younger child part.

Some of my adult patients experience their anger with the intensity of a two-year-old because a neural network from childhood gets activated. That's why a person can feel so out of control—the anger is frozen in time the way that child originally felt it.

Not all anger comes from our childhood. The trials and tribulations of daily life cause fresh anger to arise all the time. Whatever the source, people are sometimes so frightened by their anger that they bury it. When I first met Sally, who came to therapy for depression, I couldn't help but notice how meek and small she seemed despite her tall stature. She claimed that people walked all over her. She was scared to say no for fear others would get angry. As she shared her stories, she wilted like a flower in need of water. When I asked if she had feelings about what she was sharing, she said, "This is just the way it is" and then let out a big sigh. I was struck by her passivity and resignation. As I listened to stories of how her friends and family grossly took advantage of her kindness, I felt my blood boil. My vicarious anger got me curious about hers—where was it?

Sally had lost contact with her anger. But she needed her anger

SALLY'S CHANGE TRIANGLE

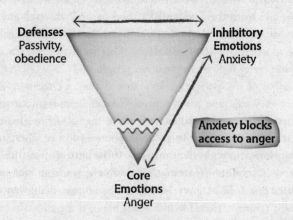

Anger was blocked by anxiety. To avoid both the anger and the anxiety, Sally became passive and obedient (the defense).

to tell her when she was being taken advantage of or dismissed. It is anger that alerts us to the fact that something is not right and needs to change. It is anger that protects us from being violated. We all need anger to tell us when something doesn't feel right or is hurtful. When we lose access to our core anger, we are at a huge disadvantage.

Sally needed to find her anger again. She needed to become aware of anger's impulses and use them for the betterment of her relationships and her life. She needed to discover alternative and nondestructive ways to satisfy her angry impulses. She needed to learn how to channel her anger into healthy assertion.

I wanted Sally to be aware of her feeling, but when I asked her about her emotions in response to a friend canceling dinner at the last minute, she said she only felt sad. Yet her body language told me that there was more to the story. When I tried to lead her toward identifying her anger, she pointedly denied it.

"Can you scan your entire body from head to toe and see if you can find even a tiny sensation that lets you know you are experiencing anger?"

She took a few moments and finally said that she felt something in her diaphragm. After sitting and observing that sensation for a minute, Sally identified it as frustration. Frustration is a very common way people thwart or constrict the anger they consciously sense but do not know what to do with.

Over the next few minutes Sally could sense anger in her body, and in time, with practice and repetition, she became comfortable experiencing it. Many of my patients have similar experiences.

You can forge an intimate relationship with anger. By imagining moving the anger to your backbone, you can assert needs, question others about their intent to cause hurt, and set limits and boundaries. Using the strength and force of assertion, not aggression, you can firmly, yet kindly, communicate your wants and needs with more calm to ensure that you will be heard.

I have also had patients on the other side of the spectrum, ones who need to gain more control over their angry impulses.

Bob grew up in a household with lots of yelling, wall punching, table pounding, and some slapping and spanking. Bob assumed that "anger" was synonymous with "acting out anger."

When I talked to Bob about the distinction between expressing impulses and simply noticing them, he was fascinated. "You mean it's like a two-step process? My father was having the emotion called anger but then he acted out his anger against our family and various household objects."

"Exactly," I affirmed. "It's a subtle but very important distinction. Anger does not hurt others or yourself. But acting out anger or turning that anger on yourself causes problems."

Almost everyone I work with struggles with their anger. They fear what their anger will do to others and to their relationships, and they fear what other people's anger will do to them. People don't like the feeling anger creates inside: the physical tightness, the hot fire in the belly, or the rush of energy up the torso. They don't know how to channel anger's energy and impulses. By working with the Change Triangle, we can change our relationship to anger. We can master its forceful and self-protective energy. Befriending anger isn't always easy, but it is always worth the effort.

The Difference Between Experiencing Anger and Acting Out Anger

Many people confuse *experiencing* anger with *acting out* anger. Experiencing anger is a purely internal experience. This stands in direct contrast to acting out anger. Acting out anger unleashes it on another person. Anger can be unleashed directly at the person who made you angry, or it may be unleashed on someone else who is just in the wrong place at the wrong time.

Acting out anger is typically destructive to others and relationships. Children who grow up in violent homes or homes with constant yelling mistakenly learn that anger = destructive action. I make a strong distinction that anger is not hitting, punching, or yelling. Anger is a core emotion identified by a body sensation and an impulse to act. Anger wants to be mean and sometimes wants to hit, punch, push, clobber, smash, stab, destroy, or shoot a weapon at someone. If we accept those impulses and discharge them safely, using fantasy, without acting them out, we gain control of our angry impulses and preserve our integrity as human beings who can solve disputes in a civilized manner.

Everything You Need to Know About Your Core Emotions

A spontaneous smile that comes from genuine delight or the spontaneous sobbing that is caused by grief are executed by brain structures located deep in the brain stem. . . . We have no means of exerting direct voluntary control over the neural processes in these regions. . . . We are about as effective at stopping an emotion as we are at preventing a sneeze.

—Antonio Damasio

WHEN I WAS younger, I remember being mystified by the powerful emotional forces that would overtake me. I remember how powerless I felt when my mind and body were kidnapped by a surge of anger, fear, sadness, guilt, or shame. In the throes of anger, most likely at a boyfriend or my parents, I have the memory of watching myself acting and behaving in ways I could not control. I hated myself when I turned into a bitch or a wimp, depending on the circumstances, but I couldn't help myself.

What were these powerful forces? Who did I become in those moments? What happened to the me I liked and recognized as myself? That me was poised, thoughtful, calm, confident, and kind. My patients, too, talk about being overtaken by their feelings, depressions, and anxieties. When we are overcome by emotions, the Self gets buried underneath a dark mood or an emotion storm that hijacks the brain. Sometimes we can hardly remember that another part of us exists. Emotions, moods, and states are pervasive and all encompassing until, magically, they pass.

To understand our ever-changing emotional landscape, we have to learn some basic properties of emotions. The basic core emotions are anger, sadness, fear, disgust, joy, excitement, and sexual excitement. While we all experience core emotions in nuanced ways, they have many common properties.

Emotions Just Are

We all have seven core emotions, which are hardwired in the brain. We cannot control our emotions and we cannot prevent the reactions they cause in our mind and body. Like an alarm system for both dangers and pleasures, emotions unconsciously turn on and ignite a cascade of physical and physiological responses to make sure we survive the moment. They have urgency to them.

Emotions just are! That's the mantra I repeat to my patients who think they shouldn't have emotions. Many people think emotions are only for weak people, but that is false. No person is able to stop core emotions from being triggered in the limbic system of the brain, where they originate.[1] "Your sadness just is," I say to my patients who judge their sadness. "It's not good or bad." Bonnie's anger just was. There was no judgment, no right or wrong response to that memory. Once you accept that emotions can't be eradicated, only thwarted, you will have the impetus to deal with them in the healthiest way possible. If we know that emotions just are, it no longer makes sense to blame one's Self or others for having them. As adults, however, we are responsible for learning to manage our emotions constructively.

Core Emotions Function Like On-Off Switches

When we sense danger or pleasure, an emotion switch in our brain flips on for one of the core emotions—fear, anger, sadness, disgust, excitement, joy, and sexual excitement. Just imagine a grizzly bear is about to attack you. What emotion do you think would turn on? Fear. Fear is ignited in the brain and, without thinking, your body responds to it. If you had to think about escaping, you would be dead before you could decide to run. Thank goodness for the force of fear. Think about any time someone has scared you and you've jumped. Fear made you reflexively move away from what your brain sensed as danger. Once safe, our neocortex—the part of the brain we think with—assesses the environment for future danger and determines what caused it and whether or not the danger is over. Despite the fact that emotions cause us major suffering, evolution saw a survival benefit to emotions that turn on automatically and unconsciously. Bonnie's father yelled at her for being "ungrateful" and *poof!*—an emotion switched on: Bonnie's anger. Thinking that we shouldn't have a core emotion or it doesn't make sense or we are bad for feeling that way serves no purpose. *Emotions just are,* and they flip on and they flip off depending on what our emotional brain senses in the environment.

Emotional Sensitivity Is a Trait that Occurs on a Spectrum

People cannot help having core emotions. But emotional sensitivity, like all human characteristics, exists on a spectrum. Some of us feel a little and some feel a lot. That's just how it is. Some of our friends or families may be sensitive souls. Some may be less sensitive. When we judge others for what and how much they feel, it says more about our capacity to handle the emotions of others.

Emotions Are Contagious

Watch what happens when one baby in a group of babies starts to cry. Before you know it, the whole group is wailing. Or think of people laughing at the movies. When you hear someone laughing hysterically, just try not to laugh.

If your partner or child is upset, it may bother you because emotions are contagious. Seeing your loved one angry, sad, or scared will evoke emotions in you. If you are not aware of this and you are not comfortable with emotions, you might become cold or defensive in order to ward off the unwanted feelings provoked by another. Some research shows that it is mirror neurons, a specialized type of brain cell, that open us to emotional contagion and give us empathy.[2]

Core Emotions Are Like Ocean Waves

Core emotions rise, reach their peak, and finally ebb, much like ocean waves. Knowing this helps prepare us for experiencing the full expression of core emotions. We must anticipate that they will at first intensify and then lessen. And we must remember to breathe deeply through the entire experience, riding the wave, allowing a couple of minutes for the intensity to diminish, before the shift occurs into relaxation and relief. It is not dissimilar to stubbing your toe. The injury happens, you anticipate the pain rising to its full force, and then it subsides. We breathe through this experience to tolerate the wave of physical pain. We can do the same thing to ride emotional waves.

Remember when Fran's grief finally broke through? She experienced several waves each lasting a few minutes. Then she experienced relief. Most core emotions, when flowing freely, last no more than a few minutes. Most of us can tolerate a few minutes of discomfort, especially if we know that relief is on the way.

Emotions Like to Be Named and Validated

We subjectively feel calmer when we know what emotions we are having. Ideally, we learn to name our emotions as children. But sometimes, for any number of reasons, we don't learn to recognize emotions. There is scientific evidence that putting language on an emotion actually changes the brain, decreasing its arousal.[3]

Craig spent a wonderful weekend with his twenty-five-year-old daughter. When she left, he felt anxious. At first Craig had no idea why anxiety came up. He had had such a wonderful weekend with her. But then after focusing inward to see what emotions he had, he realized he felt two: gratitude and joy. I think this is such a great example to illustrate the power of emotion to raise anxiety. Both gratitude and joy are wonderful, but together they can become too much at times—tipping us into anxiety and moving us up the Change Triangle from core emotions to the inhibitory emotions corner. Once Craig labeled his feelings, the anxiety went away.

I teach all of my patients to label their emotions so they feel better. Just the act of naming and validating our emotions helps our bodies and minds relax. And it's a key part of working the Change Triangle.

Emotions Are Rooted in the Body

Millions of sensory and motor neurons connect the emotional brain with all the parts of the body, including the heart, lungs, stomach, skin, small intestine, large intestine, and muscles. If you take a moment in the midst of feeling something, you will notice the experience is physical. For example, when I am sad, I feel a heavy sensation in my heart. I recognize anger as a tightening in my chest and an energy rising from my stomach that moves to my head. Fear makes me tremble. Excitement is energetic—sometimes it makes me feel tingly and I have an impulse to dance or high-five someone.

Core Emotions Are Programs for Action, and These Actions Are Meant to Be Adaptive to the Moment

Emotions drive us to act in the moment. We feel these as impulses. Be it anger, sadness, fear, disgust, joy, excitement, or sexual excitement, core emotions prime us for action. We learn about our specific impulse by tuning in to our body in the moment we are having an emotional experience. The impulse will reveal itself when we focus on the emotion. There are general impulses for each core emotion.

FIGHT OR FLIGHT

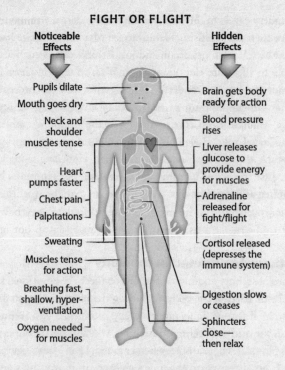

Noticeable Effects

Pupils dilate

Mouth goes dry

Neck and shoulder muscles tense

Heart pumps faster

Chest pain

Palpitations

Sweating

Muscles tense for action

Breathing fast, shallow, hyperventilation

Oxygen needed for muscles

Hidden Effects

Brain gets body ready for action

Blood pressure rises

Liver releases glucose to provide energy for muscles

Adrenaline released for fight/flight

Cortisol released (depresses the immune system)

Digestion slows or ceases

Sphincters close— then relax

- Fear's impulse is to run, hide, or sometimes to freeze.
- Anger's impulse is to fight, be aggressive, say mean things, attack, intimidate, protect ourselves/others, and catalyze change.
- Sadness's impulse is to slow us down, seek comfort and connection, and curl up.
- Joy's impulse is to smile, grow big, and share our joy with others.
- Excitement's impulse propels us toward the object of our excitement. It makes us want to jump up and high-five a friend or teammate, or scream.
- Disgust's impulse is to recoil, to move away from that which disgusts us, or to throw up.
- Sexual excitement's impulse is to move toward the object of our desire and/or seek out sexual release.

When emotions are blocked, the ability to know what impulses we are having is also blocked from awareness. Emotions and impulses tell us important information about our environment and how we are responding to our surroundings. When we lose access to emotions, we lose this valuable compass for living.

So next time you feel emotional, ask yourself, *What emotion am I feeling right now and what is it propelling me to do?* The information you discover tells you something about your emotional needs and wants, which you can then decide how to use in order to make decisions with those needs and wants in mind.

Emotions Amplify

Emotions can build in intensity and grow bigger. They have the power to overwhelm us, causing us to want to jump out of our skin or disappear. Emotions can be amplified in response to something internal or external. Self-judgment and self-criticism are internal amplifiers.

Let's say I ask a question in class that my teacher says she has already answered and I feel embarrassed. I might think to myself, *I am an idiot.* This shaming thought amplifies or magnifies my embarrassment. It gets bigger and I feel smaller. If we don't want to amplify our misery, we can stop these thoughts dead in their tracks. If we change critical self-talk to compassionate self-talk, we will feel better immediately. For example, in the schoolroom situation, thinking something like *I did not deserve to be publicly humiliated,* is showing self-compassion.

Other people can amplify your emotions too. If on the eve of a vacation I confess to my mother that I am afraid of flying and she responds by saying, "Oh God, I wish you hadn't told me that" with fear in her eyes, this makes my fear grow bigger. Now I am even more frightened. My heart beats faster, my arms tremble, and my breathing becomes shallower and more rapid.

Anger is an emotion that is easily amplified. Just think of how fights with a loved one can escalate. If you broach a problem with your partner and your partner feels accused and gets defensive, you become upset because you don't feel heard. Your partner, interpreting your upset as anger, gets angrier. From the first perceived insult, you both get angrier and angrier and more defensive, digging in your heels and leaning into self-righteous indignation. If we are not careful to de-escalate conflicts when they arise—by pausing, taking a break, and most of all resisting the pull of anger's powerful impulse to engage in a fight—then fights quickly turn into screaming matches or worse.

It gets scary when we find ourselves without the tools or abilities to calm down escalating emotional energy to a manageable level. That's why we erect defenses to cope. That's why Sara, every time her anger was triggered, had to shut it down or entertain fantasies of fleeing my office. She had no tools or skills to manage her feelings.

In contrast, we can choose to amplify positive emotions like joy and excitement by sharing them with others who will be happy and excited for us. When we share positive emotions with those who respond well, good feelings build in both partners. Amplifying joy and excitement fosters secure attachments. In fact, sharing the happy and exciting moments of our days with our partner is a great way to fuel excitement and love in our primary relationships.

Emotions Have Energy

Humans are living organisms. All living organisms need to stay in a balanced state of energy so they don't overheat or get so cold that they die. Just like a car needs gas to run, we consume food for energy to make our bodily functions run. Respiration and digestion create energy for the cells in our body. Energy enables our hearts to beat, lungs to breathe, stomachs to digest, and muscles to move. We have to balance our use and expenditure of energy so homeostasis and harmony are maintained.

If a car gets too hot, it overheats and stops working. The engine creates heat, and that heat must be released. So it is with core emotions. They create energy, and that energy needs to be released. When we use too many inhibitory emotions and too many defenses, emotional energy is blocked and we have problems.

Anxiety, guilt, and shame are the three ways that we apply downward energy to thwart core emotional expression. The inhibitory emotions help in the moment by preserving our connection to others, but there is a cost. Emotional energy gets trapped.

When Jonathan learned his dog had died, the sinking sensation of grief was suddenly palpable to him in his stomach and heart. The rush of sensation inside him spread across his body heading up to his eyes. But before the grief could reach his eyes, where he could release it by crying, he stopped it with an automatic muscular constriction in his throat. Most of us have felt the proverbial lump in the throat. Jonathan stopped his crying and told himself, *Man up!* Not feeling his sadness was one of the factors that led to his depression.

People routinely block core emotional energy. When the energy of emotions is blocked, people move up the Change Triangle to inhibitory emotions and defenses. But that energy doesn't disappear, and it causes unrest and puts stress on the mind and body. It doesn't have to be that way. We can work our way back down the Change Triangle to experience our core emotions and manage our feelings in a healthier way.

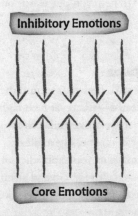

Picture a piston: core emotions arise with energetic impulses that push up and out for release. Anxiety, shame, and guilt are the emotions that squash down the energy from the core emotions that push up for expression.

Experiment: Noticing Internal Experiences

IN THE FOLLOWING exercises, we begin the practice of noticing and naming internal experiences. It is important to remember that there are no right or wrong answers when it comes to knowing yourself; only your subjective perception counts. When you need to, use the emotion and sensation word lists in the appendix (see pages 277–283) to help you put words on your emotions and your sensations.

Physical Sensations

Slow down by being still. Feel your feet on the floor and take four or five deep belly breaths—whatever feels right for you. Now, remind yourself what it feels like to be tired or hungry. Pick the experience that you can most easily recall.

What are the sensations you experience in your body that let you know you are hungry/tired? Give yourself at least thirty seconds for noticing, because body sensations take much longer to be perceived than do thoughts.

Write down one or two sensations that let you know that you are hungry/tired:

1. _____
2. _____

Scanning Your Body from Head to Toe

Keep breathing steadily and scan your body from head to toe, like putting your toe in the water before you jump in—just see what it is like. See if you can describe some sensations you notice, however subtle. Remember, if at first you perceive no sensations in your body, linger for a while in your heart and stomach area and see what an extra ten seconds brings. For example, *My body feels calm* or *I feel jittery*.

Write down three sensations you notice:

1. _____
2. _____
3. _____

If a sensation starts to build in a way that feels scary or uncomfortable, take a break. Keep breathing deeply and imagine the peaceful place you identified earlier. Then dip back in again when you are calmer and feel ready to describe the sensation(s).

Remember: Never judge what you notice. Stay curious and compassionate toward yourself at all times. If tuning in to your physical sensations, not judging yourself, remaining curious, and having a compassionate stance toward yourself feels hard or impossible, validate that. Then ask yourself what makes it that way. See if you can describe what feels weird or uncomfortable. Is it the sensation itself? Do you feel silly or indulgent? Are you judging or speaking harshly to yourself? Just notice.

Building Mental Flexibility
Between Thoughts and Emotions

To figure out which corner of the Change Triangle you are on in a given moment, you must discern the difference between a thought and an emotion. Sometimes our thoughts are helpful to us, but often they are not constructive. Ruminations, obsessive thoughts, and worries swish around in our brain. We aren't even aware that our thoughts are making us feel worse.

I don't suggest that we stop thinking. Spending all day living in vulnerable and emotional states is not practical. Most of us, however, pay attention only to our thoughts and ignore our emotions. We want to build flexibility to glide freely from thoughts to emotions and back.

Focus on your thoughts. Notice them. Maybe you are thinking, *This information is intriguing.* Maybe you are thinking, *This stuff is silly.* Maybe you are thinking about what you will eat for dinner tonight. Just notice without passing judgment on your thoughts. The goal is just to notice. It's that simple. What are you thinking right now?

Write down three thoughts you notice:

1. _____
2. _____
3. _____

Next, move down below your neck to your core. Focus there for about ten seconds. Make sure you don't hold your breath and are breathing deeply.

Can you describe either an emotion or physical sensation you notice? You might sense that you are calm, relaxed, tensed, stressed, warm, cold, happy, sad, angry, scared, excited, bubbly, numb, or fluttery.

Write down three emotions or sensations you notice:

1. _____
2. _____
3. _____

Finally, shift back to your head. Focus on your thoughts again. Ask yourself, *What did I think of this exercise?*

Write down three things you are thinking now:

1. _____
2. _____
3. _____

Then shift back down again to your core and sense what you are experiencing. Don't assume what you sensed before is what you sense now.

Write down three emotions or physical sensations you notice now:

1. _____
2. _____
3. _____

Did you sense the difference between going up into your head and thinking your thoughts versus coming down into your body and sensing emotions and physical sensations?

Checking In with Your Internal State

I recommend setting a reminder in your calendar each day that says something like "REMEMBER TO CHECK IN WITH YOUR BODY." This is how you get into the habit of slowing down and tuning in to your thoughts and your emotions. When you notice something that feels right and good, stay with it for a little while. The goal is to get to know the sensation. Stay curious.

When you notice something that feels hard, like tension, jitters, sadness, aches, and the like, see if you can find words that best describe the emotions/sensations. Can you assign a cause to what you're experiencing? Ask yourself, *What is happening that brings up this emotion/sensation right now?* See if you can identify whether you're feeling a core emotion or inhibitory emotion. Over time, you will learn which corner of the Change Triangle you are on with more and more accuracy and be more able to help yourself.

For example, Fran, knowing her tendency to block sadness, made sure she checked in with herself regularly. She knew that her brain reflexively buried or dismissed sadness, so she had to actively find it and bring it forth. When she noticed any sadness inside, she honored it. "Honoring" means prioritizing. She tuned in to the sensation(s) in her body that told her she was sad and focused on those sad sensations until they shifted or spoke to her. She tried to figure out what was happening in her inner or outer environment that evoked sadness at that moment. She approached her sadness with compassion.

Most people find it easier to put language on experiences that are uncomfortable. We seem to have more language at our fingertips to describe negative experiences, while we grasp for words that describe positive experiences. Take being calm, for example. Many people report that calmness feels like nothing. But, when we experience calm, words like soft, still, aglow, and tender apply. When you find emotions and sensations that feel pleasant, linger with those sensations and add language that fits, even if it's metaphorical. When we add language, it acts like a reference point, marking the good experience in the brain. You will more easily be able to return to these nourishing experiences as a result.

The Daily Routine

- Slow down and notice what is happening in your mind and body.
- Notice defensive thoughts and maneuvers and question their reason for being there.
- Try to move defenses aside by coming out of your head and checking in with your body.
- Try to put words on what you are experiencing.
- Validate your feelings.

By engaging consistently, you are creating positive brain change.

Experiment: Finding Your Core Emotions

SCAN YOUR BODY slowly from head to toe looking for any emotions, no matter how slight or subtle. When you find some kind of feeling, ask yourself each of the following questions to find the core emotion that best fits. Be sure to go slowly. Check for one emotion at a time. Give yourself *lots of time* (thirty seconds to scan your body for each emotion, which will feel very long).

Answer each question below and put a check mark next to each one you find right now. Just accept what you notice and resist the temptation to evaluate *if* you should have the feeling.

- Do I feel any anger?
- Do I feel any sadness?
- Do I feel any fear?
- Do I feel any disgust?
- Do I feel any joy?
- Do I feel any excitement?
- Do I feel any sexual excitement?

Pick *one* core emotion you're experiencing. Experiment with tuning in to the emotion itself; don't think about the emotion, only sense it. Stay with it for thirty seconds while taking deep breaths. What comes up as you stay with the emotion for longer?

Write down three things you notice:

1. _____
2. _____
3. _____

Complete the sentences below for the emotions you are currently experiencing. Don't judge or think, just let the emotion, as you sense it physically, tell you the answer.

I am angry at _____ because _____.

I feel sad about _____ because _____.

I am afraid of _____ because _____.

I am disgusted by _____ for doing _____.

I feel joy about _____ and feel like sharing it with _____.

I am excited about _____ and feel like sharing it with _____.

I am sexually excited by _____ and my fantasy is _____.

5

Inhibitory Emotions

Spencer's Social Anxiety

SPENCER GREW UP in a cold home. His father was a contemptuous man who had few friends and found people "annoying" and "stupid." Spencer's mother was passive and quiet; she did nothing to offset the tense and hostile atmosphere in the house. Spencer found a sense of peace through drawing and painting alone in his room.

As an adult, Spencer worked in graphic design, though his passion was painting. He was a talented artist, but, because of his shyness, he struggled to promote his art. Spencer told me, "I have to overcome my social anxiety so I can be more comfortable meeting new people and showing my work." In social situations, Spencer hesitated to do or say anything for fear of saying "the wrong thing."

In one of our first sessions I asked him, "What do you mean by 'the wrong thing'?"

"I worry I will say something stupid, or something annoying," he replied.

"And if you do?"

"That would not be good!" I could see Spencer's body react in fear.

"It wouldn't?"

"I don't want to seem like an idiot or have people get angry at me."

I noticed his left leg jiggling. "What's the movement in your left leg telling us?"

"I'm scared people will be angry at me. I can't deal with that," he said.

"What's the image you see in your mind as you share that with me?"

"Me, standing alone, with everyone looking at me, judging me and angry with me for being an idiot," Spencer said. That scene played in his head prior to entering every social interaction. No wonder he didn't want to go out.

I was impressed by Spencer from the first time we met. He was nice looking and had a kind and gentle demeanor. Always polite and thoughtful, he would bring me a cup of coffee if he came in with one for himself. My sense of Spencer was that under all that inhibition there was a really interesting guy who had a great deal to offer, if only he had more confidence. Sadly, he feared evoking judgment and anger in others. He protected himself by limiting his interactions with other people, having only a smattering of casual friendships.

Spencer's constant preoccupation with making mistakes and angering people was the way he stopped himself from feeling the intolerable anxiety generated by being with other people. If his defense could talk, it might say, *If only I could figure out exactly what someone wants from me then I could give it to them and be safe from their anger.* His brain was overactive, constantly trying to figure out how to protect himself from the imagined judgments and wrath of others.

Unfortunately, he was trying to solve an unsolvable problem. None of us can read minds. Trying to anticipate what others want takes a tremendous amount of energy that could otherwise be used for fun and engagement.

Spencer's defense was living inside his head. It took him away from the physical symptoms of his anxiety—nausea, a clenching deep in the pit of his stomach, a jittery core, a rapidly beating heart—and helped him avoid the discomfort of being in his own skin. But this strategy did not provide a long-term solution to his social anxiety.

Defenses help us to avoid what is painful: anxiety, shame, guilt, and core emotions that can be overwhelming. But they exact costs. For Spencer, the cost of that defense was the inability to relax around people. Obsessive circular thinking (also called ruminations) and worrying are pointless, not to mention tormenting. His mind was replaying this sequence over and over: *No one will like me. . . . I am a terrible person. . . . I'm going to make a mistake. . . . Everyone will be angry with me. . . . No one will like me. . . . I am a terrible person. . . . I'm going to make a mistake. . . . Everyone will be angry with me. . . . No one will like me. . . . I am a terrible person. . . . I'm going to make a mistake. . . . Everyone will be angry with me. . . .*

The costs of ruminating about how to avoid others' anger are many:

- Ruminations use energy that could otherwise be put toward working efficiently, having fun, being creative, or being curious in the world.
- Ruminations can trigger the fight/flight part of the brain into a perpetual state of alert for danger. This causes the release of stress hormones, which, over time, can damage health.
- Ruminations compromise a person's ability to solve problems. Minds don't work well when they are anxious. Ruminating and worrying make people feel like they are working on a problem, but it is inefficient work at best and, sometimes, the problem is in fact nonexistent.

About three months into treatment, Spencer described what it was like for him as a teenager. "When my father didn't like what I said, he made me feel like I was a horrible, horrible person, as if I'd stabbed him. It wasn't like he understood that I was a normal teenager who said obnoxious things sometimes. He took it to heart and said stuff like 'You hate me; you treat your dog better than me.' He constantly told me I was bad."

"So cruel." I sensed my fury at both his mother and father for their lack of empathy and care. This kind of contemptuous neglect is so damaging.

"It was?" Spencer said.

"Well, how did it feel to you?" I asked.

"Bad, but I thought it was my fault."

"What comes up for you when I tell you that your dad acted cruelly?" I asked.

"I am relieved. Thank you," Spencer said, gazing downward.

"And you are so different from them both it seems." I was recalling how he treated his dog growing up. One of the things his parents did right was buy Spencer a puppy that he raised and took care of for over thirteen years. The way he loved and cared for his dog moved me to tears.

I used his relationship with his dog, Wesley, often in our work. When I wanted to illustrate an example of what it felt like to be loved without fear, I would ask him to recall how he felt with Wesley. When he needed reminding of what it felt like to be loved and accepted, I asked him to remember how Wesley felt about him and how he felt with Wesley. I would compare how he treated Wesley to how his father and mother treated him as a way for him to see that he was not like his parents.

Spencer was empathic to others but not to himself. I wanted him to get curious about this double standard. Why could he feel for people and cut them slack for their mistakes and yet be so sure that people would not do the same for him?

I thought that a part of him might be stuck in a past memory about his father that was unconsciously replaying in the present. In other words, his brain didn't realize it was a memory he was reliving. Spencer was seeing the world through the eyes of a young part of himself. He was responding to people in the way he responded to his father. If he could process the core feelings about his dad from when he was young and help the wounded young parts of himself feel safer, then maybe he would develop more confidence, and see present-day reality and other people more clearly.

As adults, we have the power to protect ourselves from people who act mean, unlike when we were children. But Spencer kept believing that everyone would treat him as his father had or that he wouldn't be able to cope if someone now did.

Several months into our work together, Spencer had an important insight.

"I thought I was born defective and that's why my father was so miserable and mean."

"Life was so hard when you were young. You really were dealt a tough hand. It's not your fault that your dad was so tough and miserable. My guess is he was like that long before you were ever born. Do you know anything about his childhood?" I asked.

"A little. I know it wasn't good. I overheard my mother saying something to my aunt one day about my grandfather having a problem with alcohol. I think he may have even spent some time in jail for drunk and disorderly conduct. One story goes he almost killed a man in a bar brawl."

"So, it seems like your dad grew up with an angry dad. That's probably what made him angry, not you. Can you see that?"

"I get it intellectually."

"You get it up here," I said, pointing to my head, "but not down here," pointing to my heart.

"That's about right," he confirmed.

SPENCER'S CHANGE TRIANGLE AT START OF TREATMENT

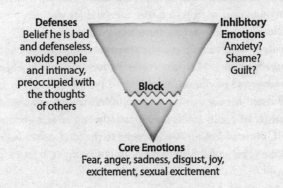

Defenses
Belief he is bad and defenseless, avoids people and intimacy, preoccupied with the thoughts of others

Inhibitory Emotions
Anxiety?
Shame?
Guilt?

Block

Core Emotions
Fear, anger, sadness, disgust, joy, excitement, sexual excitement

Healing trauma means helping the brain update its "software" to the present. We want past events to be filed in the brain as memories. When we are actually in danger, we want our survival emotions to kick in. But when we are safe, we want to feel calm so we can use our energy for living. Our work was rewiring Spencer's brain so he could learn that whatever happened to him as a child was over. Spencer also needed to learn some additional social skills like how to set limits and boundaries with kindness, since no one had modeled that for him when he was a child.

As our work progressed, Spencer slowly gained confidence. Having labeled the interactions he had with his father as abusive, he started to see himself as a survivor of small t trauma. He was beginning to feel at a deep level that the abuse was not his fault. His father, being the parent, was the responsible party. I could see his confidence developing. He spoke up about things he didn't like with more certainty. He stood taller, his shoulders back instead of hunched. His voice was deeper and louder. He even dressed a little neater, as if he cared more about himself and how he presented to the world.

During a session six months into our work, Spencer was sharing a memory of when his father had unjustly accused him of leaving a window open when the heat was on. His father was irate that it drove up the heating bill. Spencer was certain he didn't leave the window open.

"He called me an irresponsible idiot."

"That is so unfair and mean," I affirmed. "Can we be with this memory and deal with your father once and for all?"

"Okay," he said, waiting for me to guide him.

"First, I want to help you shift into your most confident Self," I said with a smile. "Can you conjure a recent memory when you felt most proud of yourself?"

I wanted his present-day Self to feel as strong and capable as possible. If he could access a memory of when he felt good about himself, positive feelings would come to the forefront of his mind and make it easier for him to relate to the younger, hurt parts.

"I guess it was when I received an award at work. I was employee of the year. They announced it at the company Christmas party. Everyone was there and I got a cash reward. But the best part was the speech they made. They called me a team player, always willing to lend a hand."

I was touched. He had never shared that with me before.

"Wow! What do you feel in your body as you remember that?"

"I feel stronger, like I'm taller and more upright." He shifted in the chair and sat up straighter.

"Did you notice the shift in your posture?" I asked so he could bring awareness to this shift.

"I sat up straight."

"So, as you stay connected both to this strong and upright sense of you and to me, let's go back to this memory with your father. Let the memory of this moment become as vivid as possible. Can you see the memory over here as if it is on an old grainy TV?"[1] I held my palm up about six feet away from him to stand in for a TV screen. I wanted Spencer's brain to gain distance from the memory in order to distance himself from the young parts and prevent the emotions they held from overtaking his sense of Self.

"Yes," he said.

"What do you see?" I asked.

"I see me and my dad in the bathroom. The window is open. He is pointing at it and yelling. My head is down."

"Now as you sit here with me in your present-day most confident strong Self, what comes up emotionally as you see this scene?"

"I feel bad for me and angry at my dad for being such an asshole," Spencer said in a stern voice. He had one foot in the present and one foot in the past, which is the way trauma is safely processed.

"Is there an impulse?" I asked.

"I'd like to protect the boy and tell my dad that he's the one who is bad for treating a kid that way." Spencer sounded confident as he said this. I could almost sense his brain changing—the old and new neural networks separating into a distinct past and present. His voice was strong and he sounded steady.

"Can you put your strong and confident adult Self into the scene and use your imagination to do what feels right?"

Spencer stared at my hand. The expression on his face was angry: lips pursed, brows furrowed.

"What's happening?" I asked after about a minute.

He shifted his gaze from the imagined TV to my eyes. "I stormed into the bathroom, called him an asshole, punched him in the nose, took my boy by the hand, and told him no one would ever talk to him like that again without consequences."

We were both quiet now, processing this incredible moment of fierce love and protection on behalf of himself.

He took a deep breath, eyes focused on me, then gazed upward, then back to me. I waited for him to share first. "That felt good," he said.

"Stay with how it feels inside."

"I mean I'm a little shaky. My whole body is tingling."

"Is it tolerable? Can you stay with it?"

He nodded, then after another thirty seconds or so he added, "It's subsiding now. I feel somehow lighter yet more solid or weighted at the same time. Wow!"

"Wow!" I mirrored.

Spencer continued. "I mean, he's my dad and I love him, but I also can't stand him. He was such a douchebag to me. I can't believe I could stand up to him like that and it wasn't so hard. He didn't even put up a fight. He folded and I just walked out with the kid. Me."

"Stay with what this all feels like inside."

"The shakiness is going down even more. I feel strong."

"Where in your body do you feel stronger?" I asked.

"It's like a solid feeling all up and down my back up to my head. But like there is an opening in front. I don't know if that makes sense but that's how it feels." He sat up straight and tall. He had a calm look on his face. He looked different to me now, somehow more grown up.

"It makes perfect sense to me. Just stay with the physical experience and see what happens next."

"I can't believe I did this!"

"You did it! What emotion goes with that?"

"I'm not sure. I guess I feel proud of myself."

I beamed. "Just notice what that's like. This is new and amazing."

"It's like my whole body feels bigger and I'm excited but not anxious. I like it, but it's kind of weird too."

"Weird? I know what weird means to me, but what does it mean to you?"

"It's like it feels good but maybe a little scary too."

"Yeah. It's good but a little scary too," I repeated, staying close with him. I wanted us to take our time here so he could feel all these newly emerging emotions deeply, allowing space for his brain and body to take it all in, to integrate it, to make a new normal. A minute elapsed.

"I feel calmer now." Spencer looked into my eyes. "Thank you," he said. "I am grateful that you encouraged me to do this."

"You're welcome," I said, feeling happy. We sat in silence for a while. Then I asked, as I typically do, "What was it like to do this together today?"

"It was amazing. I feel hopeful. If I can pretend stand up to my dad, maybe I can for real stand up to others. Maybe I don't have to fold. Maybe I can stand tall and take some risks."

"I know you can. This is just the beginning."

Spencer's Self had fully realized an openhearted state. I saw his confidence, his calm, his clarity. I felt our connection. And, most important, he had compassion toward himself.

The following week, I asked Spencer if anything had come up after that huge and important session. "Any thoughts you want to share?"

"Yes, I thought quite a bit about my childhood. Memories kept coming up. I thought about how fearful I have always been and how much time I lost because of all the hiding I have done. I don't want to do that anymore. I am not sure this feeling will last, but I do feel different. I even contacted a gallery owner that an artist friend of mine suggested I call. I only left a message but I felt good about it. Really good about it!"

"How do you understand that?" I wanted him to describe the internal changes he had experienced since last week.

"I think something about standing up to my dad changed me. Even though it was fantasy, it felt effective. I can't explain it. I just feel less scared. If someone is an asshole, that's on them, not me."

Spencer and I continued our work for another two years. We processed feelings about his mother, and as that work progressed his relationship with her improved. Spencer came to understand his mother's neglect as a result of her own childhood traumas and fears—she was scared to stand up to his father for fear of repercussions. And while he didn't exonerate her, he felt forgiveness and compassion. He and his mother forged a new, closer relationship apart from his father. Spencer flourished in his day job as a graphic designer, asking for a long overdue raise and taking on additional responsibility. He found more delight and satisfaction in his existing friendships. He started dating a lovely woman who seemed very good for him, and he landed a show at a gallery upstate.

On many occasions, I diagrammed the Change Triangle for Spencer and gave him the pieces of paper as a reference. He told me he carried one in his wallet. He referred to it at times and used it as a reminder to stay in touch with his core anger, especially at times when he felt the pull toward fear and shame. When he felt his younger parts triggered to these emotions, he immediately imagined them, checked in to what they needed, and gave it to them. Sometimes, he told me, they needed verbal reassurance that he could protect them if someone was mean. Sometimes they needed a pat on the back. At other times, he timidly admitted, they needed a big hug.

I helped Spencer cultivate compassion for his younger parts instead of contempt. Processing all his stuck emotions eventually led to relief and increased self-confidence that he could handle his feelings. He spent more and more time in an openhearted state.

Working with Anxiety, Shame, and Guilt

PAST EXPERIENCES MAY have taught us that certain core emotions were not acceptable, so when a core emotion is evoked in the present, anxiety and other inhibitory emotions can be triggered unconsciously. The inhibitory emotions act like a red light that sends the signal: *STOP. Don't feel that!* The emotional experience switches from one that is core to one that is inhibitory. Core emotions are thwarted in three different ways: with anxiety, with shame, and/or with guilt.

Working with Anxiety

I knew what anxiety was long before I became a psychotherapist. As a teenager and young adult, I felt dread on Sundays in anticipation of Mondays, and I could identify that dread as anxiety. I could say, "I am anxious about school tomorrow." My parents would often ask, "What do you think is making you anxious?" Sometimes I figured it out. But beyond that and reminding myself it would pass, I didn't know what to do to actively help myself feel better until I learned the Change Triangle.

At the first AEDP workshop I attended, the instructors made us participate in what they called experiential exercises. We had to practice what we had just learned by working with emotions on a physical level and processing those experiences. Following a lecture, we formed groups of three. One person played the therapist, the other played the patient, and the third person was the witness who kept track of the time and called on instructors for help as needed. When it was my turn to be the patient, I was asked, "What are you feeling right now?"

The words "right now" were important. Before I did anything with my emotions, I had to bring myself into the present moment, and then I had to slow myself down to a snail's pace, so I could begin to perceive my emotions and my physical sensations as they were happening, in real time.

When the student playing the role of therapist asked me what I was feeling now, I was nervous about trying these techniques for the first time, so I answered, "I'm nervous!"

Then she asked me, "How do you experience that nervous feeling in your body?"

How did I experience my nervousness, technically called my anxiety, in my body? What a novel question! I took a deep breath, tuned in to my visceral experience, and scanned my body from head to toe.

"I feel my heart beating fast in my chest. I feel a kind of vibration all over," I said.

My partner then prompted, "Can you just stay with that feeling inside for a while? Breathe and notice. Let me know when something shifts. All we are doing is noticing."

I stayed with my physical experience as instructed. Admittedly, I was frightened. I remember believing that if I focused on my quickly beating heart, it might speed up even more. I thought I would get more anxious and out of control. I was in public and vulnerable—I didn't want to lose it in front of my colleagues. Despite my fears, I summoned the courage and trust to stay focused on the thumping in my chest. Much to my surprise, my heart calmed down. As I focused inward, the vibrating sensations calmed down, too, and I felt more relaxed. This was a revelation.

Since then, when I recognize I'm anxious, I immediately shift my awareness to my body. I resist the pull to go up into my head and think, a reflexive action most of us do naturally. I hone in on the way I feel physically. I don't judge myself and I don't put pressure on myself. I just stay with the physical sensations of my anxiety, breathing slowly and deeply, until something shifts. Just like in that workshop, I calm down. Dealing with my anxiety in this way helps me feel more in control of myself. Lowering anxiety in this way is also a precursor to finding the core emotions.

PEOPLE EXPERIENCE ANXIETY IN A VARIETY OF WAYS

Anxiety comes in many forms. Some of my patients get dizzy or have an out-of-body experience. Some of my patients feel a knot or clenching in their stomachs. Some of my patients notice that their hearts beat faster and their breathing gets shallow. Some of my patients feel a tingling in their arms and legs. Anxiety is creative and can manifest itself in a variety of symptoms:

- dizziness
- spaciness
- out-of-body experiences
- confusion
- ear ringing
- blurred vision
- clenched stomach
- GI distress: diarrhea, nausea, vomiting
- hot or cold flushes
- sudden urge to urinate
- sweating
- migraine headaches
- rapid or pounding heartbeat
- shallow breathing
- shortness of breath

- chest pain
- tingling in arms and legs
- restless leg syndrome (jiggly legs)
- shakiness

When we identify that we are on the anxiety corner of the Change Triangle, the next step is to calm anxiety. Tuning in to the physical sensations, breathing, and grounding help anxiety calm down. Then the task is to figure out the core emotions underneath. Even if we can't always figure out for sure what emotions we are experiencing, merely looking for them is useful because it creates distance and perspective between our internal experiences and our Self.

CORE EMOTIONS AND ANXIETY

Anxiety should be viewed as a helpful, albeit uncomfortable, signal that we are experiencing core emotions. When you notice you're feeling anxious, that's great! You can use that cue as a call to work the Change Triangle to find, name, validate, and experience the underlying core emotions. Not only are those core emotions important in and of themselves, but by moving from anxiety to core emotions, your anxiety will diminish.

MANY EMOTIONS AND ANXIETY

Depending on what is happening in our environment, a combination of core and inhibitory emotions may arise at the same time. When many emotions arise together, we get overwhelmed and anxious. To diminish the sense of being overwhelmed, we need to break down what we are experiencing into manageable, workable bits by naming each and every core emotion we are able to notice.

When it comes to the Change Triangle, we have to work with one emotion at a time. Noticing each emotion, one by one, and imagining space between them lowers anxiety. Run through each core emotion and look for it inside yourself: *I notice excitement AND fear AND joy AND . . .* Naming each core emotion and separating it with an "and" instead of a "but" helps the brain hold your emotions while keeping them separate. Using "but" negates or diminishes everything before it. Saying, *I feel sadness BUT also joy,* for example, undermines the sadness. We need to fully own *I feel both sadness AND joy.* We tend to each and every core emotion one at a time. As you notice each emotion, name it, validate it, and sense it. Then move on to check if there are more emotions to validate.

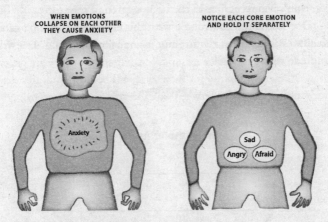

WHEN EMOTIONS
COLLAPSE ON EACH OTHER
THEY CAUSE ANXIETY

Anxiety

NOTICE EACH CORE EMOTION
AND HOLD IT SEPARATELY

Sad
Angry   Afraid

CONFLICTING EMOTIONS AND ANXIETY

It was a revelation for me to learn that we could experience opposite emotions at the same time. For example, when we love someone but they hurt us, it is not unusual to feel *I love you AND I hate you* at the same time. The emotions here would be love and anger.[1] Although love and anger occur for most of us routinely, we struggle to hold in our mind simultaneously these two opposite feelings with their two opposite impulses. The anxiety that irreconcilable conflicts cause is greatly ameliorated by remembering to validate both sides. In your mind, you would say to yourself something like *I love my partner AND right now I hate or I am so angry at him or her.* Often a small rewording like that feels much better and more manageable.

Here's an exercise: The next time you are anxious, draw a figure like the one below, leaving room to write in the figure's head and its body. Notice the anxious thoughts in your head and write some of them down. Then, turn your awareness to what you are experiencing below the neck. Try to name each and every core emotion that you find under the anxiety. Run through each core emotion one at a time: Am I feeling sad? Am I feeling scared? Am I feeling angry? Am I feeling excited? and so on. List all the core emotions you think you recognize in the body section of the figure.

Don't be afraid to struggle with this exercise again and again. Keep working it. Just the attempt is good for your brain. You will improve with practice!

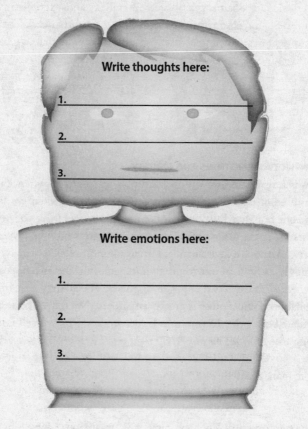

Write thoughts here:

1. _____
2. _____
3. _____

Write emotions here:

1. _____
2. _____
3. _____

Working with Shame

The mass of men lead lives of quiet desperation.

—HENRY DAVID THOREAU

Every step closer to my soul excites the scornful laughter of my devils, those cowardly ear-whisperers and poison-mixers.

—C. G. JUNG

When working the Change Triangle, loosening defenses often uncovers shame. Shame is universal, complex, and excruciatingly painful. Shame is so painful that the mind contorts in all sorts of ways (defenses) to protect us from even knowing that we have shame. We can, with some courage and mental energy, free ourselves from shame. Learning as much as we can about shame is the first step.[2]

We all have shame. Not one of us is spared. At one time or another and for one thing or another, we are all rebuffed, rejected, ignored, hear the word "no" at a time of true need, or are disapproved of by someone we rely upon.

No one wants to talk about shame. This makes sense. It's uncomfortable. Talking about shame actually triggers shame—we can begin to sense our body reacting as soon as we hear the word. Learning about shame, however, helps minimize its power.

So, what exactly is shame? How does it get created? How do we recognize it? And how do we transform our shame? Breaking shame down into two categories helps with understanding. There is a helpful kind, *healthy shame,* and a hurtful kind, *toxic shame.*

Healthy shame ensures we become good citizens of the world. Our innate self-preservation instincts have to be inhibited so we can form effective groups. Groups offer many survival benefits: help, collaboration, protection, and the like. Shame makes sure we are not too greedy, covetous, aggressive, abusive, and neglectful. Healthy shame motivates us to be good people. When we act in accordance with the values in our group, we feel good. When we don't, we feel ashamed of ourselves.

Empathy is the capacity to put yourself in the skin of another person, helping you understand and share that person's feelings. Empathy prevents us from committing acts against humanity like rape, murder, and violations of human rights because we literally feel bad when we hurt others. We imagine what it feels like to be on the receiving end, and we don't want to inflict that on anyone. Healthy shame and empathy are nature's way of helping humans feel for and care about one another so that we survive as a species.

Toxic shame is the deep sense that "I am bad, I am not good enough, I am unlovable." Toxic shame is not necessary for the survival of our species—we'd all do better without it. Yet sadly, it exists and is a root cause for much of our psychological suffering. Toxic shame leads to depression, addictions, eating disorders, personality disorders like narcissism and borderline personality disorder, and more. Shame causes perfectionism, contempt, arrogance, grandiosity, and prejudice—all defenses we use against insecurity. When we are in shame, we are not open to sharing our authentic Self. Our shame tells us we have something to hide. Shame tells us we are broken, defective, or different. Furthermore, shame tells us that if anyone finds out about what we are ashamed of we will be rejected. The good news is that there is so much we can do to prevent and heal toxic shame. But first we need to learn what causes toxic shame, recognize its symptoms, and eradicate stigmas so that we can talk honestly with one another.

At one point, I had no idea what shame was. I thought it was just about being embarrassed every now and then. Once I studied the biology and psychology of shame, I learned to see all the silent, unconscious ways shame affects people. I started to notice it everywhere. I noticed the ways people avoided sharing honestly about their lives, their feelings, and their experiences. I noticed how uncomfortable some of my friends got when I shared my hardships or asked a probing question about their lives. I noticed and began to question when and why I held my true Self back. When I discovered my shame and outed it, either just to myself or by sharing it with others, it somehow lost its power. The relief I felt was enormous.

Shame Is Not Guilt

Shame and guilt are often confused. Guilt is what we feel when we have *done* something bad. Shame is when we feel *that we are bad*! Guilt is about bad deeds. Shame is about a bad Self. Shamed parts of us often believe

I am not good enough.

I am stupid.

I am worthless.

I am flawed.

I am ugly.

I am unlovable.

I am broken.

I am unacceptable.

I am a failure.

I am a bad person.

Working the Change Triangle helps transform toxic shame. It does this in several ways:

- by reminding us shame exists and it might be keeping us stuck in our defenses
- by guiding us to actively find and acknowledge parts of us that have shame
- by guiding us to accept ourselves as we are
- by guiding us to revisit the memories that caused us to feel ashamed so we can liberate the core emotions originating from that time, like I did with Spencer

Our mission is to unravel the misconceptions that birthed our shame, understand the small t and big T traumas we went through that caused those beliefs, and experience the core emotions that arose from the insult or attack to our core sense of Self. At the end of that process, relief awaits. We are more in touch with our authentic Self. More open to others. The process is liberating![3]

Think about Spencer. He came to me because he was experiencing debilitating social anxiety, but when we started to talk about his father, Spencer held a lot of shame. Spencer believed, because his father told him so, that he was ungrateful, mean, not good enough, and a bad son. He thought his badness caused his father's behavior. On the contrary, Spencer was incredibly thoughtful (bringing me coffee) and cooperative (winning employee of the year for being a team player), and showed gratitude (thanking me for helping him), but his shame told him otherwise and kept him from seeing his father's abuse for what it was.

HOW SHAME HAPPENS

We are not born with shame; we learn it from others. When we come forward to connect with another person and we are shut down, shame is triggered. Shame is our physical and psychological response to primal rejection.

Our shame is bound to our specific life experiences. We all have suffered shame, but what makes us feel shame and why we suffer it is unique for everyone. As adults, we will likely not remember how our shame developed. But shame is always tied to specific events that taught us to be guarded or to hide. Many of our shame-forming experiences happened before we could speak, when we were babies. For example, picture a smiling, excited eighteen-month-old baby running open-armed to his mother. This baby is undefended and vulnerable. This baby's nervous system expects a mother who matches his emotions, who is equally excited, smiling, and welcoming. But when the baby gets to his mother, he finds her preoccupied. His mom is understandably tired from a long day; maybe she is struggling with a little depression, dealing with her aging parents, or facing other common hardships. She is not emotionally available. She greets her baby with a flat or even disappointed facial expression. No one is to blame for this kind of unreceptive response; the mother is doing the best she can. Still, the mother's lack of matched enthusiasm evokes shame in her child. The mismatch between a child's exuberance and his caregiver's indifference is experienced as a rejection, and the baby internalizes the sense that he was bad for being excited. Additionally, when we are rejected, core emotions like anger and sadness arise as well. After all, we do not like being rejected, so it makes sense that rejection would trigger anger, the initial protest, and then sadness for the loss of the connection between our Self and the one who caused us shame.

Anger and sadness arise naturally in response to even the slightest rejection, especially when we are young. If our sadness or anger is responded to positively, our nervous system settles down, and we return to feeling calm. If our core emotions are not responded to with empathy, and instead are met with indifference—or worse, retaliation—shame causes us to retract inward for protection. If repeatedly rejected, young minds form entrenched beliefs that it is

~~Who's to Blame?~~ Who Is Responsible?

In my experience, most people don't want to blame their parents or other family members, even when they did hurtful things and made big mistakes. Blame is not helpful. As a parent, I made many mistakes for which my children paid a price. The last thing I want is to shame parents. I do, however, like to talk in terms of who was the responsible party. Since parents are adults, they are responsible for their children's well-being. As parents, we can and must be accountable for our mistakes. We can also forgive ourselves. One way to do this is to make the shift from shame (I am bad) to guilt (I sometimes did bad things). In other words, we can say to ourselves that we didn't mean harm and we are not bad people, but still we made mistakes and did hurtful things that we regret. Then we can try to make amends, like owning and apologizing for the mistakes we made and things we did when we did not know any better.

our own fault. Shame then causes us to hide in protection, blocking the future recognition of our anger and sadness.

Of course, even the "best" childhoods include shaming. Socializing inevitably requires our parents, at times, to inhibit the expression of our feelings. Sometimes big displays of emotion are simply not appropriate, such as when a child is giggly or having a tantrum in public. We all get a "SHHHH!" once in a while. But with repeated insults, unaccompanied by a parent's attempt to repair the break in connection with the child, the child learns, "If we do A, we will feel shame." So we stop doing A.

Toxic shame is caused in two main ways:

1. when our bids for love, physical/emotional care, and acceptance are consistently met with indifference, disdain, neglect, or retaliation
2. when we subjectively sense criticism or rejection for who we are, what we need, and what we feel

Abuse and neglect always lead to chronic shame. When children are mistreated, they believe it is their fault. It is as if they assume they must *be* bad or else they wouldn't *feel* so bad. Children are too young to consider that their caregiver might be at fault.

Remember how Sara's mother shamed her, making her feel like she was bad for having basic needs and emotions? As a child, if Sara was sick and needed care, her mother yelled at her. If Sara protested at having a toy taken away from her, her mother yelled at her. Had Sara's mother been knowledgeable about the impact of shaming her daughter, she might have been more aware and perhaps worked harder to hold back her own emotional reactions.

Bonnie's father shamed Bonnie for not liking her ballet class. With a little education about the effect of shame, Bonnie's father might have paused before he reacted to Bonnie. He might have gotten curious about why he was triggered to anger by Bonnie's comment. After all, she was just a little girl with no real power. But Bonnie's harmless remark about not liking ballet had great power over him, so much so that he reacted intensely. That kind of outsized reaction should be a clue that shame might be hiding under one's anger. Her dad could have calmly let her know that while she had to continue ballet class, she didn't have to like it. The fact that he was triggered to anger says more about Bonnie's father than about Bonnie. Had he been more self-aware, Bonnie would have been spared the symptoms of her shame and trauma.

Shaming communication conveys to a child that he is bad. A nonshaming approach entails a parent taking responsibility for decisions and not blaming the child. Spencer's father, who had unresolved shame stemming from his physically abusive childhood, passed down that shame to Spencer by humiliating him for his needs and emotions. Shame is a hot potato—people unconsciously and automatically pass it on to others: "You're bad! You're weird! You're wrong!" This is how trauma and shame are handed down from one generation to the next. Talking about shame, educating one another about shame, and ultimately *healing* shame are important not only for us but for our children and generations to come.

TOXIC SHAME FROM FEELING DIFFERENT OR APART FROM SOCIETY

Shame comes from society and its institutions as well. Our cultures, our religions, our education systems, and our communities all have many rules, both spoken and unspoken, for how a person should be. We naturally experience shame when we believe we do not measure up. Even people with loving, supportive families can feel ashamed for being poor, or nonwhite, or non-Christian; for identifying as transgender or gay; or for being sick or disabled, just to mention some of the groups that still suffer stigma and injustice. For example, many parents work hard to help their daughters accept and love their bodies. But it is almost impossible to compete with the forces of our culture—magazine covers of emaciated, hairless, airbrushed women—which create shame for those of us who don't look like that. An eating disorder, as I mentioned earlier, is a symptom indicating that there is a part of that person suffering from toxic shame. To recover, shame must be addressed.

Another environment where shame is created can be school. Many people don't learn well with a teacher lecturing at the front of the room. They need to interact and experiment with their environment. Two plus two on a blackboard is a very different experience than holding two oranges and grabbing two more to learn that they add up to four. Kids who learn best from a lecture have an unfair advantage in more than one way. Not only do they learn more, but they also have less shame. Children who struggle to learn in our current system incorrectly attribute their lack of success to their lack of intelligence—they blame themselves. But it is the system that has failed them, not the other way around.

Cultural definitions of masculinity and femininity also are responsible for much of the toxic shame we have. For example, Marlboro Man culture tells us that men are supposed to be tough. Aggression and anger are manly. Men who display tender emotions like sadness or fear, who allow themselves to be interdependent with others, are labeled "wimps" or "pussies," terms designed explicitly to shame. Women, conversely, are expected not to show anger. In fact, women who display anger are labeled "bitches," a word designed to shame. In general, men are shamed for showing tender emotions and women are shamed for showing anger and sexual excitement, being called "promiscuous" or "sluts."

Janie was born with a high level of sexual excitement. Remember that sexual excitement is a core emotion and core emotions exist on a spectrum with some people feeling them a lot and some people feeling them a little. Janie wanted sex not because she had low self-esteem or for any other negative reason. She just loved sex. But our culture and her religion (she was a nonpracticing Catholic) shamed her for this genetic attribute that she had no capacity to control. *Feelings just are!* Sadly, Janie felt shame about herself. In high school, Janie was called a nymphomaniac, slut, whore, and the like, all of which affected her self-esteem. In truth, the people doing the name-calling needed to work the Change Triangle to understand what emotions (fear? sexual excitement? disgust? shame? anxiety?) were underneath their defense (aggression in the form of name-calling), which was triggered by Janie's sexuality.

Movies portray sex and relationships in an unrealistic light, and this promotes shame. We grow up believing that what we see in the movies is normal, and we measure ourselves against it. So, when our sex or relationships do not meet those standards, we feel ashamed, frequently pretending to be something we are not.

The word "normal" is a part of the problem, creating shame rather than helping. What is "normal"? Why does "normal" matter? The whole concept is a setup for creating shame. If "normal" matters to you, ask yourself why. Your answer will shed light on shame.

How do we reconcile these cultural expectations with the reality of our biology and core emotions? What do we do about the fact that we cannot realistically meet the expectations set for us? Should we accept that part of growing up is to become ashamed of our authentic Selves? Should we stand by and allow people to be shamed for who they are, what they naturally feel, for the people they love, for what they like, and for what they need?

The more you look, the more you will find shame creating standards. It is no wonder so many of us feel like we have to hide who we really are and pretend to meet ridiculous and arbitrary standards. Unless we have an understanding of shame and how to combat it, we will continue to hide, limit ourselves, and suffer the consequences of our defenses.

WHAT TRIGGERS SHAME?
Fill in the blank:

If everyone knew _____ about me, I could never show my face again.

The threat of your deepest secret being exposed triggers a danger signal in the brain. We become afraid—shame and fear go together. When others point out or get too close to seeing the things about which we are ashamed, our shame is triggered.

Here's an example: My patient Martha had a fear of being perceived as needy. "Martha is so needy," is what she heard as a child. As an adult she felt ashamed when she had needs. Martha internalized the family belief that having needs was equivalent to being bad. Both her friends and her partner tried to reassure her that they did not think she was too needy, but she could not stop feeling bad about herself. Her shame not only caused her to pull away from the people she loved but also caused her to become resentful when her needs were not met. She projected the disdain she had toward her parents for not wanting to meet her needs onto her friends and partner. The shame distorted her perception of reality and prevented her from seeing that her friends and partner were not her parents—and that they were in fact generous and giving.

The Perfection Myth

Many people I treat strive to be perfect. When someone tells me she wants to be perfect, I ask, "Perfect for whom?" No one is perfect! Every one of us has flaws. The whole notion of perfection makes no sense when you understand that we all see through a subjective lens. What is perfect to one person is probably not perfect to someone else. Usually the word "perfect" is code for: *At one time, I needed to be some specific way to get approval from someone important and avoid being shamed.* Uncovering the original someone in that scenario can help loosen the grip of a perfectionistic standard.

Difference is another great shame evoker. *I like this but you like that. I want this but you want that. I am this but you are that. I feel this but you feel that.* Why does difference cause shame? Because difference is hard for the brain. We feel unsure of what the difference means. Is one of us bad? Is one of us better? Am I threatened? Am I "normal"?

- I have a mental illness. What does that say about me?
- My child is gay. What does that say about me?
- I have cancer. How will people see me now?
- I suffer from addiction. Will I be judged?
- I have anxiety. Can anybody tell? If so, will they judge me or understand?

- What does my suffering say about me?
- What do my sexual fantasies and preferences say about me?
- What does it say about me that my mother, father, siblings, and friends are all married but I am not?
- What does it say about me that I don't want or don't have any children?
- What does it say about me that I am divorced?
- What does it say about me that I don't make lots of money?
- What does it say about me that I have a trust fund and don't need to work?
- What does it say about me that I don't have a college education?
- What does it say about me that I have a disability? How will people see me?
- What does it say about me that I have an accent or that I am an immigrant?

Can you add your own worries about being different here?

_____

WHAT HAPPENS WHEN SHAME IS TRIGGERED

Evolution is clever. It designed the emotion of shame to be excruciatingly painful, so we do almost anything to avoid it. What else could make us deny our primal gratifications and selfish needs to conform to the needs of a group?

What happens when shame is triggered? You might relate to the experience of wanting to hide, run away, or cover yourself. You might relate to feeling unworthy, bad, inadequate, embarrassed, or not fitting in. You might relate to feeling alone, isolated, or disconnected. These are all various manifestations of shame. When we are about to say or do something that we believe will get a negative response, the inhibitory emotion of shame (or embarrassment in its less intense form) sends a signal to our nervous system to shut us down. Access to core emotions and connection to people is cut off. When shame hits we feel ourselves folding inward, shrinking, and receding into nothingness. We all recognize the downward gaze of shame: we avoid eye contact because we cannot bear being seen in a negative light. Our faces flush, exposed in our shame. It's horrible.

Shame causes us to stay small, to shrink down. The mind of someone who has been burned more than once for exposing her authentic Self might say, *Let's just keep our Self as small and hidden as possible, so no one can hurt us. If we expand and reach out into the world to discover new things, we will get slammed down again. Play it safe by staying small and hidden away.* And so we do.

Another psychological response to chronic shaming is to cover the feeling of smallness with arrogance or aggressiveness. For example, children and adults who bully others have deeply ashamed parts, which likely feel so unbearable that they must be fiercely denied and defended against using the defense of aggression. Bullies also either lack empathy because they likely never received it or have blocked their empathy because it is too painful. Remember that one of the main causes of toxic shame is when caregivers lack empathy for their children and dismiss, deny, or have disdain for feelings.

Most of us have pockets of shame here and there that go undiscovered, as Bonnie's or Spencer's did, yet affect how we feel and exist in the world. We silently feel empty, disconnected, lonely, and just plain bad about who we are. Some of us sense a void in our lives that we might try to fill with material possessions or accomplishments. But this doesn't work because the void is internal. We have secrets or we pretend to be something we are not. We use vices to anesthetize our shame. Or we use character armor like arrogance and aggression to defend against our pain. The mind creates a multitude of ways to protect us from feeling the pain of shame.

THE RELATIONSHIP BETWEEN SHAME
AND TAKING IN GOOD FEELINGS

Working the Change Triangle reminds us to tune in to our internal world in the present moment and become aware of the ways we either shrink down (with shame) or allow our openhearted Self to expand and be authentic. In any given moment, we can check inside and wonder, *Am I holding myself back? Am I sharing who I am? Am I taking healthy risks in sharing myself with others? Do I feel small or big? Am I allowing myself to take up space? Am I allowing myself to deeply receive praise, love, joy, and other pleasurable feelings?* If you always indiscriminately hold your authentic Self back, if you cannot share your true feelings with others, if you never take risks to connect with others, if you feel small, if you won't let yourself take in or even notice positive experiences, you can locate yourself easily on the top of the Change Triangle.

Shame causes us to habitually dismiss good feelings (which give us the sensation that we are physically expanding) in order to maintain the status quo of staying small for protection. We stay small for two main reasons.

CULTURAL MESSAGES

There is a lack of education on the difference between healthy pride and arrogance or conceit. We have a blanket rule against showing confidence and good feelings. We receive messages like *Don't get too big for your britches* or *Don't get a swelled head.* We have neither schooling in the importance of taking in good feelings nor a model for how to experience praise viscerally. We don't have explicit permission and encouragement to do so either. Most of us, upon hearing affirming words, don't permit ourselves to physically expand with delight. Keeping our Self in a diminished state offers protection from being shamed by others who might judge us for being cocky or confident. But we can viscerally feel good and still be humble and considerate of others. Over time, the cost for not taking in affirmation is a blow to our self-confidence.

A SUBJECTIVE SAFETY IN BEING SMALL

If our primary defense is to stay small, we cannot allow our Self to deeply take in compliments, praise, and other forms of recognition. To viscerally experience these good feelings would make us feel bigger, unprotected, and vulnerable to others. The conflict between experiencing good feelings, which make us grow bigger, and shame, which keeps us smaller, cannot be reconciled. We cannot be big and small at the same time. Protection wins out. We can, however, work to loosen the grip and even heal our shame and begin relearning how to experience pride, joy, and other good feelings. This is how self-confidence is built.

THE CHANGE TRIANGLE AND SHAME

To feel better, we know we must get ourselves to the bottom of the Change Triangle. When we are blocked by shame, we must loosen shame's grip, so we can move down to our core emotions and finally back to the openhearted state. We have to separate from our shame to heal it. We must not believe what our shame tells us about us. We cannot let it rule us. We have to see our shamed parts as if they were separate from us; once a little separation is achieved, we can begin to relate to our shame in a healthier, more healing way.

Spencer's shame led him to disconnect from people, even as he deeply wanted to connect with friends and be able to network. Once Spencer identified his shame and acknowledged that he wasn't born feeling shame, he became curious about what shamed him. Once curious, the separation from his shamed part had already begun. Now he was able to communicate with his shame so he could help alleviate it.

To recover from shame, we must uncover the root. We need to evaluate our history using common sense and the knowledge we have as adults about how people's minds work. Sometimes it is helpful to look back in time to the generations who came before us. We might have just inherited their shame.

My patient George's family believed divorce was shameful. When George was miserable in his marriage and wanted to leave, he felt trapped, believing he could not get a divorce no matter what. Value judgments are subjective, not objective truths. We must challenge them and think them through.

Was George inherently bad for getting divorced? No! George

needed to understand what led his family to link divorce to shame. How did his parents come to view divorce as shameful? What did his family believe getting divorced said about a person? What did George internalize about divorce? When he asked his parents what it meant to them, they told him they feared God would judge George harshly. Once George understood the origins of shame surrounding divorce in his family, it loosened its grip. He felt freer to make a decision in concert with his values as he worked with the parts of him that struggled.

Once we are open to the possibility that our shame is not a truth (even though it may feel like it), our goal is to form a new and secure relationship to the parts of us that have suffered shame. We can learn to offer understanding, compassion, and comfort to the parts of us that suffer, for that is part of the healing process.

Sharing with nonjudgmental others also transforms our shame. Connection is a cure for shame because shame feeds on loneliness. When you share something you feel bad about with others and they respond with empathy or their own particular shame, the loneliness is undone. Vulnerability met with vulnerability creates safety and connection. *Connection is the antidote for shame,* be it a connection between your Self and your shamed part or a connection to other people who help you feel loved and accepted, despite the very things you believed rendered you unlovable.[4]

Accessing old memories that counteract shame can also help mitigate shame. Remember times you felt loved, connected, safe, and complimented. Instead of dismissing those, try to sit with them. Although this takes work and mental energy, sitting with positive affirming memories can heal shame. The brain easily forgets the good stuff, so we must actively conjure it. Just as we sit with any core emotions, we have to stay with good feelings, breathing through any anxiety that comes up and noticing shifts. As you feel yourself physically expand, know it might feel weird or even a little scary. Keep breathing and work for a few seconds at a time so the experience is manageable. Eventually your capacity to process expansive emotions will increase. You will notice you start to actually feel physically bigger with a sense that you take up more space in the world.

It also helps to learn our blind spots—situations when it is hard for us to figure out what is reality or what is the past projecting into the present. You may not be able to assess whether or not you are having appropriate shame or toxic shame. At these times, it's best to get feedback from others to help you assess the situation.

For example, I worry if I talk too much about myself, others will think that I am self-centered. So my default is to keep myself small by not talking about myself so much. Sharing this fear with my friends and listening to their feedback that in fact I don't talk enough about myself has helped me mitigate that feeling of shame. But I still struggle with it. This is my blind spot, the origins of which trace back to some of my childhood experiences.

The Change Triangle reminds us to seek out the core emotions that hide under our inhibitory emotions. Any time we feel shame we must discover the core emotions we experienced when we were shamed by someone else. Since shame feels bad, we often feel angry, even enraged, at the person who shamed us. This anger needs to be felt. When anger is safely experienced, the shame often dissipates.

As adults, we can learn how to handle shaming moments without withdrawing or flying off into a rage. We can work the Change Triangle effectively once we know our vulnerabilities and shame triggers.

Recently, I went out to dinner with Trisha, an acquaintance I wanted to get to know better. I asked her, "How are you feeling about your job these days?" Her company was undergoing some big changes that were likely making her work life tough.

She responded to my question with, "That is such a therapist question."

I was stunned at first. Then I started imploding. I felt my face flush and my body pulling inward. I was experiencing the inhibitory emotion of shame. The shame was for being me, with my therapist-like questions. Being accused of acting like a therapist was a trigger for me. Since I had heard it many times, I was sensitive to this particular critique. In retrospect, Tricia probably didn't mean it as harshly as I heard it, but I felt insulted and humiliated.

Wanting to help myself and salvage the dinner, I excused myself to go to the bathroom. There, I used the Change Triangle to move my shame reaction aside.

First, and perhaps most important, I gave myself compassion. I said to myself, "This sucks. You didn't deserve a snide comment.

MOVEMENT UP THE TRIANGLE

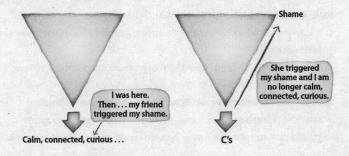

I was here. Then . . . my friend triggered my shame.

Calm, connected, curious . . .

She triggered my shame and I am no longer calm, connected, curious.

C's

MOVEMENT BACK DOWN THE TRIANGLE

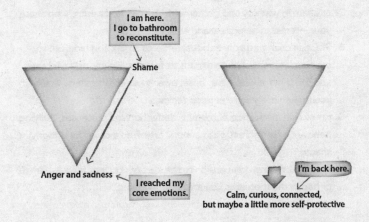

I am here. I go to bathroom to reconstitute.

Shame

Anger and sadness

I reached my core emotions.

I'm back here.

Calm, curious, connected, but maybe a little more self-protective

All you were trying to do was be nice and connect." Self-compassion helped immediately and substantially.

Then, I asked myself, "What core feelings am I having that the shame is blocking?" Just asking myself this question helped stop the shame spiral. I sifted through the core emotions and asked myself, "Am I angry?" Yes! I don't like being made to feel bad, especially when I'm just trying to be nice. "Am I afraid?" No! "Am I sad?" Yes! Trisha hurt my feelings and that saddened me. "Am I disgusted?" Slightly; I was disgusted by her behavior toward me. It was rude! Once I labeled my core feelings, I felt calmer. I could reconstitute myself and continue with dinner.

NINE WAYS TO BEGIN WORKING WITH YOUR SHAME

1. You were not born feeling shame about yourself. Know that shame is learned.

2. Know that shame is not your fault, even though our shame tells us it is.

3. Know that as adults we can learn skills and get help in handling shame like learning to manage rejection. We can gain enough confidence to take chances and come out of hiding. There is always hope.

4. Know that you can surround yourself with friends and partners who accept and love you for you. You can find people with whom you can safely share your accomplishments and failures. You can find people to share in your joy and excitement. You can find people who share your interest in being real and authentic.

5. Practice changing your habitual reflex to shrink and hide. Slowly start experimenting with expansive feelings like joy, pride, interest, and excitement when they arise, by acknowledging them. Notice if you immediately dismiss good feelings.

6. Know that arrogance, contempt, perfectionism, pretenses, bullying behavior, and aggression in general are often a cover for underlying shame.

7. Practice offering compassion to the part of you that feels ashamed or bad in the moments you are suffering most.

8. Practice working with your shamed part by asking it as though it were another person you were talking to, "How did you learn to feel ashamed? From whom or where did you get this message?" Then be patient and listen to your shamed part. It might tell you something new.

9. Practice finding and validating the core emotions you have felt as a result of being shamed either in the present or in the past.

Working with Guilt

Shame makes us feel something about our Self *is* bad, but guilt tells us when we have *done something* bad. Guilt helps ensure that we don't hurt others. Guilt also keeps us in check so we live harmoniously with other human beings. Sometimes, though, we feel guilty when we haven't done anything wrong except perhaps evoke feelings in another.

When using the Change Triangle to help with guilt, I find it useful to separate guilt into two categories: guilt for when we actually do something truly bad and guilt for when we haven't done anything objectively bad but we feel like we have or someone told us we have—for example, guilt we feel for having a particular need, preference, thought, or emotion. Knowing which of those two types of guilt we are experiencing is the first challenge. We work with each kind of guilt in a different way.

Many people experience guilt for putting their needs before someone else's. Sometimes, putting other people's needs first is the right thing to do. Most of us were raised to do just that. But often putting ourselves first is the wisest thing to do, both for our well-being and the well-being of our relationships. Consistently prioritizing the needs of others is not good for our mental health, nor is it good for our relationships, as it breeds resentment.

When I first met my husband, Jon, back in 2002, I believed I was above all a caretaker who put the needs of others before mine. My self-esteem was tied to my being a caretaker. When I told Jon during a conversation early in our relationship that I thought of myself as "all giving," he said, "Great! Because I am all taking!" I laughed, assuming he was joking. But much to my dismay, over time, I realized he wasn't joking. In fact, he was the first person I had loved who wanted, needed, and felt comfortable taking more than I could give. I was getting more and more exhausted and resentful. I realized that I had needs too. That was hard for me to admit, to say the least.

In couple's therapy, I had to come to terms with the fact that I was not all giving, like I wanted to believe. He half joked that I had pulled a bait and switch on him. Having reached my capacity for giving, we were forced to redefine ourselves. I was so ashamed of my limits and guilty that I couldn't do everything he asked of me. Physically, the guilt made me feel sick.

The process of accepting my limits was at first excruciating and then liberating. Looking back, I know that the entire process of accepting my limits and setting boundaries by saying no helped me to become a more loving and connected spouse. My gratitude and appreciation for Jon grew bigger as I felt truly loved in spite of my limits. Through the process of tolerating my guilt, Jon and I reset our standards. He is no longer all taking. I am no longer all giving. We came into balance; we had to in order for the relationship to survive.

Many of my patients feel guilty about advocating for themselves or setting limits, like saying no to requests that push them beyond their capacity. Their children, partners, and parents blame them and react harshly, pointing out their limitations or withdrawing connection. Alternatively, some people blame others for making them feel guilty. In general, we blame someone else for "making" us feel guilty rather than contend with the core emotions we have when we set limits, like fear. When we set a limit, we also need courage to allow the person hearing the *no* to have their feelings, too, like anger or sadness. Everyone is entitled to his or her feelings, but not entitled to lash out or act on them in a mean way or in other destructive ways.

Being blamed by others is one way we come to believe and accept that our emotions or thoughts are bad. We are given the message either directly or nonverbally: *Your sadness hurts me. Your anger makes me feel bad about myself. Your joy makes me feel small. Your excitement deadens me.* Eventually we feel guilty for what we feel. Some people feel guilty just for the act of existing, as if they are doing something bad to someone else just by being alive, as with survivor guilt.

What can we do to shift our guilt when it is unwarranted and doesn't serve us? We have to listen to our guilty part and find out what "crime" it believes we committed. Then we have to evaluate whether the crime was truly a wrongdoing or if we are merely trying to advocate or take care of our Self. If we feel guilty for taking care of our Self, then we need to understand the roots of our guilt and why it's hard to accept that we have limits and boundaries. Maybe the guilt is connected to shame—we have let someone down by being the way we are. Maybe the guilt serves to block core emotions—we may feel guilty for our anger.

When you ask the part of yourself that experiences guilt what crime it believes you committed and you have no answer, you must suspect the guilt is inhibiting a core emotion. To help alleviate misguided guilt, look for the core emotions underneath. Think about how Sara felt guilty for asking me a question. It felt too assertive. Sara's mother was threatened by her assertiveness. She yelled at Sara, which evoked Sara's core anger. But because it was dangerous for Sara to get angry with her mother, the anger was squashed by guilt (and shame). As an adult Sara believed she committed a crime anytime she even thought about asserting her needs over someone else's. She also internalized the sense that being assertive was a bad quality. So the mere thought of asserting her needs made her feel unbearably guilty, as well as ashamed.

When you plot your state on the Change Triangle and you have determined you are suffering from guilt, you can ask yourself, *If I didn't move to guilt, what feelings might I have toward the person who is evoking my guilt?* Guilt can arise in connection with any core emotion, depending on childhood experiences. You can feel guilty about your anger, your sadness, your excitement, your fear, your sexual excitement, your disgust, or your joy.

As adults, if we constantly put the needs of others before our own, we get depleted, depressed, anxious, and experience a variety of stress-induced health issues. We are evolutionarily wired to survive, and survival means taking care of ourselves. Core emotions evolved exactly for this purpose. We need to listen to them and honor them, gaining some clarity about what is going on beyond the guilt and finding a balance or compromise that feels good. When we begin prioritizing our own needs, we have to tolerate our guilt until it decreases (and it will) and a new normal is found.

In my work with Bonnie, she had guilt about being angry with her father. Even though she learned that *feelings just are* and no one got hurt if she experienced her anger, it still felt wrong to express her angry impulses in fantasy. By going through the process of tolerating the guilt so she could experience her core emotions, she came to understand that her emotions were okay. No one had ever taught Bonnie, like most of us, that fantasies are acceptable. Our thoughts and emotions are purely internal processes—they don't affect others unless we act on them.

We can either skillfully and diplomatically set limits and boundaries or do so in a way that can create a sense of insecurity and danger for others. How we speak when we are letting someone know our limits makes all the difference. It helps to come from a place of concern for the other, letting them know they've been heard before clearly expressing our own needs. The more we practice setting limits and boundaries, and holding the line while being clear and kind, the easier setting limits and boundaries becomes.

We all do hurtful things to others from time to time, sometimes intentionally and sometimes unintentionally. If someone says we caused hurt, we cannot deny it. Being hurt is subjective, and the victim gets to decide that it occurred. For example, if you are hurt because your partner spends too much time at work, your partner, despite working to bring home a paycheck for you both, needs to listen to your hurt. Then ideally you can decide together how to handle it. Sometimes change needs to happen. Often being heard and understood is all that is required. Some situations require an apology and amends to be made.

My patients Mara and Jack had been living together for a year. While dusting, Mara accidentally knocked over a glass figurine, which shattered against the tile floor. Unfortunately, it was an award Jack had received as an honor for his work in advertising. Mara's first impulse was to hide the evidence. She panicked about how Jack would react. She entertained fantasies of running away to avoid his anger and any other emotions he had about the broken award. Mara's second impulse was to convince both Jack and her guilty conscience that this mishap was not such a big deal. *Objects are just objects,* she told herself. *It is not as if I killed someone!* Of course, that is true, but that kind of attitude might not serve her relationship with Jack.

In truth, Mara was deeply sorry. Her third impulse was to gather the strength and courage to look Jack in the eye and say, "I broke your glass award. I know how much it meant to you. I know it's irreplaceable. I'm deeply sorry for breaking it. I understand how upsetting it must be to lose a cherished possession. If there's anything I can do to make it up to you, please tell me. In the meantime, I understand if you are angry and I am deeply sorry."

Admitting we did something wrong is a humbling experience. It takes strength to withstand the assault to our egos. Many of us pride ourselves on not making mistakes. Some of us were harshly berated for making mistakes when we were young. As a consequence, even though we are adults, we continue to berate ourselves just like someone else once did. Most of us understand intellectually that perfection is not a realistic standard, yet it can be hard, painful, and scary to own our mistakes.

The skill of knowing when and how to apologize is one that serves all of us and our valued relationships. What makes a good apology? The late Randy Pausch, in his beautiful book *The Last Lecture,* sets guidelines for the three parts of a proper apology:

1. saying you are sorry and what you are sorry for
2. showing your understanding for how your actions caused hurt

3. making amends or asking how you can make amends if you are not sure

Learning how to offer a real apology is one of the best things you can do for your relationships. It's all about accountability. When our actions cause hurt, we feel guilty. When we own the damage, whether done by mistake or on purpose, it sends a message: *I care about you more than I care about my ego.* Authentically caring about the hurt feelings we cause to those we love fosters deep love and trust. It's not easy. But a heartfelt apology has the power to heal even the deepest wounds.

Experiment: Calming Anxiety

FOCUSING AWARENESS ON physical sensations is a powerful catalyst for brain change. That's why tuning in to the sensations our anxiety evokes—like a fluttering or tightening in the chest or a knot in the stomach—decreases anxiety. It often helps to calm anxiety the minute you notice it.

Leaning into anxiety is counterintuitive. We typically avoid the sensations that bother us.

With curiosity, compassion, and zero judgment, notice your anxiety, nerves, or tension. Breathe deeply as you drop the story line or thinking going on in your head and focus only on the physical manifestations of your anxiety for about twenty seconds or until you notice something shift.

Write down three shifts you noticed for better or for worse, no matter how small:

1. _____
2. _____
3. _____

When we stop avoiding core emotions with defenses, the Change Triangle predicts that anxiety might arise. We are no longer deflecting the anxiety with defenses. If we are prepared in advance with three or four strategies that we know will decrease our anxiety, we'll have techniques at our fingertips to lower it and be able to work the Change Triangle to achieve an openhearted state.

You'll have to experiment to find the techniques that best lower anxiety for you. Below are a few suggestions. Try them all out, add some of your own, and put together a list of calming tools.

1. **Breathe:** Take four or five long, deep belly breaths. Deep breathing stimulates nerves in the heart and lungs that lead to calming. (See the instructions on page 59 for deep belly breathing to refresh your memory.)
2. **Ground yourself:** Placing both feet on the floor, turn all of your attention to the soles of your feet. Stay there for at least a minute till you have a strong sense of the ground beneath you.
3. **Slow down:** Be still while you breathe and feel your feet on the ground. Listen to the outside sounds around you. Notice the colors in the world around you. Notice the textures in the world around you. No multitasking!
4. **Put yourself in a peaceful place:** Imagine a calming place, such as the beach: feel the hot sun on your skin, hear the sound of the waves, feel the cool sand against your feet, and see the water. Find your peaceful place and bring up the image as vividly as possible.
5. **Focus on sensations of anxiety:** Tune in to the physical sensations of your anxiety, like a quickly beating heart or butterflies in your stomach. With curiosity and compassion for the feeling, stay with the sensations, breathing deeply until you feel them calm down. They will!
6. **Name core emotions:** Find all the core emotions that are evoking the anxiety. Ask yourself if you feel sad, fearful, angry, disgusted, joyful, excited, and/or sexually excited. Imagine them one at a time with space between each. Validate them by saying to yourself, *I feel* _____ *AND* _____ *AND* _____ *AND* . . .

7. **Exercise:** Physical exertion reliably diminishes anxiety.

8. **Connect:** Reach out to a friend. Tell him you are upset about something and want to talk about it. If you don't have a friend nearby, perhaps seek out a support group (Alcoholics Anonymous, Al-Anon, Narcotics Anonymous, Emotions Anonymous, etc.). Talking helps!

9. **Imagine your anxiety as a child part of you:** Offer the child part comfort by being your own good parent. Give it a hug, swaddle it in a blanket, offer it cookies and milk. Use your imagination in any way that the child part needs to feel a bit better.

10. **Try other activities that lower anxiety or help you feel more engaged in the moment:** Cook, play music, stretch or do yoga, make something artistic, read a good book, watch something funny or sad on television, take a warm bath, make yourself tea, practice juggling, take a walk, masturbate, or meditate. You might already have some things that you know work for you.

Write down the three calming tools that work best in upsetting moments:

1. _____
2. _____
3. _____

Experiment:
Shaming Messages

WE RECEIVE MANY messages from our parents and family members. Here are just some of them:

"Don't be so smart!"

"Don't be stupid!"

"Don't stick out!"

"Don't be so shy!"

"Don't act crazy!"

"Don't admit your flaws!"

"Be independent!"

"You're too needy!"

"You're too thin!"

"You're too fat!"

"Be tougher!"

"You're bad!"

"Act like a man!"

"Act like a lady!"

"Don't be sexy."

"Don't be ridiculous!"

"You're no better than anyone else."

"Be sweeter!"

"Be smarter!"

"Don't be weak!"

"Be more like your brother!"

"Don't be so sensitive!"

"Don't be so inconsiderate!"

"You're lazy!"

List three messages that you learned, either directly or indirectly, from your family about how you should be:

1. _____

2. _____

3. _____

How did each of those messages affect you and your sense of Self?

1. _____

2. _____

3. _____

We also receive many messages from our schools, peers, religions, and cultures. Here are some of them:

"Be quiet!"

"Be studious!"

"Be adventurous!"

"Don't act slutty!"

"Don't be a wimp!"

"You're too sensitive!"

"Don't be a sinner!"

"Be a mensch!"

"You're not religious enough!"

"Don't show your feelings!"

"Don't shame us!"

"Don't disrespect your family."

Write down three messages that you learned from your school, religion, and/or culture about how you should be:

1. _____
2. _____
3. _____

How did each of those messages affect your sense of Self?

1. _____
2. _____
3. _____

Finally, we receive strong messages about feeling good about ourselves:

"Don't be too big."
"Don't think you are better than anyone else."
"Don't get a swelled head."
"You think you're so great!"

These are comments that make us feel humiliated or ashamed. The message many of us receive says, *It is bad to feel good or to feel pride in your Self.*

Can you list three messages you directly or indirectly received from your family, peers, school, religion, and/or culture about feeling good about yourself and your accomplishments? (They can be positive or negative.)

1. _____
2. _____
3. _____

How did each of those messages affect your sense of Self?

1. _____
2. _____
3. _____

Experiment: The Shoulds You Encounter Daily

WHEN USING THE Change Triangle, a "should" is often a thought that is acting as a defense. What is its adaptive purpose in life?

When we use the word "should," it benefits us to be aware. Any time you say to yourself, *I should be* _____, notice that thought and get curious. Maybe you should or maybe you really should not. Ask the part of you, *Why should I be/do/feel* _____*?* Listen to how that part of you answers. Evaluate whether this thought is helpful or hurtful to you. Shame and guilt are often under those beliefs.

Examples:

I should be tougher.
Emotion underneath: Shame for believing you are weak.

I should be less sensitive.
Emotion underneath: Shame for having feelings.

I should be more accommodating.
Emotion underneath: Shame for being a person with needs. Guilt for not doing more for others.

I should be or I should want to be more social.
Emotion underneath: Guilt and shame for not being more social.

I should be thinner.
Emotion underneath: Shame for not being thinner.

I should talk more.
Emotion underneath: Guilt and shame for not being more talkative.

I should have a better-looking girlfriend.
Emotion underneath: Shame for not being enough.

I should work harder.
Emotion underneath: Guilt for not working harder. Shame for being lazy.

I should have more friends.
Emotion underneath: Shame for not being enough. Desire for more friends.

"Should" beliefs are not rooted in facts. They are learned. Sometimes they serve us and sometimes they do not.

Not all shoulds are bad. For example, sometimes they tell us to take care of ourselves (I *should* get a checkup at the doctor) and to be a good citizen (I *should* not be mean).

However, many "should"s are about meeting the arbitrary standards of our families, peers, religions, or cultures. Those beliefs are likely not serving you.

Can you write down three "should"s that you tell yourself?

1. _____
2. _____
3. _____

When you uncover unhelpful shame, it helps to have a curious, nonjudgmental conversation with it.

Shame: *I should be a better friend.*
Openhearted Self: *Really? Why should you?*

Shame: *So my friends would like me more.*

Openhearted Self: *What happened that made you think your friends don't like you?*

Shame (who is now wracking the brain trying to come up with examples): *No one has called me to go do something in a while.*

Openhearted Self (working the Change Triangle): *If you move aside shame, what core emotions come up from not being called?*

Openhearted Self identifies and validates the core emotions of sadness and anger.

Openhearted Self: *Maybe you need to reach out instead of waiting.*

Shame: *I am afraid people are too busy.*

Openhearted Self: *I hear you are afraid. That's hard. But it has nothing to do with who you are. It's okay to feel sad and angry that no one has called. Consider calling a friend to hang out with if you want companionship. If she's too busy, she will tell you.*

My patient Betsy felt lonely and neglected by her friends. In our work together, we identified the inhibitory emotions that were at the root of her failure to connect with people. Along with processing the core emotions, I encouraged her to have a conversation with herself very similar to the one above. This conversation helped Betsy diminish her shame. She learned:

1. She had a shamed part that worried that her friends didn't like her.
2. She worried that people were too busy for her.
3. She had feelings toward her friends for not calling her: mostly sadness and some anger.
4. She waited passively and formed all sorts of assumptions, when being proactive could solve the problem.
5. She had to summon courage to reach out.

BETSY MAPPED OUT HER DEFENSE, INHIBITORY EMOTION, AND CORE EMOTIONS ON THE CHANGE TRIANGLE

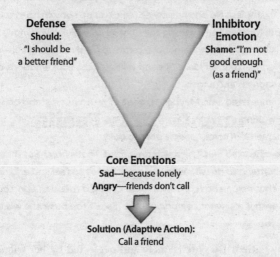

Defense
Should:
"I should be
a better friend"

Inhibitory Emotion
Shame: "I'm not
good enough
(as a friend)"

Core Emotions
Sad—because lonely
Angry—friends don't call

Solution (Adaptive Action):
Call a friend

Experiment: Guilty Feelings

SOMETIMES GUILT IS helpful. We have done something wrong and we need to be accountable and make amends. Other times guilt is unwarranted. We have not done anything wrong and the guilt serves to obscure a deeper conflict or pain, such as

- guilt for setting a limit or boundary when someone in our life is intrusive
- guilt for being alive when someone we love has died
- guilt for taking care of our own needs when we were taught that was not okay to do

Let's explore guilt. Think of the last time you felt guilty about something.

What did you do? _____

If guilt is for a "crime," what was your crime? _____
_____

Was this a crime of putting your needs in front of someone else's needs?   YES____ NO____

Was this a crime of lashing out at someone?   YES____ NO____

Was this a crime caused by lack of impulse control?   YES____ NO____

What was the motivation behind this crime?

_____

_____

_____

Have you felt guilty for this crime before?   YES____ NO____

How old were you the first time you felt guilty about this crime?

_____

Whom did you hurt? _____

How did you hurt him or her? _____

How do you know you hurt him or her? (How did he or she

communicate the hurt? With words, with actions, with a look?) _____

_____

Is an apology warranted?   YES____ NO____

Do you need to apologize to repair a broken connection with someone?

YES____ NO____

What will you apologize for? _____

How did your crime affect the other person? _____

_____

How can you make amends? _____

Do you feel guilty about having something good or about feeling

something good?   YES____ NO____

If yes, then try to consciously move your feelings from guilt to gratitude

for what you have/feel.

When you allow yourself to feel grateful instead of guilty, notice
what changes inside. Write down three internal shifts you notice:

1. _____

2. _____

3. _____

The better we get at working with our anxiety, shame, and
guilt, the more we can loosen the hold they have on us. As the
grip of our inhibitory emotions lessens, we can more easily make
our way down the Change Triangle to work with our core emotions and get to the openhearted state.

The Healing Emotions of Joy, Gratitude, and Pride in the Self

> In the midst of winter, I found there was, within me, an invincible summer.
>
> —Albert Camus

ALTHOUGH MOST OF us would be comfortable admitting we want to feel good and feel good about ourselves, most people struggle to attend to positive emotions. Psychologists have learned that dwelling on and sharing our positive emotions is good for the brain. The ability to deeply experience joy, excitement, pride in one's Self, and gratitude is healing.

For many of us, it is impossible to have a discussion about, let alone to experience, good feelings without bringing up bad feelings like shame. When I ask people to talk about their joy, accomplishments, gratitude, and love, they inevitably avoid the topic, sometimes visibly squirming. The link between good feelings and shame lies in what happens when good feelings are openly expressed and shared. If we receive affirmation in response, we feel bigger, more closely connected, and happier. If we receive judgment or scorn instead, the experience is unbearable. Because joy, pride, and gratitude have such potential for healing damage, we must work to maximize those feelings. When shared with others who support us, these feelings will amplify and energize us, bringing us closer to the openhearted state of our authentic Self.

Most psychotherapists are trained to focus on painful thoughts, negative emotions, and problems. It's a professional bias. But when you work with the mind from the perspective of the Change Triangle, it becomes evident that much of what we defend against are, in fact, emotions that feel good. This is where the contribution of Diana Fosha, the developer of AEDP, cannot be overestimated. Diana, and AEDP, have taught us the enormous healing potential there is in learning to feel, and fully feel, our positive feelings: love, gratitude, joy, tenderness, confidence, and belief in our own intrinsic goodness.[1] When, rather than defend against these healing emotions, we instead feel them, and feel them fully, the feelings of well-being that arise deepen and expand, and resilience grows. Furthermore, scientists now also tell us that in addition to expanding our resilience and well-being, fully feeling our positive emotions, like love and gratitude, rewires our brains and strengthens our immune systems.[2]

When I invite my patients to stay with emotions that make them grow bigger inside, anxiety and shame shout, "No!" My patients, in the course of a session, will often mention something good that happened or a good feeling they've experienced. But when I ask them to deeply feel that affirmation, their defenses pop up. When I ask them to speak from the defenses that just arose, they say things like "It's not nice to dwell on my accomplishments." "It feels weird and wrong." "I don't deserve to feel good." "It's no big deal and not that great."

Most of us have never deeply experienced either pride or gratitude. My patients use shrugs, eye rolls, or other nonverbal communication that lets me know that pride and joy have been blocked. Unless we work to process the anxiety, shame, or guilt that arises when we viscerally feel good about ourselves, these defenses will block us from expanding. We think that they are protecting us from the exposure that comes when we feel bigger because at one time in our past, it wasn't safe to be big. If we work to become aware of our defenses and calm our inhibitory emotions, joy, pride, love, and gratitude will come forth. Over time, a fresh capacity to enjoy these good feelings builds. Confidence results.

Every person has a unique story about his or her relationship with positive feelings. Bethany, for example, was successful in her career. Yet she would not share the joy and pride her accomplishments brought. "I am scared I will be judged as selfish and self-absorbed." As a little girl, Bethany was annoyed with her mother for working long hours to build her career. She was not aware of the connection between her anger at her mother and her fear of anger from others. All Bethany knew was that she longed to share her accomplishments with someone. She longed to be recognized by her family. She fantasized about getting attention and praise, but the thought of actually telling someone about her accomplishments made her sick to her stomach from a cocktail of anxiety, dread, and shame. The risk of igniting jealousy and anger far exceeded her wish to share. So she held back, remaining alone with her success.

Mary, in contrast, needed constant compliments and reminders that she was liked. No matter how much affirmation she received, it did not stick. She felt good when she received praise, and then the feeling vanished. Like someone addicted, she would need another fix. Mary had learned to block incoming good feelings. It was as if she had a hole in her self-esteem bucket and the bucket could never fill. She would fish for a compliment. She'd get one. Pride, joy, and gratitude would rise, but then anxiety was triggered and defenses cut off any further emotional experience. That is why no matter how much she was praised, it never went deep enough to stick and effect change in her brain.

We need to learn to experience pride, joy, and gratitude in such a way that it transforms our sense of Self. By working the Change Triangle, we can deepen good feelings. But first, we must notice when we are defending against a good feeling. The next time something good happens to you, pause to take notice of your internal response. Do you bask in the glory or move away to some other thought or task? Notice your body posture, as well as what you say. Once you notice the move to a defense, fight against it. Lean in to any positive feeling that comes up, even if it is just a molecule or two. Notice it, don't diminish it, and see what happens next.

Some of my patients have an identity crisis when they feel good. They have been down or small for so long, they don't recognize themselves when they feel big. Feeling big can make younger parts feel alone and disconnected from their family because they have never had the experience of feeling big and worthy in connection with that group. Feeling big and confident can also bring up survivor guilt, especially when other family members or friends aren't doing so well. Sadly, many of us have complicated feelings about being confident and coming out of hiding. Staying with and tolerating new experiences of self-confidence and self-worth can slowly establish a new internal normal. We can learn what it is like to be big and still be connected to those we love and need.

Pride in the Self is a natural response to accomplishing something we feel good about. Unfortunately, it is often misunderstood, confused with conceit or arrogance. I don't want you to boast or become self-aggrandizing at the cost to someone else's self-worth. The healthy pride I want you to experience is a purely internal feeling where you enjoy the natural, biological sense of expansion that occurs when you feel good about yourself or something you have done. Pride makes us feel like we are growing taller. Pride has energy. Experiencing pride in the Self is good for us.[3]

Pride is feeling good about the Self. Gratitude is the experience of being touched by what someone else has done for you. When someone is kind, affirming, or complimentary, gratitude arises. Often gratitude comes after we have expressed our emotions with someone who wholeheartedly received them without judging or trying to fix us. I may be moved to hug the person who made me feel so good. Certainly I feel moved to thank the person. Most people say that their heart feels warm when they experience gratitude toward another.

Some people feel that acknowledging gratitude demeans them. This is often a result of how gratitude was modeled in the past. There is no question that the expression and reception of gratitude between two people deepens the relationship and adds to their affection and intimacy. Building the courage and capacity to let good feelings flow is healthy, but it is hard.

Pride and gratitude are deeply physical experiences. Both enrich our lives. When we are ready and able to move our defenses aside, pride, joy, and gratitude are available for discovery. They are nourishment for the mind, body, and our relationships with ourselves and with others. Access to these emotions heals low self-esteem, loneliness, depression, anxiety, and more.

I use the Change Triangle to bring awareness to my reaction when someone affirms or compliments me. Practice noticing your reaction to affirmation. Do you end up on the defense corner, the inhibitory emotion corner, or at the bottom of the Change Triangle, where you viscerally experience joy, pride, and gratitude? Can you identify and fight against avoidance so you have a new opportunity to experience these nourishing emotions? Can you practice taking in little manageable bits of joy, pride, or gratitude by focusing on their physical manifestations and staying with them for a few seconds, noticing the wave as it builds? If so, you should detect energy moving through you. You will feel yourself grow, elongate, solidify, and enliven as your pride, gratitude, joy, and excitement expand, unencumbered by inhibition. This is truly a gift you can give yourself.

Experiment: Joy, Gratitude, and Pride in the Self

Viscerally Experiencing Joy

Think of something real or imagined that brings up joy.

Name one sensation associated with joy you sense inside:

_____

Bringing up joy might also bring up inhibitory emotions and defenses. Notice any that come up during this experiment. Can you name them?

Write down three things you notice inside and identify the corner of the Change Triangle where they belong:

1. _____
2. _____
3. _____

Gratitude

It's hard to get into the practice of noticing gratitude. This is a capacity that has to be exercised, just as you go to the gym to build your muscular strength.

Find a container and label it "Things I Am Grateful For."

At the end of every day, recount and write on a piece of paper three things, no matter how small, that happened that you feel grateful for. Put the paper in the container. After three weeks, notice and write down how you feel in response to this experience.

Viscerally Experiencing Gratitude

When someone gives you a compliment or does something nice for you, check inside to see if you experience gratitude. If you cannot sense gratitude, see if you can conjure it. Imagine what it might feel like.

Once you have even a glimmer, notice what sensations inside your body tell you that you are feeling gratitude.

Stay with this physical experience and notice what happens after about thirty seconds.

Name one or two sensations you recognize as gratitude:

1. _____

2. _____

Noticing Good Things About Yourself (Pride)

Find a container and label it "Things I Am Proud of Myself For."

At the end of every day, write down three things that you are proud of. You might feel proud of getting out of bed because that takes so much energy. You might feel proud of getting a good grade at school, of getting through a hard day at work, of something you made or cooked, or of the kindness or compassion you extended to someone else or to your Self. Don't judge or compare your accomplishments with others' accomplishments.

Every day for three weeks write down your three accomplishments and put them in the container. We are taking advantage of neuroplasticity here. By repeating this new process every day, it will strengthen the neural networks and teach them to look for things you feel good about.

After three weeks, notice how you feel in response to this experience.

Write down three things you notice:

1. _____
2. _____
3. _____

Viscerally Experiencing Pride

When you receive praise or validation, check inside to see if you experience pride.

If so, what inside your body tells you that you are feeling pride? Stay with the physical experience and notice what happens after about thirty seconds.

Name one or two sensations you recognize as pride (use the appendix list of sensations on page 277 if you need help):

1. _____
2. _____

Notice what happens, without judging, when you receive praise or affirmation.

Next, try to name any blocking emotions and thoughts you notice. Some common blocks are embarrassment, anxiety, guilt, fear, disbelief, or judgment toward you or the person praising you.

Noticing blocks helps your inner experience become more conscious. Awareness creates the potential for change and healing.

Write down three things you notice:

1. _____
2. _____
3. _____

If you're feeling brave, try to set aside any blocking thoughts or feelings and allow some of the good feelings to grow inside you.

Feel yourself expand—even a tiny bit of internal expansion builds this new emerging capacity. Breathe deeply if anxiety starts to arise. The anxiety is just there because you are doing something new.

Describe what you notice without judging yourself:

_____

_____

_____

Defenses

Mario's Story: Moving Through Trauma to Peace

I MET MARIO early on in my career when I was practicing according to more psychoanalytic principles. He was assigned to me as a patient by the intake worker at the institute where I was training. His symptoms included depression, irritability, avoidance of intimacy with his wife, low sex drive, and dissatisfaction with his career (he worked as an editor for a local newspaper).

As I was trained to do, I began the session by sitting down and waiting for Mario to speak. Analysts believe that how the patient begins is important information. The patient leads the sessions. The problem was that Mario talked to fill the awkward silences; he thought that was what he was supposed to do. While this approach gives a patient unlimited space to think and speak, there is a downside. Very few people gravitate to scary, painful, or shameful emotions, especially with a neutral therapist with whom safety has not been established.

I was unhappy with the progress Mario was making. I had been using a psychoanalytic/interpretive approach. I listened to the content of his stories and tried to make connections between what he told me and his unconscious. For example, I would say

217

**MARIO'S CHANGE TRIANGLE
AROUND A TRAUMATIC EVENT
WHEN HE WAS FOUR YEARS OLD**

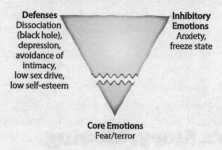

things like "Maybe you can't move past this trauma with your father because it keeps you connected to your family." But whether or not these were helpful interventions, they felt hit or miss to me. I tried to be supportive by listening and trying to understand. But deep down I felt that wasn't enough.

For more than a year, he talked and I listened, empathetically. My support helped him tolerate the daily demands of life but he was not thriving. Mario's depression didn't seem to lift. His childhood had been very tough, with a suicidal mother and a father who was prone to rages. In an early session he recalled, without much feeling, a time when he witnessed his father beat his older brother savagely. This memory came up often, and he described it as the "scenery" of his life. It haunted him. He felt, on a gut level, that this memory was somehow related to his depression, but his insight didn't change his depressed mood.

Since many of the patients I saw had a history of traumatic events in their childhoods, I read as many books as I could find on trauma treatments and attended workshops in AEDP and models like eye movement desensitization and reprocessing (EMDR), Somatic Experiencing (SE), Sensorimotor Psychotherapy, and Internal Family Systems therapy (IFS). About a year after I started work with Mario, I had received formal training in AEDP. AEDP and other healing models like EMDR and IFS teach active ways to change and heal traumatic states so they don't continue to haunt the sufferer. I decided to alter my approach with Mario, moving from a psychoanalytic model to a trauma model.

Each session, I started by inviting Mario to slow his mind down. I modeled slowing down by speaking . . . very . . . slowly . . . and calmly. People respond to this invitation automatically with slowed thoughts and a sense of dropping down from the head into the body. Mario found this very calming. In general, when people slow down, emotions and sensations make themselves known. This is good news and bad news. If we have the knowledge, understanding, and tools to work with our internal experiences, we are prepared to process these emotions and sensations and feel better. If we don't understand what is happening to us, we will likely move to the top left corner of the Change Triangle, utilizing defenses to cope. Did you ever meet someone who can't stop moving, working, talking, or being productive? If so, it is probably because he doesn't like it when he becomes aware of emotions.

I would wait for a nod, a look, or a word that told me Mario had accepted my invitation to relax and slow down. Then I would continue to coach him. "Just let yourself sense the ground beneath your feet, your body being supported by the chair, and let's also take a few deep breaths together."

Mario had a knack for tuning in to his emotional world, for noticing and putting language on physical sensations, and he was very open to using fantasy. We had a pivotal session in which he finally addressed the trauma that had defined much of his life.

That afternoon, about two years into our work together, Mario walked into my office with his blue eyes big and an eager smile.

"Can we notice how you are in this moment as we begin?"

He nodded positively.

"Great! So, just tune in to yourself below the neck and begin to notice, one by one, any emotions you are aware of and how you sense them physically. Remember we are just noticing with a stance of compassion and curiosity in yourself. Try not to judge what you notice."

He told me he noticed anxiety. I could now see some pain reflected in his eyes.

"Where do you feel it physically?"

He pointed to his heart area.

"Can you describe what you sense? How big is the area? Is it solid like a stone or hollow like a balloon? What do you sense? Just stay open to whatever words come. Trust your intuition." I spoke slowly and softly.

He paused for about a minute.

He said, "It's this big and round." He demonstrated what he sensed with his hands, which rose up to his chest, forming a circle about the size of a honeydew melon.

"Does it have a color?" I asked.

"It's black," he said.

We hold, in our bodies, pockets of experience that come in all sorts of colors, shapes, sizes, and sensations.

I asked, "Can we find a way to be with this round black experience that feels safe?"

"I don't know. Can we?" he asked with a smile. Mario had a great sense of humor. He was teasing me. We had established trust and safety together. Our relationship had already given him the confidence to explore some tough places.

"I think we can do it. Let's go slowly and stay in contact so we can stop if anything feels too much."

He nodded.

I guided him. "Can you tune in to this black round thing and notice where you are in relation to it?"

"I see a huge cavern and I'm about ten feet from the edge."

"You're doing so great. Can you move closer so you can peer into it?"

I think of black holes as the physical sense of traumatic experiences that were so overwhelming at the time of the trauma that the mind went black, metaphorically, to deal with it. Black holes often form when an event causes so much conflict and overwhelming emotion that it cannot be integrated and understood by the mind. My job is to connect with the patient so he feels safe to explore the black hole and help make the conflicts and emotions tolerable so they can be processed.

As adults, our traumatic experiences can be understood in a new way, whereas they were incomprehensible to us as children. In Mario's case, my hope was that if we could safely explore this black hole, it would help alleviate his depressed mood. Exploring what is in a black hole often leads us back through the brain's memory networks to the scene of the original trauma. We illuminate the darkness in the black hole by imagining a flashlight, for example, to see what it contains.

"I'm scared to go closer; I'm scared I'll fall in," he said.

"What would make you feel safer? How about if you imagine we are both holding a rope and I will hold it tightly to prevent you from falling in as you go closer?" I suggested.[1]

"No," he said. "You're not strong enough!"

"What do you need to feel safe? Can you imagine it?"

"A big old tree with a huge trunk. The rope is tied to the tree then you hold the rope." He knew exactly what he needed.

"Great idea!" I said. Once people get into these kinds of emotional, physical, and imaginal (the use of imagery) experiences, our minds create solutions in the service of getting well. The brain reacts to fantasy as though it is reality, and that can have huge implications for healing in psychotherapy. For example, I can guide a patient to imagine fighting back against a perpetrator or escaping the very attack that originally caused the trauma. Imagination can lead to a visceral sense of relief as if it really happened that way.

We can know intellectually that we survived a trauma and not know it emotionally. Unless our emotional brain feels safe, it will continue to trigger our body into fight, flight, and freeze states that cause suffering. The emotional brain learns that real danger is over and we are now safe when old emotions are processed and a narrative without gaps is integrated into our personal history. Trauma becomes a memory: "This happened to me but it is now over."

Mario walked to the edge of the hole and looked in but he couldn't see anything. It was pitch-black. I asked him if he would go in and look around knowing that he was securely tied to me and I was securely tied to a giant tree.

He was willing to try.

Mario forged ahead. He imagined a flashlight so he could see what was in the hole. Objects from his childhood home spontaneously appeared swirling about like he was in a tornado.

All of a sudden, and much to my surprise, he landed on the ground. "I am in the basement. My father is beating my brother!" We had talked about this memory frequently but he had never experienced it in this real way where emotion and sensation accompanied the image in his brain. I had never traveled down a black hole before with someone actually landing in the original scene of his trauma.

He cried.

I was a little frightened by the intensity of what was happening. I thought back to my basic trauma training. *The patient can process the trauma if he has one foot in the present while experiencing the past.* I checked in with him. "Is a part of you still here with me?"

"Yes," he said.

"Good. What are you feeling now as you see yourself in the basement?"

"I am scared. I'm scared. I want to run away."

We had accessed his fear, the blocked core emotion. Next, I wanted to elicit fear's adaptive impulse, the one originally thwarted.

"What in your body tells you that you want to run?"

"My legs are trembling!"

"Feel that as you run," I whispered, not wanting to startle him. "Feel your legs running. See yourself running. Run until you are safe."

I waited a little while then checked back in with him.

"What's happening now?"

"I ran out of the basement and through the backyard and I'm running down the street in my neighborhood but now I'm scared and I don't know where to go." He started to cry again.

I asked, "Where can you go that's safe?"

"I don't know," he cried.

"Mario, who is a safe person, who can provide comfort?"

"I don't know. I don't know. I'm scared."

He needed help. This made sense, since he was so young and scared in this state.

"I am talking to the adult Mario now who is sitting here with me. Can you imagine your adult self in the scene now with little Mario? Can you be your own good father to that little Mario?" I suggested, hoping that would provide some comfort so little Mario would not be alone.

I could have suggested that he put me in the scene or his wife or anyone else he felt safe with, but I wanted to first suggest that the safe person be himself so he would always have internal comfort available.

Adult Mario said, "I am on the street with the boy. I open my arms so he can run to me. He does. I am hugging him."

Mario was crying hard now. I was tearing up, too, deeply touched by what I was witnessing.

I was quiet. Knowing that little Mario was now safe with adult Mario, I felt more able to take a step back and give him space to cry, now perhaps less from fear and more from relief.

Mario sniffled as his crying subsided. He took a deep breath, gazed upward, and reestablished eye contact with me.

"I'm calming down," he said.

"What do you notice inside now?" I asked.

"I feel a little shaky, like I am trembling a bit all over."

"Let's just stay with the trembling sensation and see what happens."

I wanted the trembling to resolve naturally—not have him thwart it. The body is wired to heal from trauma if we let it without interruption. The trembling sensation associated with fear is natural and normal. Letting it dissipate all the way is akin to letting all of fear's energy release, so Mario would feel much better.[2]

Mario was silent, but I sensed we were closely connected even as he turned his attention away from me and back to his body. After about thirty seconds he reported, "It's lessening."

"Good! Just stay with it all and notice what comes up next."

When Mario was little and witnessed his father's rage, he was terrified. He was so terrified that he could not run. His attachment needs, which biologically drew him toward his family, dictated that he stay close to home. His core emotions and body, however, had a natural and adaptive survival impulse to escape danger.

The impulse to stay and the impulse to run clashed and created a massive internal conflict. He was frozen in fear. The part of his mind that held the conflicting emotions in this memory stayed cordoned off from consciousness, but the black hole was the placeholder, so to speak, for the emotions that were there but could not be experienced. As he grew into an adult, the black hole marking the trauma stayed as it was. He matured around this trauma, yet it exerted unconscious influence, causing his depression.

The work of this session allowed the frozen impulses to thaw. His body and mind, now safe with me, could in essence pick up where they left off, primed to run and escape the danger. In the fantasy we had in the session, he was able to complete the thwarted impulse to run, thereby releasing the energy that was locked inside, causing the scene to be stuck in time.

I asked Mario what he was experiencing now.

"I can't believe my father was such an animal! He tormented

MARIO'S CHANGE TRIANGLE:
GUILT AND ANGER
(MURDEROUS RAGE)

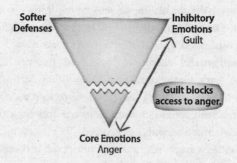

all of us, and we had to be on edge all the time, watching what we said and did, so we didn't upset him."

"As you share these huge insights with me, what emotion do you have toward your father for what he did to you and your brother?"

"I am furious," he said, his eyes wide.

"And how do you feel that inside right now?" I asked.

"Energy is running through my body from my gut all the way up. I want to kill him."

"How do you want to kill him?"

After what he just did using fantasy, I wondered if he could do it again, only this time honoring his fury instead of his fear.

"I want to shoot him in the head," Mario asserted.

"Can you let yourself imagine that? Make it into a vivid movie. Tell me what you see."

"I would . . ." he started, but I quickly interrupted him.

"Not what you *would* do, but imagine you're doing it right now. I want you to see it like it is happening in the moment just like we did before, with your fear."

Taking my direction, he said, "I see his face. I raise my gun. I cock it." He stopped.

"What's happening now?" I said after we had sat in silence for a few moments.

"I don't want to kill him," he said, looking quizzically at me, his head lowered a bit and cocked to the side.

"What are you feeling inside as you say that?"

Mario answered immediately: "Guilt."

"Yes, that makes total sense. That's because you're not a sociopath," I said, smiling. "You have a conscience and you're not a murderer. But this is pretend. You're not really killing your father, so do you think you could ask the guilty part of you to step aside so you could go back to honoring just what your anger wants to do? That way, you won't have all that energy stuck inside you."

"Okay," Mario replied. "I'll try."

"Let's check back in to your body and see if the anger toward your father is still there," I suggested. Anger fantasies should originate from the physical sensations of the anger to be maximally effective. The body holds the knowledge of what needs to be done to release the anger. We must follow the body, not thoughts. It should feel organic, not made up or like one is performing.

"Yes, I feel it, especially when I think of the memory of what he did to my brother and me that day."

"Good. If you check in to the physical sensation of anger, what does it want to do now?" I asked.

"It wants to shoot him in the head again."

"Stay with it and let me know what happens."

"We are about three feet apart. I am aiming the gun at his head. He puts his hands up and screams, 'No!' and I shoot him right between the eyes. My heart is racing."

"Look at your father," I urged. "What do you see?"

"He's on the floor. Half of his head is blown open. The left eye on his face is open, staring up."

"Good. Now check back in to the anger sensation in your body. What do you notice now seeing him dead on the floor?" If there was still anger, it meant there was another impulse to imagine.

"The anger is gone," he said, his eyes softening and facial expression changing to sadness.

"What emotion is coming up now?" I asked.

"I feel sad," he replied.

"Just make room for the sadness—let it come up so you can be done with this once and for all," I said gently and lovingly. "You deserve to have all these feelings."

Tears overflowed onto his cheeks. His body softened. He was still looking at me.

"What's this sadness for? Can you say?" I asked.

"I feel bad for what we all went through back then. It was terrible. No one should have to live in fear of their parent hurting them." He corrected himself. "*I* shouldn't have had to live in fear. It's just very sad."

"Yes it is," I affirmed. "So very sad."

We sat together in silent respect. He was mourning for himself, for all he had endured and all the subsequent difficulties it caused him.[3] He started to cry again.

"You have been holding in so much pain for so long. Don't hold it back. It's okay here. You were so little. It's good to let this out." I talked as he cried to let him know I was here. A few minutes passed.

He finished crying and took a deep breath. This told me the wave of the sadness, another core emotion, was over.

I asked, "How do you feel inside now?"

"Tired but better. Calmer." He looked at me again; our eyes met and I felt the click of connection.

"You were so amazing. I am so deeply touched by your courage today," I said.

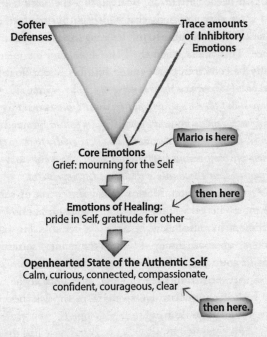

Softer Defenses

Trace amounts of Inhibitory Emotions

Mario is here

Core Emotions
Grief: mourning for the Self

then here

Emotions of Healing:
pride in Self, gratitude for other

Openhearted State of the Authentic Self
Calm, curious, connected, compassionate, confident, courageous, clear

then here.

Core emotions of rage and grief are finally unblocked and experienced. Healing begins, the past is perceived by the brain as truly past, and gratitude and pride in the Self emerge.

We processed the work we did together, and his relief turned into pride in himself and gratitude toward me. We stayed with the physical experience of these healing emotions, pride and gratitude, for as long as time and his stamina allowed. I believe in exploring healing emotions for as long as possible—they are elixirs for the human brain.[4] Finally, we reflected together on the power and importance of the work we just did, another healing step, and the session ended.

Working with Mario's emotions and physical sensations transformed his depression for the better. For years Mario had taken antidepressants and medications like Xanax for anxiety. Like many palliative medications, they only covered up his symptoms without healing the underlying cause.

My goal was to help Mario find the traumatic states inside him that needed attention. By exploring the black hole, we liberated three core emotions that had been buried: fear, anger, and sadness. Mario was able to put language and meaning to the experience. This transformed the black hole, and his memory could finally be consciously integrated into his brain: *When I was four years old, I experienced the trauma of my father beating my brother. Now I understand that I was terrified by what I saw, afraid for my brother and myself, despairing, and angry with my father. Having now felt these feelings, I know both intellectually and emotionally that it is finally over. I know my brother and I survived. I know I was not crazy for being so overwhelmed, as I was only a child and left unprotected.*

After this session, Mario's mood improved. He reported he had more energy for his wife and friendships. His professional fulfillment increased as he became less irritable. His boss and coworkers, who once annoyed him to the point of making him not want to go to the office, didn't seem so bad anymore. When his mood darkened from time to time, as is normal, he didn't sink into such deep sadness. He spent more time in an openhearted state. He generally felt lighter and happier.

Defenses

ALL PEOPLE HAVE defenses. They come in all shapes and sizes, tailor-made according to genetics, temperament, and environment. They are brilliant adaptations the mind makes to help us cope with and manage unbearable feelings and conflicts. Defenses are adaptive in their original environment. Over time, however, they become entrenched. We are not able to give them up. When the current environment calls for a new response but we continue to maintain our old defenses, they are no longer helpful and often become hurtful. As adults, our defenses can impede life in many ways. Most particularly they block our connection to our core sense of Self, as well as our connection to others.

Defenses Need to Be Honored and Respected for How They Once Helped Us

I always honor and respect defenses, and I teach my patients to do the same. When Griffin came to see me, he was so mad at himself for not being able to assert his opinion on the job, especially with his boss. I showed Griffin the Change Triangle. I wrote the core emotions at the bottom, the inhibitory emotions on the top right corner. On the top left I wrote, "Not Asserting." I explained that not asserting was a defense against whatever must have happened when he had asserted himself a long time ago. Asserting oneself is adaptive. You need something, you ask for it, you get it or you don't. It's straightforward and effective.

I suggested to Griffin that we explore how his defense of not asserting was, at one time, protective. We could learn what its original purpose was and help him find a new and more adaptive way to satisfy the same purpose.

"What was it like for you as a child when you spoke up or asserted your opinion?"

"Are you kidding me?" he replied. "I got slammed by my dad."

"What do you mean slammed?"

"My dad would always say, 'You don't know what you're talking about. Who cares what you think?'"

After validating how mean and hurtful that was, I offered up, "It was smart of you to stop asserting your thoughts."

"Yeah," he said. "I figured out pretty quickly that I could avoid his contempt by shutting up."

We honor defenses by validating that they were constructed to deal with life at the time when they were needed. When we were young, using defenses was the best way we had to protect ourselves, given the limited resources of a young brain and the genetic, familial, and cultural hand we were dealt.[1]

Griffin had already begun working the Change Triangle. By placing his lack of assertiveness on the defensive corner, its origin and meaning could now be understood. He knew he had to move this part aside and find his buried core emotions.

"Griffin, as you sit here in present time with me and think back to when your father showed you contempt, what emotions do you have toward your father now?"

Griffin was angry. When someone hurts us, being triggered to anger makes sense. Having studied the Change Triangle, Griffin learned to ask himself what he was feeling whenever he noticed he was defending against his desire to assert. Then he remembered that he could protect himself by recognizing his core emotions and using words to set limits and boundaries if someone responded hurtfully, like his dad used to.

The Change Triangle helps move us from defensive states to states of peaceful, calm, and authentic living. We do this by building an awareness of the defenses that cause us stress or trouble. We then learn their original purpose. We can ask the defense, *How are you trying to help me right now?* The defense knows the answer and can communicate it. Our defenses work hard to protect us even when the threat that originated them is long gone. Our program needs to be updated. When we connect to our true feelings by working the Change Triangle and develop confidence that we can safely navigate and use our emotions out in the world, defenses melt away, as they are no longer needed.

Defenses are mostly unconscious until we work to recognize them. Since we can often see others more easily than we can see ourselves, you will likely notice the defenses of others before you notice your own. For example, I notice that my parents are critical before I notice that I keep myself small to defend against criticism. I notice someone else having one too many drinks to escape from life's pain before I notice the habits I use to avoid discomfort or pain. We have to be quite tenacious in our self-awareness to evaluate our actions, thoughts, and feelings and determine if we are in defensive modes.

To loosen the hold our defenses have on us, it helps to understand what we fear will happen if we give them up. For example, before Bonnie could be more direct and give up her vague defense, she had to be confident that she could handle conflict and anger constructively. Defenses don't mind relinquishing their hold when we have other ways to help us feel safe in the world. A big part of this process is a willingness to experience the tender or protective emotions we defended against. The Change Triangle is our guide.

We have to learn to listen to what our defenses are communicating. When I notice a defense in someone, like intellectualizing, making a joke, or rolling one's eyes (a nonverbal defense), I invite the person to speak from that defensive part. I say, "Did you notice you just rolled your eyes when you told me how your daughter insulted you? If you speak from the part of you that rolled your eyes, what would it say?" Or, "Do you notice how you are smiling as you share this very sad story? Can you ask the smiling part of you what its protective purpose is right now?"

The answers defenses give are varied. Here are just a few:

I protect you from feeling pain.

I am protection from fear.

I am a wall protecting you from hurt.

I am a barrier to grief that I think you can't bear.

I protect you from the anger that wants to kill someone.

I protect you from being abandoned because no one can deal with your true feelings.

I protect you from feeling bad about yourself.

I hide your true Self because if other people find out how crazy you are, you will be all alone.

I am vigilant for anything you do that isn't perfect, because if you're not perfect, you won't be loved.

I force you to work because you're naturally lazy.

I make you overeat so no one will want to have sex with you and hurt you again.

Sophia was a patient who noticed she was not looking forward to seeing her close friend, Denise. She was struck by her desire to not see her. Sophia wondered about this shift in her sentiments. Plotting herself on the Change Triangle, Sophia found her internal dialogue sounded something like this: *I am avoiding my friend Denise right now. Avoiding is a defense. I must have feelings about Denise.*

Having recognized her defense, she could put it aside. She asked herself what core emotions she had toward Denise. She soon realized, by imagining being with Denise and noticing what feelings came up, that the thought of seeing Denise raised her anxiety. Sophia tuned in to her body. She felt her heart beating in her chest, and it was uncomfortable. Knowing that anxiety is an inhibitory emotion and a signal that core emotions are pushing up, she thought about each core emotion until she found the one(s) that fit. Sophia realized she was angry.

Still using the Change Triangle as a map, Sophia decided to work with her anger. She dove into her body to be with the sensations her anger brought up. She noticed an energy emanating from a tension in her belly. Spontaneously, a memory emerged of their last dinner out. She recalled how Denise had upset her by implying that Sophia's new boyfriend wasn't very smart. Sophia was insulted, but they never spoke about it. Sophia had put aside her anger, hoping it would go away. Now, however, she validated it. She stayed with the sensation of anger long enough for its impulse to come forth. It wanted to tell Denise, "Lay off! I am done being your friend!" Sophia only now realized how angry she was at Denise. Defenses are really good at what they do—which is why, until Sophia took the time to tend to her anger, she didn't realize how intense it was.

With this clarity, Sophia felt calmer. She felt ready to think through the best way to handle her anger at Denise. One option was to tell Denise how upset she was about her comment and ask for an apology to repair the rupture in their relationship. Sophia also considered not saying anything. She could attempt to process the anger on her own and avoid an awkward confrontation. Maybe she could then let it go. Ultimately, Sophia felt it was better for their relationship to talk it through. When she did, the conversation went well. Denise clarified that she didn't know Sophia's boyfriend very well and obviously jumped to the wrong conclusion. She then apologized for upsetting Sophia. Sophia felt much better after they spoke. The rupture in their connection was repaired.

Sophia's defense was avoiding her friend. But with her self-awareness she was eventually able to recognize this defense. She then made a conscious decision to work the Change Triangle to help herself and her relationship. Deciding not to avoid her emotions and linger in her defenses, she recognized her anger at Denise, processed it on her own until she had clarity, and finally chose to have a positive conversation from a calm and openhearted place. That's how so many people use the Change Triangle in everyday life.

Caleb, a patient who also used the Change Triangle on a daily basis, worked in an unfriendly office environment. A co-worker named Don often looked directly through Caleb without acknowledging that he existed. When this happened, Caleb experienced a physical jolt. Yanked out of his normal state, he experienced a sudden clenching in his stomach. He thought, *Don is such an asshole. He snubbed me!* He recognized the thought as blame, a defense against his anger. We all tend to blame others who hurt us. But the problem with blame is that it leads to a stalemate, not resolution. Physical tension is not released when we get stuck in a blaming state. Plus, blame erodes relationships.

To reach beyond the blame, Caleb tuned in to his body and recognized his anger. He checked in with the anger and listened to who and what triggered it. He stayed with its visceral sensations. The anger turned to shame—Don made him feel insignificant. Caleb felt himself small under all that angry bluster. Feeling small was familiar. He'd felt this way with many of his girlfriends when they ignored him. Caleb had felt ignored by his parents as a child. His childhood experiences made him sensitive to the amount of attention he received from others. So when Don failed to acknowledge Caleb, Caleb felt deeply unimportant. All it took was a slight reminder of a past traumatic experience to light up the old neural networks from childhood. Don represented Caleb's mother and father in that moment, and Caleb was experiencing the world through a four-year-old part of himself.

Just from tuning in to his anger at a visceral level, Caleb gained insight that helped him feel better. He reminded himself that even if Don was rude, it felt a lot worse because it was lighting up old neural networks. Knowing this calmed him down. Since he valued taking the high road and not engaging in conflict, he gave himself permission to experience the anger at Don and imagined telling him what a "fucked-up rude asshole" he was.

Caleb felt a release, took a deep breath, then gave himself some compassion, both for what he had gone through in the past and for having to deal with rude people at work.

Caleb knew that the thought *I am being snubbed* was a defense against the underlying anger, shame, and sadness of being ignored when he was little. Making the connection that something from the past is influencing the present situation is crucial for us all if we want to live in reality. In reality, Don was probably preoccupied, shy, or busy. Caleb's triggered four-year-old part was too quick to conclude that Don's actions had something to do with Caleb.

Of course, sometimes the past has nothing to do with it. Sometimes people are rude, preoccupied, insensitive, or clueless. Sometimes people have bad intentions. But mostly people just don't realize the effect they are having on others. As an adult, especially when we are coming from a calm, openhearted state, we can deal with rude or insensitive people in many constructive ways that don't feel bad or toxic to us. Caleb learned that if someone is truly rude and has an intent to hurt him, that says everything about that person's character and nothing about Caleb.

Thoughts, emotions, and behaviors can all act as defenses. To help figure out whether we are in a defense, we should check in frequently and reflect on what we are doing, thinking, and feeling. Keep in mind that core emotions help our species survive. To help figure out if an emotion is being used as a defense or if it is core, we can evaluate our response and judge if it seems appropriate and adaptive for the situation.

Core emotions stem from events:

- If I experienced a loss, I can expect to feel sad.
- If I was hurt by someone, I can expect to feel both sad and angry.
- If I was violated by someone, I can expect to feel disgusted, angry, hurt, and frightened.

- If someone was wonderful to me, I can expect to feel joy.
- If someone brought me a pleasant surprise, I can expect to feel happy and excited.
- If someone I am attracted to comes on to me, I can expect to feel sexually excited.

Often our core emotions are hidden by defensive emotions in those same situations. In the following examples, another defensive emotion is evoked instead of the more adaptive core emotion.

- If I experienced a loss, I can expect to feel sad (core) but instead I feel angry (defense).
- If I was hurt by someone, I can expect to feel both sad and angry (core) but instead I feel ashamed (defense).
- If I was violated by someone, I can expect to feel disgusted, angry, hurt, and frightened (core) but instead I feel only sadness (defense).
- If someone was wonderful to me, I can expect to feel joy (core) but instead I feel disgust (defense).
- If someone brought me a pleasant surprise, I can expect to feel excited (core) but instead I feel scared (defense).
- If someone I am attracted to comes on to me, I can expect to feel sexually excited (core) but instead I feel scared and angry (defense).

Even when emotions are used defensively, they still need to be honored. We need to understand the defense by finding out the purpose it is serving in the moment. Additionally, we need to access and process the underlying core emotions in order to feel better.

The energy it takes to maintain our defenses is so much better used for living courageously, engaging with the things and people we enjoy. No matter what kind of life you have, working the Change Triangle transfers the energy used for avoidance to energy for authentic, openhearted living.

Experiment:
Noticing Your Defenses

WRITE DOWN THREE things you do to cope with stress:

1. _____
2. _____
3. _____

Write down three ways you avoid a confrontation:

1. _____
2. _____
3. _____

Write down three mean things you have said and why:

1. _____
2. _____
3. _____

Write down three things you are judgmental about:

1. _____
2. _____
3. _____

Write down three ways you avoid doing things you don't want to do:

1. _____
2. _____
3. _____

Write down three self-destructive things you have done:

1. _____
2. _____
3. _____

Write down three ways you deal with difficult emotions:

1. _____
2. _____
3. _____

Review your answers and put a check mark next to the things you think are defenses.

Pick one of your defenses above (the one you'd most like to stop doing) and circle it to use for a later exercise.

Try to Notice More Defenses

Ask yourself the following questions from a stance of curiosity. Have compassion for yourself and don't judge. Write down the answers:

What behaviors do I have that cause me general problems?
What behaviors do I have that cause me problems in my
    relationships?

What behaviors do I have that cause me problems at work?

What behaviors do I have that cause me problems for myself?

Do I engage in dangerous behaviors?

How do I avoid conflicts?

How do I avoid emotions?

How do I avoid anxiety?

How do I avoid feeling bad about myself?

Am I aware of my flaws? Can I share them?

Am I aware of my good points? Can I share them?

Do I feel rigid in thought or flexible?

Do I judge others a great deal?

Do I judge myself a great deal?

Am I constantly moving and doing things?

Do I feel uncomfortable slowing down?

Do I use too many drugs or too much alcohol?

Do I think I am better than everyone else?

Do I share my thoughts and emotions with anyone?

Do I spend all day in my head?

Again, pick one or two of the above that cause you to feel bad or have problems in life and that you'd like to change. Circle them. Save these answers for a later exercise and for future work you may want to accomplish using the Change Triangle.

7

The Openhearted State

Sara Redux:
The Authentic Self
and Openhearted State

YOU'LL RECALL THAT Sara was a gentle woman who needed help asserting. Years of verbal abuse by her mother left her perpetually hiding in states of anxiety and shame. She feared core emotions, especially anger, both her own and others'.

This session occurred five months after the one where she experienced her anger toward me. I saw the fruits of our work in her increasingly calm demeanor. Although she was taxed by the demands of a new job, she managed them with grace and a sense of humor. She now was able to freely complain about work without worrying about displeasing me. Mostly, I was aware of how different and more relaxing it felt to be with her.

Sara could now name her feelings, wants, and needs. Additionally, she developed the courage to set some limits and boundaries with people around her when she felt it necessary.

In this session, Sara shared that she'd found herself curious about how her body responded to her mother's temper when she was little. "I was actually lying in bed last night working the Change Triangle and trying to notice my body sensations. I started to think about how I felt in those moments when she turned from 'normal mom' to 'crazy mom.' Once the switch happened, there was no going back. It caused a very specific feeling in me. I was trying to figure out what that feeling was and trying to work with it. There was pressure in my chest. Something was bearing down on my heart.

"I felt safe enough because I was in my bed. When I imagined Mom screaming, I felt a squeezing sensation around my heart, like my heart was having trouble beating."

I tried to imagine what that squeezing sensation would feel like in my heart and in my body. "Painful!" I said.

"And scary," she added.

"Yes, and scary." I was pleased Sara added her own words to reflect exactly her experience and not mine.

The ability to think and feel simultaneously, a reflection of a brain that is well integrated, is optimal for dealing with life's challenges. That is what the openhearted state is all about.[1] When we are in the C's, we are aware of our thoughts and sense our feelings as they are occurring in the moment.

"My mother was *so* scary!" Sara emphasized.

"So not only is there the sensation in your heart, but also fear comes up. Can you tune in to the fear? Keep me as close as you need."

I had taught Sara about maintaining dual awareness when she worked with old emotions held by her child parts. One part of her stayed in the present moment with me and another part of her mind connected to the past to communicate with the young part that held the fear. The goal was to witness and learn about the young part's fears, so we could figure out what it needed to heal.

"I think the fear was just knowing that if she was in a bad mood, I'd be at her mercy until she snapped out of it or exhausted herself. In a rage, she might force me to do meaningless chores for hours on end just so I couldn't play or have any fun. Or she would go through my room throwing things out if it was messy. If I got a bad grade, she'd rip up my schoolwork. Whatever her tantrum of the moment, it was horrible. I had to work so hard to figure out how to stop her or, better yet, to not get her started."

As Sara shared her memories, I noticed that Sara's Self was in control. Sara was calm as she told her story.

In the early years of our work, this discussion would have evoked a traumatic reaction. Just thinking about her mom's tirades could trigger a vivid flashback. We often had to stop and calm the massive amounts of anxiety and fear coming up inside her, which would trigger a freeze reaction, like what happens to animals in the wild when they think they are about to be eaten by a predator. This was an apt analogy. Sara's nervous system interpreted her mother's onslaught as a near-death experience. While she appeared still on the outside, if Sara had been hooked up to an electrocardiogram, the test would have shown a rapid heartbeat and other signs of high arousal. In a freeze state, the nervous system is highly activated.

"You went through so much," I said.

"I'm just thinking about how that was quite the ordeal almost on a daily basis. I mean, it was a lot. It's kind of amazing I was able to get through it," Sara said.

There used to be parts of Sara that would not permit or were unable to tolerate any self-compassion. Now those parts, transformed and integrated, no longer blocked her self-compassion. Instead, they allowed her to more freely offer compassion to her suffering young parts, increasing her overall calm.

"Amazing," I said. "Just amazing."

"I guess I didn't have an option. It is not like I could go away, because I was little. But yeah . . . What the *fuck*!" she suddenly said, with more force and anger than I'd seen before.

Sara was taking a big risk by allowing me to see her so enraged.

I didn't want her to feel shame and so I matched her emphasis. "Right! What the *fuck*?" I wanted her to know I was with her. I had her back.

Explicitly talking about what it feels like to share is a way to undo the utter aloneness that helped create her small t traumas.

"What's it like to share this all with me—the horror of what you had to go through as such a little girl with a delicate nervous system being taxed to the brink of what you could take?" I asked.

"It feels good to share it with you and for you to understand and recognize the severity of it. It's really nice to have you understand the impact of something like that."

"And how does that register for you that I understand the impact? What happens inside you, emotionally, in your sensations, or energetically?" I wanted her brain and nervous system to register this new way of being with me as different from the old ways of being with her mom, where her entire subjective experience had to be disavowed for Sara to survive.

"I feel calm. I don't feel that urgency that I used to feel with you. The urgency for attention and for nurturing is much less than it used to be. I feel much less desperate."

I wanted her to find positive language for this experience.

"And, instead, what do you sense?" I asked.

"More stability. That you are there for me. That there is consistency. Does that make sense?" she said.

"Yes, it does. And can I push you a little more? How do you recognize physically that you have stability and consistency, that you don't have to do it alone?"

She paused then replied, "When I used to feel like I needed you and I felt an uncertainty about you being there for me, I felt a panic or fluttering in my chest. But now that is not there. If I feel like I need you, I can calm it much more easily either using fantasy or reminding myself I will see you in a few days or that I can reach out to you."

"Yes! I hear you saying that you know that I am there and you trust I'll be consistent. What's it like inside to know that?"

"A solid calmness."

She nailed it! We were now rooted firmly in her body. Sara dropped down into the C's of the openhearted state.

"Does that feel right as you say it?"

"Yes, as right as it ever feels." Sara preferred questions that had an objective truth to them, that were either right or wrong, black or white. Sara, like some others, struggled with the whole

SARA'S TRIANGLE
FROM JOY TO THE OPENHEARTED SELF

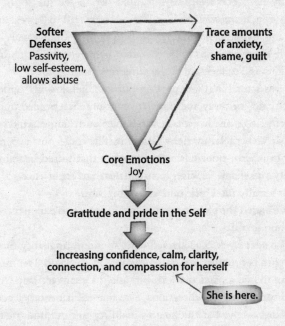

notion of body sensations being subtle, subjective experiences with no right or wrong answers.

"You are speaking about such tender and poignant experiences of safety and connection. It is huge. What is it like?"[2]

"It's amazing!" She allowed herself to feel this now without defending her core emotional experience.

"Tell me."

"It makes me want to smile, and I feel happy."

"Can you let yourself smile as big as the feeling guides you? Don't hold back that beautiful smile; let me see it." I had noticed tension around her lips constricting her expressiveness. I wanted Sara to notice it, too, so she could relax those muscles and unleash her smile.

I continued, "And as you see me smiling at you, seeing your

joy, and you seeing my joy on your behalf, what is that like?" I was bursting inside with feelings of joy and pride for Sara. Trying to amplify her good feelings, I wanted her to see me seeing her. Being seen, being matched, and being connected makes expansive emotions like joy and pride grow bigger. It is a universally pleasurable experience not to be thwarted by defenses and inhibitory emotions and to feel safe at the same time.

I was stretching Sara now on purpose, helping her build her capacity for intimacy and positive emotions. She needed to tolerate pride, joy, and intimacy for longer and longer stretches of time. It was crucial for her well-being. She could now experience these expansive emotions sometimes with only trace amounts of anxiety and shame kicking in to mitigate the experience.

"It's really nice," she said with a big smile.

We ended the session on that lovely note, and Sara left feeling calm and joyful.

The next week, Sara arrived with an interesting story. She had been with her mother at a museum over the weekend. Her mother, hoping to find a particular exhibit, asked a guard for help. As the guard was giving her directions, Sara noticed her mother getting tense and annoyed at the guard's inability to communicate effectively.

"Then I started to tense up," Sara reported. "My anxiety was rising and my mind started racing about how I could fix it before my mom went nuts." I felt Sara's anxiety rise as she recounted the memory. "All of a sudden I could see what was happening. I realized I was reacting to my mother the way I had reacted when I was a kid. I could observe this part of me feeling like I was trapped, at her mercy. I could feel my body wanting to freeze just like I automatically did when I was little. But then I remembered I was an adult. I am not little anymore. I am big. I had the power to walk away, or to step in and help, or do whatever I needed. I wasn't trapped."

"Wow!" I said.

"That calmed me down," she said with a big smile.

"What comes up as you share that with me?" I asked, wanting her to name the emotions.

"I feel proud."

Pride on behalf of the Self, a healing emotion, is another indicator of healing and of growing self-confidence. On the Change Triangle, pride in the Self and gratitude, another healing emotion, are located somewhere between core emotions and the openhearted state.

"Can we be with pride for just a few minutes?" I asked sheepishly, aware of being predictable when it came to asking Sara to stay with positive feelings.

"Okay . . ." she said.

"What is happening inside your body right now that tells you that you feel proud?" I asked.

Sara's head cocked sideways; her eyes gazing up, she focused inward. Then she looked at me, bright eyed and smiling. "Well, I feel strong and long in my core like I have a steel beam in my spine. I notice I am sitting up tall and I notice I am looking at you right in your eyes."

"Wow! I hear that you feel strong and tall, like you have steel in your spine. You noticed, too, that you are looking right at me," I repeated.

"Yes, and I feel energy moving from my lower stomach up and out across my chest and arms."

"Does this energy have an impulse? Check in with it."

"Yes, it wants to dance and celebrate." That was the impulse of her joy and pride. Sara looked relaxed. She was smiling.

"Yes! How lovely! Follow the energy. Can you imagine it, make it into a fantasy? What does the feeling want to do now?" My invitation was designed to help her stay in the moment and deepen these healing emotions while letting their energy release in an active fantasy.

"As strange as it sounds, I see the both of us together, dancing in a circle around a maypole. We are holding hands and circling it, around and around, laughing."

"I can see it too," I said and paused, savoring the moment and allowing it to hang suspended between us. After thirty seconds or so, I noticed a shift, a softening in her face. That was my cue to ask, "What's it feel like to see us like this?"

"Happy, and now calmer. Just being." The wave of energy had peaked and ebbed. Sara was again in the openhearted state.

In therapy, Sara learned to access her C's—calm, curious, connected, compassionate, confident, courageous, clear. After this session and beyond, she continued to notice when she was in an openhearted state or when she was in old, familiar, unassertive states that felt bad. Sara played an active role in her moment-to-moment well-being. Realizing she was out of sorts, she would use the Change Triangle, exercise, take walks, watch fun television shows, and participate in other activities that were calming and restorative. Sara could also be her own good mother. She could give herself compassion and care.

Sara changed how her brain functioned. Using the Change Triangle, Sara got in touch with her blocked emotions. She developed a relationship with the young parts of her that had suffered trauma. She communicated with and calmed her anxiety, shame, and guilt. She noticed, validated, labeled, and processed her core emotions. She used imagery and imagination for healing actions, just like she had learned to do with me. Access to her authentic Self continued to grow. These gains are permanent and the practices can help Sara for the rest of her life.

The Self,
the Openhearted State,
and the C's

Only the True Self can be creative and only the True Self can
feel real.

—D. W. Winnicott

The Relationship Between Our
Self and Other Parts of Us

The authentic Self's natural state, when it is not obscured by
trauma or overtaken by emotions, is the openhearted state.

Self = Openhearted State = C's

In an openhearted state we are **calm**; **curious** about our mind, the
minds of others, and the world at large; **connected** to our body
and to the hearts and minds of others; **compassionate** to ourselves and to others; **confident** in who we are; **courageous** in
action; and **clear** in thought. Emotions and parts of us still exist
and are noticeable, but they don't overtake us. The Self, which we
are born with, and our parts, which develop from life experiences,
coexist. Which one is in the foreground and which one is in the

background can change from moment to moment. When we get triggered and emotions and parts get activated or evoked, the Self can be temporarily obscured by the emotional urgency of the moment. To regain access to the openhearted state, we work the Change Triangle.

Through our work, Sara was able to shift into her openhearted Self. From that perspective, she was aware of a variety of childhood parts representing many ages from birth to her teenage years. After practicing the Change Triangle consistently, over time, Sara could be in contact with her calm openhearted Self while she also felt the upset parts of her.

Gordon was a patient who shared memories of himself as a four-year-old. I asked Gordon how he saw that little boy in his mind's eye. Gordon saw himself in his mother's kitchen. He saw what his younger part was wearing and the expression on his little face. When I'm working to help someone access a young part, I often ask if the young part is aware that we are here working to help it. Sometimes the part is aware, which means we can communicate with it. Sometimes the part is not aware, in which case we work to build a connection by communicating with it and seeing what it needs to feel better.

It is from the perspective of the Self that we relate best to younger and traumatized parts. Gordon, with practice, was able to maintain enough distance from triggered young parts to prevent them from overtaking him and obscuring his access to his Self. Instead, he related to wounded childhood parts as they arose. He validated their feelings and gave them compassion.

The Self can notice what's going on inside the mind and body. We can strive, over our lifetime, to become more and more aware. With awareness comes benefits. There is so much in our lives we cannot control. One thing we can control, however, is how we react to ourselves, treat ourselves, and choose to act in the world. Using self-awareness and the Change Triangle as a guide to return to the openhearted state, we can be the directors of our own lives. Living with purpose, we can work to make good things happen.

LINES OF COMMUNICATION BETWEEN
THE SELF AND INTERNAL PARTS

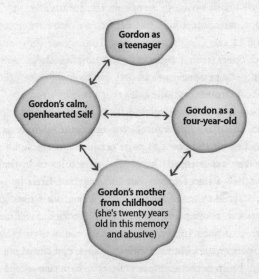

**The Self learns to communicate with other parts and helps build
communication between parts. In neuroscience terms, we are integrating
dissociated neural networks. As a result, the nervous system calms down
and is not as easily triggered.**

We can lead constructive lives. We can work to have loving relationships that nurture our souls. Being the architect of our lives—
taking control—gives us our best chance to thrive.

The Self notices our defenses, inhibitory emotions, and core
emotions. *I am aware that I am thinking about what the weather will
be tomorrow* or *I am aware that I am angry at my boss and I feel an
impulse to call him names* or *I am aware that I have butterflies in my
stomach as I think about public speaking.* Practice using your Self to
notice your defenses, thoughts, feelings, impulses, and body sensations. The Self assimilates all that information to use for our
greater good. When the Self is compromised, which happens
when we are triggered by overwhelming emotions and young
parts, it must work extra hard to regain the openhearted state.

The Openhearted State

How do we know we are in an openhearted state?

For one, we subjectively feel better. We also have access to at least some of the C's: calm, curious, connected, compassionate, confident, courageous, and clear. Memorizing these words is a great idea because then you can actively look for these states and try your best to shift into the ones that you can.

For people who have suffered from much adversity and who still suffer the effects of trauma, the openhearted state is sometimes blocked by traumatized parts or stuck emotions. Once core emotions are experienced, however, what follows is the openhearted state—a transformational state characterized by insight. We have a sense that the past is over. When one drops into the openhearted state after processing a deep emotional trauma, a coherent story of one's life emerges, just as it did with Fran, Sara, Bonnie, Spencer, and Mario. With the stuck emotional energy released, the brain becomes more coherent. Experience and understanding come together, which overall calms the nervous system. The brain becomes integrated. That's why this kind of personal work is transformational.

Openhearted states are the opposite of traumatic states. Traumatic states bring us in contact with reactive, highly stressed parts. In traumatic states, we are in fight, flight, and freeze modes. Our emotional brains are going wild preparing us for defensive action. In these states, thinking, problem solving, and rationality are compromised, if not shut off entirely.

The more we process old and stuck emotions, the easier it is for us to access our C's and the openhearted state and the more time we stay there. This is because when our brains are more integrated they are more stable. Our brain, given the choice, prefers stability.

There are two main ways to get to the openhearted state: first, by experiencing our core emotions. Fran, Sara, Bonnie, Spencer, and Mario dropped into their openhearted states following their experience of emotions that had been blocked by childhood parts.

The second way to access the openhearted state is by looking for your C's and seeing if you can make a conscious shift into being them just by being aware and applying your emotional energy.

For example, when I am in a bad mood and perhaps get on my husband's case about something petty, even though it may feel awkward and forced at first, I will make myself remember things that bring on my compassion for him. Or I might bring up a memory of when I felt very connected to and appreciated by him. Or I might instead get curious about my impulse to criticize. It's not easy by any means, but shifting into the C's often feels much better. Often I can sense a real softening in my physical tension.

The openhearted state is the place where we can understand and process the ways our friends and family sometimes disappoint us. The openhearted state is the place where we can appreciate our Selves for our efforts and we can forgive our Selves for our mistakes. In the openhearted state, we see others more accurately, not through a distorted historical lens. Because the openhearted state is calm, we can think straight, solve problems, and deal with challenges and differences with our peers.

Not everyone feels comfortable in the openhearted state. Some people can't tolerate calm, believe it or not. There are many people who grew up in chaotic households. All they knew growing up was agitation and anxiety. If you grew up with constant drama and excitement around you, for better or for worse, states of calm might feel flat, dead, or boring. Feeling calm or content might cause you an identity crisis: *Who am I when I am calm?* Or the calm might initially trigger agitation because it's an alien experience— too unfamiliar.

If you have difficulty with the openhearted state and want to change, you must work to establish a new normal. This is possible but requires working the Change Triangle to arrive in the openhearted state as often as possible and tolerating the discomfort that change always brings.

Working the Change Triangle around and around again over a

lifetime leads us back to this openhearted state with regularity. With practice, we can arrive here more quickly and more often.

Check if you are in an openhearted state by asking yourself the following questions:

- Am I physically *calm*? If not, am I willing to pause and do things that calm me down like taking a walk outside, breathing, feeling my feet on the floor, or remembering some of my positive qualities and those of my companion(s)?
- Can I get *curious* in my reactions to the world and people around me? If I notice that either my partner or I am in a defensive mode, can I get curious about the emotions underneath? Am I curious to map myself, or my companion, on the Change Triangle to understand more about what is happening?
- Am I feeling *connected* to myself emotionally? Am I feeling connected to the people around me? If not, can I make a shift toward connection?
- Can I access *compassion* toward myself? If I am not alone, can I access compassion toward my companion(s)? Can I access compassion now even though I may also be having other emotions like fear, sadness, or anger?
- Am I *confident* that I am basically safe right now? Am I confident in my abilities to find resources and get help when I need it? Am I confident that I can take care of myself?
- Am I willing to be *courageous* and lead with vulnerability?
- Is my mind *clear* so I can think? If my mind is not clear, am I aware of that so that I do not make important decisions until I am able to access more clarity?

If you answer no to any of these questions, don't judge yourself. Check in to your body and notice all that you can. Search for your deeper emotions, hurts, and vulnerabilities. Give the parts of you that are suffering (experiencing core and/or inhibitory emotions) or working hard to protect you (defenses) all the compassion you can muster. Then, work the Change Triangle.

Some of us spend a great deal of time in the openhearted state. Some of us are rarely in an openhearted state. The rest of us fall in between. Regardless, the Change Triangle is our map and prescription for spending more time there as we grow by getting to know ourselves in ever deepening ways. If you are putting pressure on yourself to be in the openhearted state all the time or beating yourself up for not achieving it enough, you are misunderstanding the point and purpose of this pursuit. The important thing is to recognize what state you are in. By knowing where you are—in defense, anxiety, shame, guilt, core emotions, or an openhearted state—you'll know what to do next.

At the very least, you'll know if it is the right or wrong time to make thoughtful, important decisions or have a productive conversation. If you are not in a good place and don't have the strength or desire to do anything about it at the moment, that's not only fine but even a normal and natural way to feel at times. Working the Change Triangle and improving ourselves is a lifelong practice. It is always there for us when we want it.

How to Stay in an Openhearted State in the Face of Life's Challenges

Notice when you are triggered, and try to maintain calm through breathing, grounding, and imagining your safe place.

Listen to your body so you can notice and name the emotions and parts of you that are upset. Communicate with those emotions and parts.

Validate that you are upset and that you first need to care for yourself.

Offer compassion to yourself; don't listen to judging or critical thoughts.

Identify what you need to feel better and remind yourself that whatever you feel is temporary. The feeling will pass.

Experiment:
Finding Your C's

What the C's Bring Up for You

Write down the C words on a piece of paper:

- calm
- curious
- connected
- compassionate
- confident
- courageous
- clear

As you write each one, say the word out loud. Notice and write down one thought, one emotion, and one physical sensation that each C word brings up for you. For example, "calm" might elicit the thought, *I want to feel calm more often.* It might bring up the feeling of joy and a sensation of warmth. "Compassion" might elicit the thought, *It doesn't feel right to give myself compassion.* It might bring up anxiety, which causes your stomach to clench. "Confident" might elicit the thought, *I will never be confident.* It might bring up fear and make your heart race.

Finding Your C's

Knowing at any given moment if you are near or far from your openhearted state is important. Ask yourself the following questions. Answer, based on how you feel right now in the present moment, without judgment. The main goal is to be aware. If your answer is no to any of these questions, try to get a sense of what thoughts, emotions, or parts may be blocking you from access to each C. Get curious but not judgmental. Don't pressure yourself. See what you can learn by noticing, validating, and listening to your thoughts, emotions, and sensations. Notice whatever feels right to you.

Do I feel **calm**?
YES_____ NO_____
If no, what is blocking me from feeling calm?

_____

Do I have **curiosity** about myself, other people, my work, my hobbies, and other aspects of my circumstances, even if I am struggling?
YES_____ NO_____
If no, what is blocking me from being curious?

_____

Do I feel **connection** to something—i.e., other people, nature, God, or myself?
YES_____ NO_____
If no, what is blocking me from feeling connected?

_____

Do I feel **compassion** for others AND for myself, even though I may also be having other thoughts and emotions like anger and judgment?
YES_____ NO_____
If no, what is blocking me from feeling compassionate?

_____

Do I have **confidence** that I can handle my life?

YES_____ NO_____

If no, what is blocking me from feeling confident?

_____

Do I feel **courageous** to try new things, be myself, stretch out of my comfort zone, or relate in new and more vulnerable ways with people?

YES_____ NO_____

If no, what is blocking me from being courageous?

_____

Do I have some **clarity** about who I am, what I like, want, need, don't want, and don't need, and what is important to me?

YES_____ NO_____

If no, what is blocking me from feeling clear?

_____

If the experiment brings up upset or distress, try to name the emotions you are experiencing now:

_____

_____

_____

Give yourself compassion.

Experiment: Plotting Yourself on the Change Triangle

MOST OF US first become aware of our emotional states when we are upset. At the moment you realize something is wrong, you'll be at a three-pronged crossroad. One road avoids what you are feeling by turning away from whatever is upsetting you. Another leads you to react impulsively. The third road takes you toward your inner experience—lean in to it and work the Change Triangle. For example, you can get curious and ask yourself, *What just happened that triggered me?* Then you can further inquire, *What feelings does it bring up for me?*

Slow way down with breathing and grounding. Tune in to yourself now, giving yourself lots of time to notice. Locate to the best of your ability where you are on the Change Triangle. Are you on the inhibitory corner experiencing shame, anxiety, or guilt? Are you already at the bottom of the Triangle in a core feeling of sadness, fear, anger, disgust, joy, excitement, or sexual excitement? Are you in the openhearted state feeling one or more of the C's: calm, curious, connected, compassionate, confident, courageous, and/or clear? Are you in a defensive mode, blocked off from your emotions and the openhearted state?

Name what corner of the Change Triangle you think you are on right now:

_____

Write down what it is you just noticed about your internal experience that helped you figure out what corner you are on. For example, *I recognized that I am on the defense corner because I feel numb, bored, and want a drink.* Or *I recognized that I am in the inhibitory corner because I am anxious and tense and I feel small and inadequate.* Or *I recognized that I am on the bottom of the Change Triangle because I'm experiencing sadness and my body feels heavy and I feel like I have to cry.* Or *I know I'm in an openhearted state because I'm calm and I feel at peace with myself and others.*

Now you try:

_____
_____
_____

Experiment: Working the Change Triangle

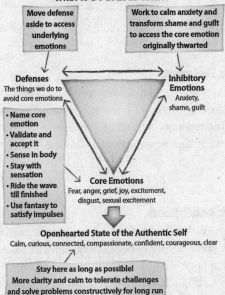

THE CHANGE TRIANGLE
What to Do at Each Corner

Move defense aside to access underlying emotions

Work to calm anxiety and transform shame and guilt to access the core emotion originally thwarted

Defenses
The things we do to avoid core emotions

Inhibitory Emotions
Anxiety, shame, guilt

- Name core emotion
- Validate and accept it
- Sense in body
- Stay with sensation
- Ride the wave till finished
- Use fantasy to satisfy impulses

Core Emotions
Fear, anger, grief, joy, excitement, disgust, sexual excitement

Openhearted State of the Authentic Self
Calm, curious, connected, compassionate, confident, courageous, clear

Stay here as long as possible!
More clarity and calm to tolerate challenges and solve problems constructively for long run

This is a summary or "cheat sheet" for what to do to work the Change Triangle. Each corner you find yourself on requires you to do something to move to the next corner going clockwise so you end up in the openhearted state of the authentic Self as much as possible.

Notice what you are experiencing now, and to the best of your ability write down where you think it goes on the Change Triangle below.

**WHERE AM I
ON THE CHANGE TRIANGLE?**

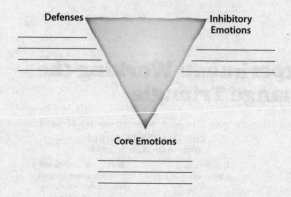

Corner 1: Defense

If you locate yourself on the defense corner, ask yourself, *If I wasn't using this defense, what might I be feeling right now?* You are trying to discover what emotion or conflict the defense is protecting you from. Now write that down where you think it goes on the Change Triangle.

Corner 2: Inhibition

If you are on the inhibitory corner it means you have figured out that you are experiencing either anxiety, guilt, or shame. Can you discern which one?

If you're feeling anxiety, calm it down by grounding your feet on the floor, use deep belly breathing, and consciously remind yourself that this is anxiety. Accept everything you notice and work to muster a compassionate stance toward yourself. Simultaneously to calming anxiety with the above techniques, try to name all the underlying core emotions you feel. Write them on the bottom of the Change Triangle diagram, above.

If you sense a part of you is holding shame, imagine that shamed part coming out of you and sitting several feet away. You want to try to visualize the part of you that holds shame. This helps to prevent the shame from overwhelming you and makes it possible to communicate with and soothe your shamed part. Talk to your shamed part like a good parent would, with a stance of curiosity and compassion. Ask, *What are you ashamed of?* or *What does what happened say about you?* Once you know what the shamed part is reacting to, give it love and compassion. Be your own good parent and try to intuit what that part needs to feel better. Use imagination to give the part what it needs. Most shamed parts need to feel connected, secure, safe, calm, loved, and accepted.

Now try to find your core emotions toward the person who originally caused you shame or taught you to be ashamed of that quality. To help find your core emotions, try asking yourself these questions: *If I felt strong and confident in myself, what emotions would I have toward the person who first shamed me? What emotions would I have on behalf of my best friend if he was hurt or shamed the way I was?* If they are core emotions, write them on the bottom of the Change Triangle diagram. If they are inhibitory, write them on the inhibitory corner.

If you are experiencing guilt, ask your guilt, *If guilt is for a crime, what's my crime right now?* If you hurt someone, prepare an apology and make amends.

If you did nothing wrong, your goal is to tolerate the guilt that setting limits and boundaries cause. Then try to notice what core emotions were blocked toward the person who originally would not tolerate your limits and boundaries.

If you feel guilty for being lucky or having something someone else lacks, move from guilt to gratitude. You can choose to be compassionate and give back in concrete ways. Being guilty doesn't do anything positive for you or the person evoking the guilt.

Corner 3: Core Emotion

If you locate yourself on the core emotion corner or you worked the Change Triangle to get there, it means you are experiencing sadness, anger, fear, disgust, joy, excitement, sexual excitement, or a combination of them. Validate each emotion separately by saying, *I feel* _____ *AND I feel* _____. Name them all. Write them down at the bottom of the Change Triangle diagram.

At this point, if you feel comfortable with further experimentation, try to stay with one core emotion. Notice and name the physical sensations it brings up. Stay with the sensations in your body as you breathe nice, long, deep belly breaths. Stay with those sensations until something shifts or you notice an impulse. Use fantasy to imagine what the emotional impulse wants to do. Ride the emotional wave until you feel calmer.

Finally, which if any of the C's do you have access to right now? List them here:

_____

_____

_____

_____

_____

_____

_____

Congratulations! You have just worked the Change Triangle. Remember, the Change Triangle is a map and a tool to use for the rest of your life. With practice and experimentation both on your own and with others, you will get better and better at recognizing where you are, where you need to go, and how to get there.

Final Words

AS YOU'VE LEARNED, psychological symptoms, like depression and a myriad of others I've mentioned throughout this book, lead us back to core emotions. We always have the choice to either let ourselves experience emotions or use defenses to avoid them. At this point in my life, when I am feeling a core emotion, I know I need to make room for it. If I can do that, no matter how much it hurts, I always feel better.

No one is perfect at working the Change Triangle. Really, no one. I still have to remind myself to work the Change Triangle. I still have trouble sometimes figuring out what corner I'm on and how to help myself or one of my patients. But with that said, I cannot imagine life without this guide.

The process of working the Change Triangle does not have an end point. It is instead a lifelong practice. The goal is to continue to know yourself and to spend more time in the openhearted state.

Across our lifespan, we can continue to grow, learn, and become more alive and comfortable with who we are, flaws and all. With ever-increasing awareness, we can notice when we shift into a state that doesn't serve us or our relationships. We can work our way back down the Change Triangle with the skills and knowledge we have acquired. With hard work, we will become masters of this process. We will feel better, we will be wiser, and our lives will be easier and fuller.

If, after reading this book, you can locate your current state on the Change Triangle, you have accomplished a great deal. Just the act of noticing where you are on the map helps create emotional distance between your Self and what is upsetting you. Noticing your emotions, moods, states of mind, thoughts, physical sensations, beliefs, or anything about your experience while you are having the experience is exercise for the brain. Dual awareness of your Self and whatever you are experiencing leads to harmony, calm, and the perspective that you are more than your feelings, thoughts, and symptoms.

As you move toward vitality and authenticity, your ability to tolerate challenges will grow. Pain, anxiety, and fear will still arise, but emotions won't be as debilitating or scary as they were before. We are not powerless to change or at the mercy of our minds.

The power of the Change Triangle is huge. Think of an ocean. Waves knock us down and pull us under. Sometimes it might feel as if we are drowning. But if we are prepared, if we know what to do when a wave topples us, if we build strength and balance, we can find our way back to the surface each time with less effort and more confidence that we will survive the next wave that comes.

If you remember one thing from this book, remember: *emotions just are!* Judging yourself is not useful. Believing you can stop emotions from happening is false. Instead, focus your mental energy on dealing constructively with them. Use the Change Triangle. Get to know what you are experiencing. Learn what your experience is trying to tell you. You don't have to act on emotions, and in most cases you won't, but the information those impulses give you is important. If nothing else, emotions make us feel alive.

Slow down every once in a while. Because anxiety speeds up the brain, actively slowing our thoughts and actions is calming. Slowing down allows us to connect. Slowing down enables self-reflection. And, of course, we must slow down to work with our emotions.

Get curious about your internal world before you judge or draw conclusions about it. Stay curious about the minds of others before you draw conclusions about another person's intent. Pausing requires discipline, but it is well worth the work. In that space you can ask yourself, *I wonder what emotion she was experiencing that made her do X, Y, or Z?* Pausing to understand the deeper emotions affecting behavior before you jump to conclusions will help all your relationships.

Lastly, whether for your sake or for the sake of someone you love, remember that emotions need to be validated for our body and mind to feel right. Stop judging and start validating. Every relationship you have—especially the one you have with your Self—will benefit.

Acknowledgments

THERE ARE SO many people I want to thank, beginning with Richard Abate for seeing something in me that I didn't see. He made it possible for me to realize this longtime dream of sharing the Change Triangle far and wide.

Thank you to Julie Grau and Laura Van der Veer for their amazing editing. Thank you to Mengfei Chen, Beth Pearson, copy editor Amy Morris Ryan, Debbie Glasserman, Christine Mykityshyn, Jessica Bonet, Linda Friedner Cowen, and the rest of the team at Random House and Spiegel & Grau for taking this project from a proposal to a book.

I want to acknowledge James Ryerson, my editor at *The New York Times,* for coming up with the title *It's Not Always Depression.*

I want to thank Diana Fosha for developing AEDP and writing the foreword. Her courage and genius in synthesizing current research into a healing and transformational psychotherapy model in which love and authenticity are explicitly valued have changed the course of the way people treat and approach those suffering from psychological distress. I have so much love and gratitude for you, Diana.

I have had many gifted AEDP teachers that I want to acknowledge, including: Eileen Russell, Natasha Prenn, Kari Gleiser, Jerry Lamagna, Jeanne Newhouse, Steve Shapiro, Sue Ann Piliero, Barbara Suter, David Mars, Karen Pando-Mars, Gil Tunnell, Jenna Osiason, and Ron Frederick. I want to acknowledge all my psychoanalytic supervisors, especially Marc Sholes, Claire Herz, Ann Eisenstein, and Dodi Goldman, for not only teaching me how to be a boundaried and skilled psychoanalyst, but for tolerating me and encouraging me as I challenged them with "You gotta learn about this new model (AEDP). I think it is the wave of the future!"

I have to single out my primary supervisor, teacher, and mentor, Benjamin Lipton, who made me the psychotherapist I am today. His heart and mind are in every one of these clinical stories, as my technique and way of being are largely derivative of him and what he has taught me. Thank you, Ben.

I want to thank my oldest friend, spiritual guide, and marketing genius, Monica Schulze Hodges. Since we were both nine years old, we've forged life together, stronger because we had each other. Her support has been invaluable. From encouraging me and embracing the Change Triangle herself, to suggesting I start a blog and editing the posts each month, to coming up with the name the Change Triangle, to capturing the essence of what I am doing with words and pictures, to helping me with my website, to encouraging me to be courageous every step of the way, her hands-on help has allowed me to reach so many people, and the gratitude I feel is beyond words. And I want to thank my dear friends Lucy Lehrer, Tracey Pruzan, Heidi Frieze, Natasha Prenn, Betsy Kavaler, and Lisa Schnall for always being kind, loving, and supportive.

I need to acknowledge my mother, Gail Jacobs. Her patience, love, affirmation, and support have no limits. And thank you for hammering me about not using jargon in my writing.

My deepest gratitude and thanks go out to my sister, Amanda Jacobs Wolf. I couldn't imagine life without her and the great love, wisdom, and friendship she bestows on me every day.

To my children, Samantha and Brackets, who inspire me to

grow and be a better person, I love you more than you'll ever know and I love being your mom. To Jessica and Naomi, my stepdaughters, I'm grateful for our special relationships.

Jon Hendel, my husband and partner in life, spent literally hundreds and hundreds of hours reading and rereading this book. Thank you for being the most loving, thoughtful, wise, fun, and caring partner—you are perfect for me.

Finally, I am grateful to every person who let me have the honor and privilege of being their psychotherapist. I learned and grew from every one of you. A special thanks to those people whose permission I received to share our work so that others might be helped. You have given a life-changing gift.

Resources

FOR THOSE PEOPLE wanting to learn more about trauma, experiential psychotherapies, and professional training, below is a short list of websites. With the exception of my blog, these websites offer free articles and information, therapist directories, and much more. For a constantly updated list with many more resources, please visit my website: hilaryjacobshendel.com.

- My blog: hilaryjacobshendel.com/hilarys-blog
- AEDP (accelerated experiential dynamic psychotherapy): aedpinstitute.org
- IFS (Internal Family Systems therapy): selfleadership.org
- EMDR (eye movement desensitization and reprocessing): emdria.org
- SE (Somatic Experiencing): traumahealing.org
- Sensorimotor psychotherapy: www.sensorimotorpsychotherapy.org
- Healing Shame workshops: www.healingshame.com

Appendix A

List of Sensation Words

THE BRAIN FEELS better when we find language that fits our experiences. When we find the right word, like "bruised," for example, that goes with our experience of feeling hurt, there is a "click" of recognition that feels good and right.[1]

The lists of sensation and emotion words below and in Appendix B are to help you find the right words for your experiences. Note that I organized the words into categories to help make it easier to find the word or words that best fit your experience. You might see the same word twice under different categories. You might find the right word for your experience under another category. Words not listed here might also come into your mind. Trust your experience and use the word that best fits your internal experience, regardless of category.

Angry

burning	explosive	impulsive
clenched	fiery	knotted
constricted	heated	prickly
energized	hot	red-hot

Anxious

clammy
clenched
constricted
damp
dizzy
dry
faint
floating
fluttery
fuzzy
guarded
headachy
heart-pounding
jumpy
knotted
queasy
spacey
tingly
trembly
twitchy
vibrating
tense
shallow breath
spinning
panicky
tight

Ashamed

alone
contracted
cut off
dark
deadened
deflated
disappearing
disconnected
empty
flushed
frozen
hiding
imploding
invisible
numb
receding
small

Constricted

armored
blocked
clenched
closed
cold
congested
contracted
cool
dense
knotted
numb
paralyzed
prickly
pulsing
stuck
suffocating
tense
thick
throbbing
tight
wooden

Depressed

alone
contracted
cut off
dark
deadened
dense
disappearing
disconnected
drained
dull
empty
heavy
numb
thick

Disgusted

acidic
bilious
clenched
cringing
gagging
grossed out
knotted
nauseated
poisoned
queasy
sick
tense
tight

Excited

activated
breathless

bubbly
bursting
buzzy
electric
energized
expanding
expansive
floating
fluid
flushed
itchy
nervy
pounding
pulsing
radiating
shimmery
streaming
tingling
twitchy

Expansive

growing
inflated
luminous
puffed up
radiating
shimmering
strong
tall
tremulous

Fearful

breathless
chaotic

clammy
cold
dark
frantic
frozen
jittery
jumpy
icy
shaky
shivery
spinning
sweaty
trembling

Guilty

buzzy
constricted
dropping
jittery
sinking
tense

Happy/Joyful

aglow
cozy
energized
expanding
expanded
expansive
floating
full
moved
open
smiling

smooth
sunny
tender
touched
warm

Hurt

achy
bruised
cut
open
fragile
jagged
pierced
prickly
raw
searing
sensitive
sore
wobbly
wounded

Openhearted

airy
alive
awake
calm
connected
expanded
expansive
flowing
fluid
full
light

open

peaceful

relaxed

releasing

shimmering

smooth

spacious

still

strong

vital

warm

Sad

blue

burdened

down

empty

heavy

hollow

untethered

weighted

Tender

aglow

bruised

cozy

flaccid

fragile

jagged

melting

moved

soft

throbbing

touched

warm

Vulnerable

brittle

exposed

fragile

open

quivery

raw

sensitive

Appendix B

List of Emotion Words

Angry

aggressive
covetous
critical
disappointed
disapproving
distant
enraged
frustrated
furious
hateful
hostile
hurt
infuriated
irate
irritated
jealous
mad
pissed
provoked
resentful
sarcastic
selfish
skeptical
violated

Anxious

agitated
avoiding
confused
constricted
hidden
indifferent
nervous
tight
tingly
uptight
withdrawn

Ashamed

alienated
devastated
disrespected
embarrassed
empty
inadequate
inferior
insecure
insignificant
isolated
powerless
ridiculed
victimized
vulnerable
withdrawn
worthless

Confident

amazing
appreciated
creative
courageous
discerning
important
invincible
powerful
proud
strong
successful
valuable
worthwhile

Disgusted

averse
disapproving
grossed out
rejecting
repulsed
revolted
turned off

Distrustful

astonished
disillusioned
jealous
judgmental
loathing
perplexed
provocative
sarcastic
skeptical
suspicious

Excited

activated
amazed
awed
courageous
eager
ecstatic
energized
expansive
faithful
high
interested
liberated
surprised
wondrous

Fearful

afraid
anxious
bewildered
confused
discouraged
dismayed
frightened
helpless
hesitant
inadequate
insignificant
overwhelmed
rejected
scared
shocked
startled
submissive
terrified
worried

Guilty

apologetic
avoiding
contrite
meek
remorseful

Happy/Joyful

amused
cheerful
courageous
creative
daring
energetic
excited
fascinated
hopeful
joyous
optimistic
playful
sensual
sensuous
stimulated
wonderful

Hurt

- awful
- exposed
- humiliated
- ignored
- insecure
- pained
- raw
- rejected
- sensitive
- submissive
- threatened

Openhearted

- aware
- brave
- calm
- clear
- compassionate
- confident
- connected
- courageous
- creative
- curious
- fulfilled
- hopeful
- inquisitive
- inspired
- loving
- nurturing
- open
- pensive
- philosophical
- playful
- respectful
- responsive
- sensitive
- strong
- tender
- thankful
- thoughtful

Peaceful

- accepted
- calm
- clear
- compassionate
- connected
- content
- creative
- curious
- grateful
- relaxed
- secure
- serene

Sad

- abandoned
- alone
- apathetic
- ashamed
- bored
- depressed
- despairing
- disappointed
- droopy
- empty
- flat
- ignored
- indifferent
- isolated
- lonely
- remorseful
- sleepy
- tired
- withdrawn

Vulnerable

- defensive
- exposed
- protective
- raw
- scared
- skittish
- weak
- withdrawn

Bibliography

WHILE I AM providing a detailed bibliographical reference section, before that I want to highlight people who have influenced me immensely, without whom this book and my work would not be the same. I'll mention some of their books below, but for full citations, please see the list of references that follows.

First and foremost, I want to acknowledge the work and brilliance of the developer of accelerated experiential dynamic psychotherapy (AEDP), Diana Fosha. Diana synthesized an enormous body of research and clinical work on neuroscience, emotions, attachment, transformation, and trauma and developed a new and highly effective approach to help people heal from psychological wounds. For those of you who want to dive further into the theory and practice of AEDP, I encourage you to read her seminal text, *The Transforming Power of Affect.* For a deep and fascinating exploration of emotions by various renowned clinicians and researchers, I also recommend *The Healing Power of Emotion: Affective Neuroscience, Development and Clinical Practice,* edited by Diana Fosha et al. More information can be found on the AEDP website, aedpinstitute.org.

Although it was Diana Fosha who first introduced me to the

Change Triangle, which she called the Triangle of Experience, I have to acknowledge the work of David Malan. In fact, the Triangle is often referred to among professionals as Malan's Triangle because he was the first to publish a book explaining "the Triangle of Conflict," as he called it. If you want to read more about Malan's work, his book *Individual Psychotherapy and The Science of Psychodynamics* provides an in-depth read.

Throughout this book I have referred to "parts," "Self," and "the C's." The idea that humans are made up of various states, parts, or personalities as opposed to one unified whole is not new. Freud and the object relations theorists routinely wrote about ego states and introjects. Richard Schwartz, however, stands out as someone who has greatly influenced my work and writing. The way he writes about parts, the Self, and the C's are all reflected in this work. Richard developed an entire model on how to work with parts to heal symptoms of psychological distress and trauma. For clinicians who are interested to learn more, I recommend reading *Introduction to the Internal Family Systems Model* and *Internal Family Systems Therapy*. His book *You Are the One You've Been Waiting For: Bringing Courageous Love to Intimate Relationships* is written for the general public. To learn more, go to the IFS website: selfleadership.org.

References

Ainsworth, M. (1978). *Patterns of Attachment: A Psychological Study of the Strange Situation.* Hillsdale, NJ: Lawrence Erlbaum.

Aposhyan, S. (2004). *Body-Mind Psychotherapy.* New York: W. W. Norton and Company.

Badenoch, B. (2008). *Being a Brain-Wise Therapist.* New York: W. W. Norton and Company.

Bowlby, J. (1988). *A Secure Base: Parent-Child Attachment and Healthy Human Development.* New York: Basic Books.

Brown, B. (2010). *The Gifts of Imperfection.* Center City, MN: Hazelden.

Coughlin Della Selva, P. (2004). *Intensive Short-Term Dynamic Psychotherapy: Theory and Technique Synopsis.* London: Karnac.

Cozolino, L. (2002). *The Neuroscience of Psychotherapy.* New York: W. W. Norton and Company.

Craig, A. D. (2015). *How Do You Feel?: An Interoceptive Moment with Your Neurobiological Self.* Princeton, NJ: Princeton University Press.

Damasio, A. (1994). *Descartes' Error: Emotion, Reason, and the Human Brain.* New York: Penguin Books.

——— (1999). *The Feeling of What Happens: Body and Emotion in the Making of Consciousness.* New York: Harcourt Brace.

Darwin, C. (1872). *The Expression of the Emotions in Man and Animals.* London: John Murray Publisher.

Davanloo, H. (2000). *Intensive Short-Term Dynamic Psychotherapy: Selected Papers of Habib Davanloo, MD.* Hoboken, NJ: John Wiley & Sons.

——— (1995). *Unlocking the Unconscious: Selected Papers of Habib Davanloo, MD.* New York: John Wiley & Sons.

Doidge, N. (2007). *The Brain That Changes Itself.* New York: Penguin Books.

Fay, D. (2007). *Becoming Safely Embodied: Skills Manual.* Somerville, MA: Heart Full Life Publishing.

Fonagy, P., Gergely, G., Jurist, E., and Target, M. (2004). *Affect Regulation, Mentalization, and the Development of the Self.* New York: Other Press.

Fosha, D. (2017). How to Be a Transformational Therapist: AEDP Harnesses Innate Healing Affects to Re-Wire Experience and Accelerate Transformation. In J. Loizzo, M. Neale, and E. Wolf (eds.), *Advances in Contemplative Psychotherapy: Accelerating Transformation.* New York: Norton.

——— (2013). Turbocharging the Affects of Healing and Redressing the Evolutionary Tilt. In D. J. Siegel and M. F. Solomon (eds.), *Healing Moments in Psychotherapy.* New York: Norton.

——— (2009). Positive Affects and the Transformation of Suffering into Flourishing. In W. C. Bushell, E. L. Olivo, and N. D. Theise (eds.), *Longevity, Regeneration, and Optimal Health: Integrating Eastern and Western Perspectives.* New York: Annals of the New York Academy of Sciences.

——— (2004). "Nothing That Feels Bad Is Ever the Last Step": The Role of Positive Emotions in Experiential Work with Difficult Emotional Experiences. L. Greenberg (ed.), *Clinical Psychology and Psychotherapy* 11 (Special Issue on Emotion), 30–43.

——— (2000). *The Transforming Power of Affect.* New York: Basic Books.

Fosha, D., Siegel, D., and Solomon, M. (2009). *The Healing Power of Emotion: Affective Neuroscience, Development and Clinical Practice.* New York: W. W. Norton and Company.

Fosha, D., and Yeung, D. (2006). AEDP Exemplifies the Seamless Integration of Emotional Transformation and Dyadic Relatedness at Work. In G. Stricker and J. Gold (eds.), *A Casebook of Integrative Psychotherapy.* Washington, DC: APA Press.

Frederick, R. J. (2009). *Living Like You Mean It: Using the Wisdom and Power of Your Emotions to Get the Life You Really Want.* San Francisco: Jossey-Bass.

Fredrickson, B. L. (2001). The Role of Positive Emotions in Positive Psychology: The Broaden-and-Build Theory of Positive Emotions. *American Psychologist* 56, 211–26.

——— (2009). *Positivity: Groundbreaking Research Reveals How to Embrace the Hidden Strength of Positive Emotions, Overcome Negativity, and Thrive*. New York: Random House.

Gallese, V. (2001). Mirror Neurons, Embodied Simulation, and the Neural Basis of Social Identification. *Psychoanalytic Dialogues* 19: 519–36.

Gendlin, E. T. (1978). *Focusing*. New York: Bantam Dell.

Herman, J. (1992). *Trauma and Recovery: The Aftermath of Violence from Domestic Abuse to Political Terror*. New York: Basic Books.

Hill, D. (2015). *Affect Regulation Theory: A Clinical Model*. New York: W. W. Norton and Company.

James, W. (1890). *The Principles of Psychology*. New York: Henry Holt & Company.

Kaufman, G. (1996). *The Psychology of Shame*. New York: Springer Publishing Company.

Korb, A. (2015). *The Upward Spiral: Using Neuroscience to Reverse the Course of Depression One Small Change at a Time*. Oakland, CA: New Harbinger.

Lamagna, J. (2011). Of the Self, by the Self, and for the Self: An Intra-Relational Perspective on Intra-Psychic Attunement and Psychological Change. *Journal of Psychotherapy Integration* 21 (3): 280–307.

Lamagna, J., and Gleiser, K. (2007). Building a Secure Internal Attachment: An Intra-Relational Approach to Ego Strengthening and Emotional Processing with Chronically Traumatized Clients. *Journal of Trauma and Dissociation* 8 (1): 25–52.

Lerner, H. (2005). *The Dance of Anger*. New York: HarperCollins.

Levenson, H. (1995). *Time-Limited Dynamic Psychotherapy*. New York: Basic Books.

Levine, A., and Heller, R. (2010). *Attached: The New Science of Attachment*. New York: Penguin Group.

Levine, P. (1997). *Waking the Tiger: Healing Trauma*. Berkeley, CA: North Atlantic Books.

Lipton, B., and Fosha, D. (2011). Attachment as a Transformative Process in AEDP: Operationalizing the Intersection of Attachment Theory and Affective Neuroscience. *Journal of Psychotherapy Integration* 21 (3): 253–79.

Macnaughton, I. (2004). *Body, Breath, and Consciousness: A Somatics Anthology*. Berkeley, CA: North Atlantic Books.

Malan, D. (1979). *Individual Psychotherapy and the Science of Psychodynamics*. London: Butterworth-Heinemann.

McCullough, L., et al. (2003). *Treating Affect Phobia: A Manual for Short-Term Dynamic Psychotherapy*. New York: Guilford Press.

Napier, N. (1993). *Getting Through the Day*. New York: W. W. Norton and Company.

Nathanson, D. (1992). *Shame and Pride: Affect, Sex, and the Birth of the Self.* New York: W. W. Norton and Company.

Ogden, P., and Fisher, J. (2015). *Sensorimotor Psychotherapy: Interventions from Trauma and Attachment.* New York: W. W. Norton and Company.

Ogden, P., Minton, K., and Pain, C. (2006). *Trauma and the Body: A Sensorimotor Approach.* New York: W. W. Norton and Company.

Pally, R. (2000). *The Mind-Body Relationship.* New York: Karnac Books.

Panksepp, J. (1998). *Affective Neuroscience: The Foundations of Human and Animal Emotions.* New York: Oxford University Press.

———— (2010). Affective Neuroscience of the Emotional BrainMind: Evolutionary Perspectives and Implications for Understanding Depression. *Dialogues in Clinical Neuroscience* 12 (4): 533–45.

Pausch, R. (2008). *The Last Lecture.* New York: Hyperion.

Porges, S. (2011). *The Polyvagal Theory: Neurophysiological Foundations of Emotions, Attachment, Communication, and Self-Regulation.* Norton Series on Interpersonal Neurobiology. New York: W. W. Norton and Company.

Prenn, N. (2009). I Second That Emotion! On Self-Disclosure and Its Metaprocessing. In A. Bloomgarden and R. B. Menutti (eds.), *Psychotherapist Revealed: Therapists Speak About Self-Disclosure in Psychotherapy.* Chapter 6, pp. 85–99. New York: Routledge.

———— (2010). How to Set Transformance into Action: The AEDP Protocol. *Transformance: The AEDP Journal* 1 (1). aedpinstitute.org/wp-content/uploads/page_How-to-Set-Transformance-Into-Action.pdf.

———— (2011). Mind the Gap: AEDP Interventions Translating Attachment Theory into Clinical Practice. *Journal of Psychotherapy Integration* 21 (3): 308–29.

Rothschild, B. (2000). *The Body Remembers.* New York: W. W. Norton and Company.

Russell, E., and Fosha, D. (2008). Transformational Affects and Core State in AEDP: The Emergence and Consolidation of Joy, Hope, Gratitude and Confidence in the (Solid Goodness of the) Self. *Journal of Psychotherapy Integration* 18 (2): 167–90.

Russell, E. M. (2015). *Restoring Resilience: Discovering your Clients' Capacity for Healing.* New York: Norton.

Sarno, J. (1999). *The Mind Body Prescription.* New York: Warner Books.

Schwartz, R. C. (2004). *Internal Family Systems Therapy.* New York: Guilford Press.

———— (2008). *You Are the One You've Been Waiting For: Bringing Courageous Love to Intimate Relationships.* Oak Park: Trailheads Publications.

———— (2001). *Introduction to the Internal Family Systems Model.* Oak Park: Trailheads Publications.

Shapiro, F. (2001). *Eye Movement Desensitization and Reprocessing: Basic Principles, Protocols, and Procedures.* New York: Guilford Press.

Shore, A. (2003). *Affect Regulation and the Repair of the Self.* New York: W. W. Norton and Company.

Siegel, D. (1999). *The Developing Mind: Toward a Neurobiology of Interpersonal Experience.* New York: Guilford Press.

————— (2010). *Mindsight: The New Science of Personal Transformation.* New York: Bantam Books.

Stern, D. N. (1998). The Process of Therapeutic Change Involving Implicit Knowledge: Some Implications of Developmental Observations for Adult Psychotherapy. *Infant Mental Health Journal* 19 (3): 300–308.

Subic-Wrana, C., et al. (2016). Affective Change in Psychodynamic Psychotherapy: Theoretical Models and Clinical Approaches to Changing Emotions. *Zeitschrift für Psychosomatische Medizin und Psychotherapie* 62: 207–23.

Tomkins, S. S. (1962). *Affect, Imagery, and Consciousness. Vol. 1: The Positive Affects.* New York: Springer.

————— (1963). *Affect, Imagery, and Consciousness. Vol. 2: The Negative Affects.* New York: Springer.

————— (1989). Emotions and Emotional Communication in Infants. *American Psychologist* 44 (2): 112–19.

————— (1998). Dyadically Expanded States of Consciousness and the Process of Therapeutic Change. *Infant Mental Health Journal* 19 (3): 290–99.

Van Der Kolk, B. (2014). *The Body Keeps the Score.* New York: Viking.

Yeung, D., and Fosha, D. (2015). Accelerated Experiential Dynamic Psychotherapy. In *The Sage Encyclopedia of Theory in Counseling and Psychotherapy.* New York: Sage Publications.

Notes

Foreword

1. Fosha, D. (2008). Transformance, Recognition of Self by Self, and Effective Action. In K. J. Schneider (ed.), *Existential-Integrative Psychotherapy: Guideposts to the Core of Practice.* New York: Routledge, pp. 290–320.
2. Bowlby, J. (1988). *A Secure Base: Parent-Child Attachment and Healthy Human Development.* New York: Basic Books.
3. Porges, S. W. (2011). *The Polyvagal Theory: Neurophysiological Foundations of Emotions, Attachment, Communication, and Self-regulation.* New York: Norton; Carter, C. S., and Porges, S. W. (2012). Mechanisms, Mediators, and Adaptive Consequences of Caregiving. In D. Narvaez, J. Panksepp, A. L. Schore, and T. R. Gleason (eds.), *Human Nature, Early Experience and the Environment of Evolutionary Adaptedness.* New York: Oxford University Press, pp. 132–51; and Geller, S. M., and Porges, S. W. (2014). Therapeutic Presence: Neurophysiological Mechanisms Mediating Feeling Safe in Clinical Interactions. *Journal of Psychotherapy Integration* 24: 178–92.
4. Schore, A. (2012). *The Science of the Art of Psychotherapy.* New York: Norton.
5. Gendlin, E. T. (1981). *Focusing.* New York: Bantam New Age Paperbacks.
6. Fosha, D. (2004). "Nothing That Feels Bad Is Ever the Last Step": The Role of Positive Emotions in Experiential Work with Difficult Emotional Experiences. In special issue on emotion, L. Greenberg (ed.), *Clinical Psychology and Psychotherapy* 11: 30–43.
7. Fosha, D. (2009). Healing Attachment Trauma with Attachment (. . . and Then Some!). In M. Kerman (ed.), *Clinical Pearls of Wisdom: 21 Leading*

Therapists Offer Their Key Insights. New York: Norton, pp. 43–56; also Fosha, D. (2009). Positive Affects and the Transformation of Suffering into Flourishing. In W. C. Bushell, E. L. Olivo, and N. D. Theise (eds.), *Longevity, Regeneration, and Optimal Health: Integrating Eastern and Western Perspectives.* New York: Annals of the New York Academy of Sciences, pp. 252–61.

8. Fredrickson, B. L. (2001). The Role of Positive Emotions in Positive Psychology: The Broaden-and-Build Theory of Positive Emotions. *American Psychologist* 56: 211–26; also Fredrickson, B. L. (2009). *Positivity: Groundbreaking Research Reveals How to Embrace the Hidden Strength of Positive Emotions, Overcome Negativity, and Thrive.* New York: Random House.

9. Fosha, D. (2013). Turbocharging the Affects of Healing and Redressing the Evolutionary Tilt. In D. J. Siegel and Marion F. Solomon (eds.), *Healing Moments in Psychotherapy.* New York: Norton, pp. 129–68; also Russell, E. M. (2015). *Restoring Resilience: Discovering Your Clients' Capacity for Healing.* New York: Norton.

10. Fosha, D. (2017). How to Be a Transformational Therapist: AEDP Harnesses Innate Healing Affects to Re-wire Experience and Accelerate Transformation. In J. Loizzo, M. Neale, and E. Wolf (eds.), *Advances in Contemplative Psychotherapy: Accelerating Transformation.* New York: Norton, chapter 14.

What This Book Will Do for You

1. At that conference it was called the Triangle of Experience. I adapted the Change Triangle from the academic literature. Originally written about by David Malan in 1979, he called it the Triangle of Conflict. In 2000, Diana Fosha, PhD, developer of accelerated experiential dynamic psychotherapy (AEDP), renamed it the Triangle of Experience. I nicknamed it the Change Triangle to introduce it to the public. Malan, D. (1979). *Individual Psychotherapy and the Science of Psychodynamics.* London: Butterworth-Heinemann; Fosha, D. (2000). *The Transforming Power of Affect.* New York: Basic Books.

2. In the emotion and neuroscience literature there are differences among researchers when it comes to what emotions they include as core and how they name them. I choose these seven to teach the Change Triangle because they are most important and useful clinically and for personal use. For example, surprise is sometimes called a core emotion, but it is such a fleeting experience. In my practice, I don't personally see blocked surprise causing trauma like I see with the core emotions on the Change Triangle.

3. Stojanovich, L., and Marisavljevich, D. (2008). Stress as a Trigger of Autoimmune Disease. *Autoimmunity Reviews* 7 (3): 209–13.

The Story of Me

1. I want to make it clear that I am not averse to taking medication for depression or any other mental illness. In fact, I refer patients to psychiatrists when their depression or anxiety is so intense that they cannot function, do

their work, or make use of psychotherapy. Antidepressants can act as a scaffolding to prevent a feeling of bottoming out. However, medication alone often treats the symptoms without addressing the underlying causes, especially where trauma is concerned. I am a proponent of using medication when necessary and simultaneously getting good therapy to treat the underlying causes.

2. A word to explain the name "accelerated experiential dynamic psychotherapy." "Accelerated" refers to the fact that big change can happen quickly. "Experiential" means the therapist works experientially, taking advantage of the healing power of emotions—"mining the gold"—until the waves are over and the experience now feels good. "Dynamic" refers to how the past influences the present, how attachment experiences get internalized, and how new experiences with safe and loving others lead to healing.

The Change Triangle Basics

1. I first learned about the C's from Richard Schwartz when I began studying Internal Family Systems therapy. Anytime I talk about the C's, I credit Richard. Schwartz, R. (2004). *Internal Family Systems Therapy*. New York: Guilford Press.

2. I understand that some depressions and other mental illnesses are true biologically based diseases and not defenses. But people who suffer biologically based mental illness, like all of us, also block emotions and can benefit from working the Change Triangle. We work the Change Triangle within the limits of our mental and physical health to reduce as much stress and anxiety as possible with the hopes of enhancing overall wellbeing. Everyone working the Change Triangle has some "dis-ease" that they are trying to undo, whether the root cause is trauma, stress, environmental stress like poverty, chronic physical health challenges, and/or genetic and biologically based mental illnesses. No matter the root cause, the Change Triangle can help manage emotions that illness and life circumstances bring up.

3. Lieberman, M. D., Eisenberger, N. I., Crockett, M. J., Tom, S., et al. (2007). Putting Feelings into Words: Affect Labeling Disrupts Amygdala Activity to Affective Stimuli. *Psychological Science* 18: 421–28.

Fran's Panic, Anxiety, and Grief

1. Fran's story and the other stories in this book show steps that are central to an AEDP treatment. There are four steps that the therapist guides the patient through: 1) moving out of defensive states; 2) making contact with and processing the underlying core emotions; 3) processing the experience of processing core emotions (called metatherapeutic processing); and 4) arriving in and processing the experience of core state, the technical name for what I call the openhearted state. All the stories show people working the

Change Triangle. For clinicians wanting to learn more or to be trained in this method, see Diana Fosha text on AEDP *The Transforming Power of Affect* (2000) and visit the AEDP Institute online.

2. Kandel, E. (2013). The New Science of Mind and the Future of Knowledge. *Neuron* 80 (3): 546–60.

3. "Once you become aware of them, internal sensations almost always transform into something else." Levine, P. (1997). *Waking the Tiger: Healing Trauma*. Berkeley, CA: North Atlantic Books, p. 82.

4. Identifying the need to pay attention and describe carefully the sensations associated with change-for-the-better is one of Diana Fosha's most important contributions. Reference to Fosha (2013).

5. Whereas most emotion-focused models deal with suffering, AEDP has introduced a whole lexicon not only for the emotions of trauma but for the healing emotions, like gratitude, joy, feeling moved, and the ones that Fran was experiencing. Reference to Fosha (2009).

You Can Change at Any Age

1. Siegrid Löwel, Göttingen University. The exact sentence is: "Neurons wire together if they fire together." Löwel, S., and Singer, W. (1992). Selection of Intrinsic Horizontal Connections in the Visual Cortex by Correlated Neuronal Activity. *Science* 255: 209–12.

2. The four components of an experience come from the theory and practice of EMDR (eye movement desensitization and reprocessing). EMDR is a trauma psychotherapy developed by Francine Shapiro. See Shapiro, F. (2001). *Eye Movement Desensitization and Reprocessing: Basic Principles, Protocols, and Procedures*. New York: Guilford Press, p. 57.

Experiment: Slowing Down

1. These breathing instructions are adapted from New York City–based licensed acupuncturist Sharon Wyse.

2. Inhaling sometimes makes the heart beat a little faster, especially when you first start practicing belly breathing. This is normal. On the exhale is where the heartbeat diminishes. As you practice and play with breathing to find the rhythm and depth that feels most relaxing for you, you will find it to be a reliable way to both calm anxiety and get through a wave of core emotion.

Sara's Depression and Navigating Conflict

1. Asking a defense like confusion to step aside in service of accessing an emotion is pure AEDP.

2. This is specific language that Ben Lipton taught me and continues to teach his AEDP supervisees. He deserves mention here.

3. Some mothers might be put off by the thought of their babies being angry.

It is not that a baby is angry with his or her mother. It is that core anger is triggered in response to a basic need not being met. Anger elicits a loud protest—crying and screaming—to make sure Mother or another person meets the need. Remember, emotions are survival programs.

4. This idea comes from Schwartz, *Internal Family Systems Therapy* (2004).

We Are All a Little Traumatized

1. In distinguishing between different types of trauma, it is important to know that there is no judgment about one kind of trauma being worse or being more important than another. Trauma is trauma. Drawing attention to small t trauma is meant to validate people who suffer symptoms but didn't previously understand why. People who have suffered small t trauma often blame themselves for their symptoms. My hope in explaining small t trauma is to ameliorate, if not eradicate, shame and stigma for people who suffer symptoms of any trauma.

2. Narcissistic personality disorder and borderline personality disorder are terms coming out of favor. There is some consensus that these disorders are caused by childhood traumas of abuse and/or neglect.

3. Dissociation is a psychological process that causes a break in connection to one's emotions, thoughts, body sensations, sense of self, and/or memories. It can range from mild, like in daydreaming, to severe, like one sees in a diagnosis of dissociative identity disorder (DID).

4. It is common for transgender people/gender-nonconforming individuals to use gender-neutral pronouns. Using they/them/their is one of many gender-neutral options available to individuals who do not identify with the traditional man/woman binary and for whom the binary options, he/him/his or she/her/hers, do not apply.

We Are Wired for Connection

1. Jaak Panksepp is known for his research on the drive to seek. Panksepp, J. (2010). Affective Neuroscience of the Emotional BrainMind: Evolutionary Perspectives and Implications for Understanding Depressions. *Dialogues in Clinical Neuroscience* 12 (4): 533–45.

2. Donald Winnicott, MD, a renowned and respected psychoanalytic thinker and writer, put it another way. He said mothering did not have to be perfect, just "good-enough."

3. Bowlby, J. (1988). *A Secure Base: Parent-Child Attachment and Healthy Human Development.* New York: Basic Books.

4. Main, M., Hesse, E., and Kaplan, N. (2005). Predictability of Attachment Behavior and Representational Processes at 1, 6, and 18 Years of Age: The Berkeley Longitudinal Study. In K. E. Grossmann, K. Grossmann, and E. Waters (eds.), *Attachment from Infancy to Adulthood.* New York: Guilford Press, pp. 245–304; Main, M., and Solomon, J. (1990). Procedures for

Identifying Infants as Disorganized/Disoriented During the Ainsworth Strange Situation. In M. T. Greenberg, D. Cicchetti, and E. M. Cummings (eds.), *Attachment in the Preschool Years: Theory, Research and Intervention.* Chicago: University of Chicago Press, pp. 121–60.

Bonnie's Rage

1. Habib Davanloo is a Montreal-based psychiatrist who developed an experiential way of working with emotions, which he called "portrayals." The use of portrayal is a technique to help the patient focus on how an emotion is experienced in the body, and use fantasy to fully explore the actions associated with that emotion. His most notable contribution in that realm is how to work with anger and to be comfortable exploring in fantasy the actions through which that anger is expressed, as well as exploring, in fantasy, the physical consequences of those actions. Diana Fosha studied with Davanloo in the 1980s and incorporated his innovations into AEDP. The historical source of how I work with anger, which plays such a central role in healing Bonnie (Chapter 4), Spencer (Chapter 5), and Mario (Chapter 6) is Davanloo's work, which Ben Lipton taught me specifically in supervision.

2. Pally, R. (2000). *The Mind-Body Relationship.* New York: Karnac Books.

3. Credit to Ben Lipton for teaching me this specific intervention of "holding up a microphone" to let the feeling speak.

4. Again I want to credit Ben Lipton for this intervention of changing a question to a statement to help the patient own his or her wants and needs.

Everything You Need to Know About Your Core Emotions

1. There is debate on exactly where emotions originate in the brain. Many researchers, including Maclean (Maclean, P. D. [1952]. Some Psychiatric Implications of Physiological Studies on Frontotemporal Portion of Limbic System [Visceral Brain]. *Electroencephalography and Clinical Neurophysiology* 4 [4]: 407–18) and Panksepp (Panksepp, J. [1998]. *Affective Neuroscience: The Foundations of Human and Animal Emotions.* New York: Oxford University Press) stand by the limbic system and amygdala as the site of origin. But other areas are involved with emotion processing as well, like the orbitofrontal cortex (Bechara, A., Damasio, H., and Damasio, A. [2000]. Emotion, Decision Making and the Orbitofrontal Cortex. *Cerebral Cortex* 10 [3]: 295–307) and insula (Gu, X., Hof, P. R., Friston, K. J., and Fan, J. [2013]. Anterior Insular Cortex and Emotional Awareness. *The Journal of Comparative Neurology* 521 [15]: 3371–88).

2. Rizzolatti, G., and Craighero, L. (2004). The Mirror-Neuron System. *Annual Review of Neuroscience* 27 (1): 169–92.

3. In one fMRI study, appropriately titled "Putting Feelings into Words," participants viewed pictures of people with emotional facial expressions.

Predictably, each participant's amygdala activated to the emotions in the picture, but when subjects were asked to name the emotion, the ventrolateral prefrontal cortex activated and reduced the emotional amygdala reactivity. In other words, consciously recognizing the emotions reduced their impact. Korb, A. (2015). *The Upward Spiral*. Oakland, CA: New Harbinger.

Spencer's Social Anxiety

1. The suggestion to visualize a memory on an "old grainy TV" came from NYC-based hypnotherapist Melissa Tiers. I learned it at her workshop in integrative coaching of the unconscious mind in New York City.

Working with Anxiety, Shame, and Guilt

1. I don't include love as a core emotion on the Change Triangle but I do think of it as a core experience. I include love, in another category of relational emotions, happening between two people.
2. In addition to what I have shared about shame, I recommend three books to learn more about shame: *The Gifts of Imperfection* by Brené Brown, *The Psychology of Shame* by Gershen Kaufman, and *Shame and Pride* by Donald Nathanson.
3. For another example of how I work with toxic shame, see my *New York Times* article "It's Not Always Depression" (March 10, 2015).
4. For more on shame and vulnerability, I recommend the books and Ted Talks of shame researcher Brené Brown.

The Healing Emotions of Joy, Gratitude, and Pride in the Self

1. For those of you interested in learning more about this, I recommend reading the following articles: Fosha (2013), Fosha and Yeung (2006), Russell and Fosha (2008), and Yeung and Fosha (2015).
2. For more on the role of positive emotions, I recommend the following: Fredrickson, B. L. (2009). *Positivity: Groundbreaking Research Reveals How to Embrace the Hidden Strength of Positive Emotions, Overcome Negativity, and Thrive*. New York: Random House.
3. Diana Fosha deserves credit for introducing the idea to me of deepening pride in the Self and other healing emotions to foster radical transformation.

Mario's Story: Moving Through Trauma to Peace

1. I credit Ben Lipton with the technique of using a fantasy rope and sometimes a real rope to help stay interpersonally connected in a more literal way.
2. Peter Levine's excellent book *Waking The Tiger* explains this phenomenon in more detail. His methodology is based on observing animals in the wild and how they physically recover from near-death experiences. Animals

tremble after trauma. If the trembling is uninterrupted, the animal recovers, gets up, and walks away. If the animal's trembling is interrupted, the animal shows symptoms of trauma. So it is with humans.

3. I credit Diana Fosha with ideas around "mourning for the self" as a vital part of healing, as well as describing and naming the healing affects of joy, pride, and gratitude, all of which move people toward healing and transformation.

4. I must give credit here again to Diana Fosha. This is pure AEDP and among other things what makes this method so unique and powerful.

Defenses

1. The AEDP approach to defenses is in contrast to psychiatric models that pathologize defenses and inadvertently create shame. Creating shame in a psychotherapeutic context actually increases defenses. Reframing them as adaptive at the time they were formed helps decrease shame and increase curiosity.

Sara Redux: The Authentic Self and Openhearted State

1. What I call "the openhearted state" reflects AEDP's teachings on core state and IFS's teachings on the Self. For more information on core state, see Fosha (2000), and for more information on IFS definition of the Self, see Schwartz (2004).

2. A hallmark of AEDP treatment is asking the patient, "What was it like to do this work together today?" Fosha calls this *metatherapeutic processing*. For those clinicians who want to learn more about the theory and practice of metaprocessing, I refer you to Fosha's text *The Transforming Power of Affect* (2000).

Appendix A: List of Sensation Words

1. The "click" of recognition is a phrase I learned from Diana Fosha. It explains the experience when you find a word that fits your experience. It *clicks* in.